Chicken Soup
for the Soul.

Read,
Laugh,
Repeat

Chicken Soup for the Soul: Read, Laugh, Repeat
101 Laugh-Out-Loud Stories
Amy Newmark

Published by Chicken Soup for the Soul, LLC www.chickensoup.com
Copyright ©2021 by Chicken Soup for the Soul, LLC. All Rights Reserved.

The publisher gratefully acknowledges the many publishers and individuals who granted Chicken Soup for the Soul permission to reprint the cited material.

Front cover and interior photo courtesy of iStockphoto.com/Antagain (©Antagain)
Back cover and interior photos: posing meerkat courtesy of iStockphoto.com/gemredding (©gemredding), standing meerkat courtesy of iStockphoto.com/AaronAmat (©AaronAmat), two baby meerkats courtesy of iStockphoto.com/Cloudtail_the_Snow_Leopard (©Cloudtail_the_Snow_Leopard)
Photo of Amy Newmark courtesy of Susan Morrow at SwickPix

Cover and Interior by Daniel Zaccari

Distributed to the booktrade by Simon & Schuster. SAN: 200-2442

Publisher's Cataloging-In-Publication Data
(Prepared by The Donohue Group, Inc.)

Names: Newmark, Amy, compiler.
Title: Chicken soup for the soul : read, laugh, repeat : 101 laugh-out-
      loud stories / [compiled by] Amy Newmark.
Other Titles: Read, laugh, repeat : 101 laugh-out-loud stories
Description: [Cos Cob, Connecticut] : Chicken Soup for the Soul, LLC,
      [2021]
Identifiers: ISBN 9781611590753 | ISBN 9781611593150 (ebook)
Subjects: LCSH: American wit and humor--Literary collections. | American
      wit and humor--Anecdotes. | LCGFT: Anecdotes.
Classification: LCC PN6165 .C45 2021 (print) | LCC PN6165 (ebook) | DDC
      817.6--dc23
Library of Congress Control Number: 2021930727

PRINTED IN THE UNITED STATES OF AMERICA
on acid∞free paper

30 29 28 27 26 25 24 23 22 21   01 02 03 04 05 06 07 08 09 10

Chicken Soup for the Soul.

Read, Laugh, Repeat

101 Laugh-Out-Loud Stories

Amy Newmark

Chicken Soup for the Soul, LLC
Cos Cob, CT

Changing the world one story at a time®
www.chickensoup.com

Table of Contents

Introduction...1

❶
~Domestic Disasters~

1. A Twin Bath, *Shannon McCarty*.....................5
2. Hungry Like a Wolf, *Tina Koenig* 8
3. No Need for Carving, *Gail Molsbee Morris*.....................11
4. A Plague of Joy, *Heidi Allen* 15
5. Confessions of a Lunch Maker, *Kim Reynolds*.....................18
6. The Wrong Bag, *Kimber Krochmal* 20
7. A Bittersweet Victory, *Becky Lewellen Povich* 23
8. Mending Fences, *Robert Campbell* 27
9. Making a Splash, *Kathleen Gerard* 30
10. Pickled Egg Surprise, *Jeannie Dotson*.....................33

❷
~Happily Ever Laughter~

11. Challenged, *Toni-Michelle Nell*.....................36
12. Surviving the Honeymoon, *Robin Jankiewicz*.....................39
13. The Getaway, *Caleb Jennings Breakey*.....................43
14. Taking His Measure, *Tsgoyna Tanzman* 47
15. The Lottery, *Robert Campbell*.....................50
16. Put On Something Else, *Cindy D'Ambroso Argiento*.....................53
17. Perfect, *Ernie Witham*.....................55
18. Social Secretary, *Ilah Breen*.....................58
19. Married to a Metrosexual, *Delia Lloyd*.....................61

20. Husband Instruction Manual, *David Martin* 65
21. It Takes a Licking, *Manley Fisher*...............................68

❸

~I Can't Believe I Did That~

22. Too Hot for Chicken, *Pamela Gilsenan*..........................72
23. Incident at Elk Lake, *Rachel Dunstan Muller*...................75
24. The Scam, *Barbara LoMonaco* 78
25. The Art of Parenting, *Jane M. Choate*..........................81
26. The Moonlit Kayak, *Marta A. Oppenheimer*.......................83
27. The Most Expensive Bike Ever, *Barbara Nicks* 88
28. Ooh La La, *Adrienne Townsend*...................................92
29. Adventure for Two, *Emily Oot*...................................95
30. A Day at the Beach, *Barbara LoMonaco* 99
31. Nowhere to Go, *J.M. Penfold*...................................102

❹

~Doggone Funny~

32. The Great Table Caper, *Ann Denise Karson* 106
33. I Saved a Dog, *Julie Theel* 110
34. Masked Bandits, *John M. Scanlan* 113
35. Bringing Up the Rear, *Gail MacMillan* 116
36. Lead Me Not... *Joei Carlton Hossack*............................119
37. The Battle for the Sheep Pillow, *Sally A. Breslin* 120
38. A Hot Dog, *Jennifer McMurrain* 123
39. Wonder Dog, *Jan Bono*...125
40. Cold Crime, *Sharon Love Cook* 128
41. Tim Russell Is in Hiding, *Jane Marie Allen Farmer*.............131

❺
~My Crazy Family~

42. Matt, Mitts and Magic, *Mary Shotwell*.................................. 135
43. The Zamboni, *Michael Sullivan* 138
44. Men in Training, *Barbara LoMonaco*............................. 142
45. Body Language, *Amy Newmark*..................................... 145
46. The Ugly Elf Tradition, *Karen M. Leet* 147
47. Last Laugh, *Cheryl MacDonald* 149
48. Number Two, *Carrie M. Leach* 153
49. The Gift of Love, *Janell Michael*................................... 155
50. The Ballot Box, *Felice Prager* 157
51. Almost Perfect, *Heather Rodin* 160

❻
~Holiday Hiccups~

52. Home Invasion, *Monika LaPlante* 165
53. O Wholly Overwhelming Night, *Katie O'Connell* 168
54. It's the Thought that Counts, *Mike Morin*..................... 171
55. The Ghost of Turkeys Past, *Joyce Laird* 174
56. Having Mercy, *Teresa Ambord*....................................... 177
57. Ho Ho Ho, Ouch! *D'ette Corona* 179
58. Wild Kingdom, *Joyce Laird* 182
59. Striking Chaos, *Shannon Kernaghan* 186
60. How I Spent My Christmas Vacation, *Cindy Hval*............... 189
61. Cops and Mummers, *Annabel Sheila* 192

7
~That Was Embarrassing~

62. Green Salami, *Patty Hansen* 197
63. Bad Hair Day, *Heather Davis* 201
64. Damaged Goods, *April Knight* 203
65. The Smell of Love, *Rae Mitchell* 206
66. Click, *Cathi LaMarche* 209
67. Badger Meatloaf, *Mitchell Kyd* 212
68. Clueless, *Gretchen Schiller* 214
69. Field Trip Fiasco, *Ron Kaiser, Jr.* 217
70. My White Christmas Sleigh, *Joyce MacBeth Morehouse* 221
71. I Love Lucy, *Gina Farella Howley* 223

8
~Getting Catty~

72. At the Mall, *Heather Rae Rodin* 228
73. The Great Escape, *Eileen Melia Hession* 231
74. Yoga Cat, *Dena Harris* 235
75. Tommy Bangs Shampoo, *Karla Brown* 238
76. Crazy Cat Lady, *Liane Kupferberg Carter* 241
77. Frankie and Squirrelzilla, *Butch Holcombe* 244
78. Guilty Steps, *Harriet Cooper* 247
79. Trick or Feat, *Janet Ramsdell Rockey* 250
80. A Tale of Two Suckers, *Leslie C. Schneider* 253
81. This Is Who I Am, *Marijo Herndon* 257

9
~Senior Moments~

82. A Dog's Prayer, *Harriet E. Michael* 261
83. Another Mega-Sized Idea, *Ernie Witham* 264
84. The Great Escape, *Mary Lovstad* 267
85. The Reluctant Triathlete, *Brian Staff* 270

86. The Other Toy Story, *Alison Shelton* 274
87. What Goes Up, *Jeanie Jacobson* 277
88. Personal Magnetism, *Linda S. Clare* 281
89. Tunnel of Love, *Marianne Fosnow* 284
90. A Second Chance at Love, *Gwen Daye* 287
91. Road Trip, *Julia M. Toto* 289

❿

~It's All Relative~

92. Catastrophe, *Jody Lebel* 294
93. Papa's Arms, *Del Howison* 298
94. What's so Funny? *Peggy Purser Freeman* 300
95. The Wrinkled One, *Patt Hollinger Pickett* 302
96. A Traditional Norwegian Christmas, *Mark Leiren-Young* 305
97. All's Fair... *Sara Matson* 308
98. Canadian Winters Are Not for Fashionistas,
     Sheri Gammon Dewling 312
99. Glam-ma's Red Christmas Suit, *Francine L. Billingslea* 315
100. Grandparents' Day, *Miriam Hill* 318
101. Manners Mishap, *Stephanie Davenport* 320

Meet Our Contributors 323
Meet Amy Newmark 336
About Chicken Soup for the Soul 338

Introduction

Laughter is the sun that drives winter
from the human face.
~Victor Hugo

When we published our first humor collection last year, it was a roaring success. Our team started reminiscing about the funny stories we've managed to include in *all* our books. We decided to put some of our favorites together in one volume — laugh-out-loud stories that were scattered throughout our past books, the ones that were not specifically identified as "humor" collections.

Our associate publisher D'ette Corona, senior editor Barbara LoMonaco, and I had so much fun revisiting these stories. And now we present them to you, at the end of a pretty stressful twelve months, for your own enjoyment.

If laughter is the best medicine, then this book is your prescription. Turn off the news and spend a few days *not* following current events. Instead, return to the basics — humanity's ability to laugh at itself.

No one is safe from our writers, from spouses, to parents, to children, to friends, to other relatives. And of course, the funniest of all are the stories our contributors tell about their own mishaps and misdeeds. No one is holding anything back.

Chicken Soup for the Soul is often the place you turn to for advice — on positive thinking, forgiveness, gratitude, self-esteem, raising kids, caring for the elderly, etc. This time, we're not providing any of that — this is just plain fun.

There's a special twist to this collection, too. The contributors who wrote these stories have selected several charities they want to support with the royalties from this book. We'll be providing royalties on their behalf to four nonprofits that bring laughter to places where it's most needed — to hospitals and hospices — helping people of all ages who need a reason to smile.

So enjoy the sunshine these stories will bring to the cloudiest of days. And if you have your own funny stories that you'd like to share, visit our website at www.chickensoup.com and click on Submit Your Story. Maybe your own laugh-out-loud story will appear in our next humor collection.

— Amy Newmark —
Author, Editor-in-Chief, and Publisher
Chicken Soup for the Soul
February 8, 2021

Domestic Disasters

A Twin Bath

Childhood is that wonderful time of life when all you
need to do to lose weight is take a bath.
~Author Unknown

y son had screamed his way through six months of life when I declared to my husband, "We need to have our second child now." He thought I was crazy, but I explained that having two babies close together would surely help our situation because the two children would entertain each other. Therefore, there would be less screaming. Less screaming was our immediate goal, so we went forth with "The Plan."

I got pregnant immediately, and as life would have it, twin girls were on the way. My fourteen-month-old son was still screaming when they arrived. We knew they were ours because the girls screamed just as much as our son did. They screamed at each other, they screamed at their new brother, and they screamed at us. My son reacted by screaming. I screamed at my husband, and he gently reminded me of "The Plan." Oh, yes, "The Plan."

We loved our little screamers, and as time passed, the screaming did subside, and they did entertain each other. They entertained each other so much, though, that they were never very interested in my words, especially when they were used to try to put a stop to any of their entertainment. Big people are not nearly as entertaining as little people we learned, and my voice never seemed to penetrate their eardrums. In fact, my constant "Don't, don't, don't…" was met with an immediate need by them to perform the action following the word "don't."

* * *

So here I am one day, home alone with the three. An afternoon bath is needed after the highchair feeding frenzy. The girls are about eighteen months, and my son is two-and-a-half. All three have to be in the bath at the same time because, if not, the free-range child left out of the bath will surely find some furniture to pull down or a ceiling fan to ride. So all three are in the bath, wet and naked. Ding dong! Someone is at the door. I run the ten feet from the bathroom to the door, grab the package from the UPS man and turn to slam the door. However, one of the naked, sudsy little people scampers by my leg, running full speed into the front yard. It's the boy. I run to grab him, yelling, "Don't you run out there!" It takes both my arms to wrangle his slippery little body back to the door. The sudsy twins only hear, "You run out there!" Remember, they are compelled to perform the action after the word "don't." So they, too, slip past me and streak down the street.

Panic sets in. The choices aren't good. Do I run the current wet one into the house, taking my eyes off the twin runaways? I can't lock the door because I'll lock myself out. But if I don't lock it, the initial escapee will reopen the door. I go with Plan B: run after the twins, carrying Offender #1 in my arms.

We are ten houses down the street now, and they are still running, screaming their little naked heads off. I am running after them yelling, "Don't! Don't!" carrying my son like a foamy, kicking football under one arm. I catch up to them. Their twin mind reading goes into action, and they immediately sprint in opposite directions.

Where is everyone? I need help! Please, someone come out of your house and help! Don't you see two streaking twins running by your windows followed by a crazed, wild-eyed mom carrying a naked football?

One girl makes a dash for the street, and I decide to go for that one. I tackle her, but her wet body squirts from my grasp. I do a Jet-Li–style karate move and pin her in between my legs, still holding the squirming boy. I yell a futile, "Don't! Don't!" at the last free child, and she mocks me by running figure eights in a nearby yard.

Then, for some strange reason, the free twin stops running and screaming. A puzzled look takes over her face. All of a sudden, she is contemplative. I see her bend her legs ever so slightly and assume a wider stance. Oh, no. Please, no. But, alas, she uses the yard as her own personal potty, defacing the yard that Stella, the owner, proudly prunes and preens every weekend. Right as this is happening, help arrives in the form of Stella emerging from her front door. Everyone freezes and looks at her. She stares in amazement. The pottying twin continues her "business" on the yard. "Help!" I squeak.

Looking back, I remember Stella watching the kids as I cleaned up her yard with the dog's pooper-scooper. Then she helped me walk all three of my naked hoodlums back to my house. Fortunately, she was also a mom, and she told me stories of her parenting adventures. She assured me that, especially with twins, there would be many more adventures around the corner. Boy, was she right!

—Shannon McCarty—

Hungry Like a Wolf

*Fun fact: Australian Shepherds, unlike Australian
Cattle Dogs, aren't actually Australian; the breed
was developed in the United States.*

My husband Michael has the equivalent of a preschool education when it comes to food preparation. He knows the basics, like how to spread Nutella on rye. His food pairings are imaginative and desperate. He shouldn't be in the kitchen in the same way a color-blind person shouldn't be an art director of a fashion magazine.

Michael does know his way around a refrigerator filled with leftovers though. The key to his survival has always been his prowess at warming up said leftovers in the microwave.

This brings me to the most sacred day of leftovers: Yom Kippur, the holiest day of the year for Jewish people. Many non-Jewish people know it as the annual Jewish observance of fasting. The fast begins at sundown on the night known as Kol Nidre and continues to sunset the next day. There is always an extravagant feast on Kol Nidre before sunset to hold everyone over for twenty-four hours of starvation.

I love all the Jewish holidays because my mother-in-law does the cooking. The agreement we have is that I set the table and she provides the food. This has served us well through the years, and was negotiated on a table napkin one year after an especially challenging cooking experience. As part of the deal, I even get to keep the leftovers.

Notwithstanding the Jewish holiday contract, I am still entrusted with the care and feeding of the entire family and that includes taking care of our Australian Shepherd, Slugger Free Spirit Red Sox Koenig, who does not participate in the Yom Kippur fast.

Slugger is a purebred Aussie, a stunning red merle with a soft coat in shades of white, tan and reddish brown. Unfortunately, as Slugger has aged, he has developed a throat condition. He often gags as if something is caught there. So one September, around the time of Yom Kippur, I tried changing his food from dry pellets to wet food. I hoped it would be less harsh on his throat. So it wouldn't be wasted, I spooned his uneaten moist food into a plastic container and put it in the refrigerator.

As she does every year, that Kol Nidre my mother-in-law brought a complete holiday dinner to my house. We rushed through eating so we could get to temple in time for the evening service. We stuffed chopped liver, brisket, and noodle pudding into plastic containers to be eaten the next day when we would break the fast on Yom Kippur.

That year, as he does each year, Michael fasted the entire day. His ritual is to break the fast at exactly 5:00 p.m., even if the sun has not set. He is fond of saying "It's always sundown somewhere in the world."

While Michael struggled through the last half-hour of his fast, I took Slugger for a walk. When I returned home twenty minutes later, I saw that Michael had pulled a container of leftovers out of the refrigerator. The top was removed from the container and placed next to a box of crackers on the center island in the kitchen. Dry, beige crumbs littered a blue disposable plate. A dirty knife rested on the black granite countertop.

How nice, I thought. Michael has helped himself to some chopped liver.

"How are you doing?" I asked.

No response. He pointed to a mouth full of food.

Michael had moved on from the appetizer portion of the evening to a warmed plate of beef brisket and kugel, which are egg noodles baked in soft cheese and sugar. He was watching a movie with a TV tray in our family room.

I picked up the plastic container to put it back into the refrigerator, but something didn't look right. I took a closer look at the contents. I showed it to Slugger, who raised his nose into the air. Sniff, sniff, and sniff. He licked his chops.

I sniffed the contents, too. I imagined what Slugger must be thinking, "Why is Michael eating my food?"

"Yeah, that's what I'm wondering, too," I said aloud. "But thanks for sharing. You're a good dog."

I wasn't sure what to do next. Should I tell Michael that he had just broken his holiday fast with dog food? Or should I call all the family members on my contact list and tell them the story? After a twenty-four-hour fast, some entertainment is needed.

"What do you think, Slugger?" I said. "Call the relatives? Post the story on Facebook?"

Slugger cocked his head to the side.

"That's what I thought. You're such a bad dog."

I looked at Michael happily enjoying the rest of his dinner. I decided that if the dog food was good enough for Slugger, then it was good enough for my husband. I spooned the rest into Slugger's bowl, grabbed my cell phone and called anyone who would answer the phone. Like food, this was a story best served fresh.

— Tina Koenig —

No Need for Carving

*One of the things that binds us as a family
is a shared sense of humor.*
~Ralph Fiennes

Soon after we married, I told my husband, "I'd like to host the family Christmas dinner."

Well aware of my limited cooking experience, he paused before he asked, "Seriously?"

"If I organize and plan it to a T, it'll be the perfect day."

To ensure success, I called my mother for her traditional holiday recipes. With pen and paper in hand, I dialed her number. Eager to end the initial chitchat, I blurted out my plan. "I'm cooking Christmas dinner for my in-laws." I thought the phone line had been disconnected.

Then I heard her chuckle. "Are you sure?"

When she realized I meant it, she suggested we compile a menu. After we made a list of what to serve, she dictated a detailed grocery list. Pumpkin spice? I had to ask where to find it. Extra cans of turkey broth? I thought it came from the turkey pan. She explained each item to me and after she hung up, I stared at the five pages in my hand. What had I gotten myself into?

When I braved the jam-packed grocery store, the items piled up. At the checkout, my cart looked like a dump truck — filled to the brim and ready to tip.

At home, I arranged ingredients according to each dish. Marshmallows, Karo syrup and brown sugar sat by the canned yams.

Rosemary and sage lay by the package of cornbread dressing mix. Flour and cornstarch were ready for milk and turkey broth. Even the refrigerated items sat in groups.

I'm a detailed person — especially in uncharted territory. My method guaranteed there would be no chaos. And, I certainly needed a plan for this day.

I taped my mother's recipes to the kitchen cabinet doors and assessed what I could prepare ahead of time. I've never enjoyed dinners where the hostess serves the meat at room temperature, the veggies lukewarm and the rolls ten minutes later. Most assuredly, mine wouldn't be one of those. Everything would be ready at exactly the right time.

On Christmas Eve our house buzzed with activity. The smell of pumpkin pie hung in the air. My centerpiece complemented the red-berried holly leaves on the china; my festive mulberry candles waited to be lit, and my evergreen crystal goblets were shiny and bright. I placed the pristine sterling silverware on the just-bought linen napkins that matched the rich maroon tablecloth.

I instructed my husband, "No nibbling the appetizers on the lower refrigerator shelf. You can have the not-so-pretty ones on the top."

Eager for the perfect day, I slept little that night.

Christmas morning arrived with the sound of "Jingle Bells" from the radio alarm. I hit the off button and bounced out of bed… all ready to execute the plan.

"Need help?" My husband opened one eye.

"Nope. I've got it under control. Go back to sleep."

He rolled over and snored before I even shut the bedroom door.

In the hub of activity, I wrapped the seasoned turkey in foil and placed it on its assigned oven rack. A checkmark went on my to-do list. I added torn pieces of dried bread to the crumbled cornbread dressing. Check. Peeled and diced Idaho potatoes. Check. I scooped green and black olives into crystal serving bowls. Stuffed celery sticks lined a crystal dish. Check, check.

At the assigned times, I added the broth to the dressing and placed the pan below the already-cooked turkey. The yams had enough brown sugar to zap us into a sugar high. Every dish adhered to my schedule.

As guests arrived, I calculated where their food items fit into my plan. In the last thirty minutes before mealtime, I hummed as I finished the final tasks. Whipped potatoes steamed from their pan. Toasty brown marshmallows melted over the yams. I removed the foil from the roasting pan and slid the turkey back in the oven to turn it golden brown. My table would look like the delicious dinner pictured in the Poultry section of the *Betty Crocker Cookbook*.

I sighed and stepped away from the kitchen cabinet and then went to the living room to chat with guests while the turkey browned. From across the room, my husband winked at me. Everything was right with the world.

Then it happened.

A loud bang from the direction of the kitchen made everyone jump. My mother-in-law paled. Had she been shot? No, no, there was no blood.

"Sounded like a gunshot to me." My brother-in-law offered his two cents as he looked out of the street-side windows.

Nervous laughter and murmurs filled the room.

In the dining room, I surveyed the candles. Had a votive glass become too hot and burst? No, there was no evidence.

My husband took a few steps toward me. "I think it came from the kitchen."

We headed to the kitchen with a gaggle of relatives trailing behind.

Every dish looked exactly as I'd left it a few minutes earlier. I raised the lid on the stovetop items to take a peek. No one saw anything amiss.

"Who knows what it was." I shrugged my shoulders and erased my worry.

As we stood in front of the oven, I decided to baste the turkey once more. Ready for my in-laws to be awed, I reached for the hot pads and opened the oven door. Like synchronized swimmers, each of us leaned back as an extraordinary amount of steam rose.

And the source of explosion made itself known.

Pieces of turkey greeted me — on the inside of the door, on the sides of the oven, and… in the dressing. The marshmallow-topped yams were dotted with brown turkey pieces. The legs hung by thin sinews. More skin draped over the edge of the roasting pan. Parts unknown dripped from the oven ceiling and turkey skin sizzled on the bottom burner.

There was absolute silence — until I couldn't help myself. I laughed. Everyone joined in. Once the cackling subsided, I placed the roasting pan on a trivet. My mother-in-law peered at the bird's remains, patted my back and sighed.

My shoulders drooped as I bit my lip. Now they all knew my cooking skills were limited. My husband stopped laughing and wiped tears from his eyes. Then, he noticed the look on my face.

He kissed my cheek and returned the electric knife to its box. "Folks, let's head back to the living area and give my wife some space." As he herded the chuckling clan toward the living room, I mouthed a "thank you." Tears stung my eyes.

I surveyed the damage. Pieces of turkey were everywhere. I grabbed a fork and popped a piece in my mouth. Hmm… tasty. A strutting Tom turkey decorated a large platter, a gift from my mother-in-law. I smirked as I covered it with salvaged pieces from the exploded bird. The veggies were scooped to bowls, the gravy bowl filled to the brim, and rolls nestled in a basket.

When I announced "time to eat" wide eyes greeted me. Although hesitant, everyone gathered at the table and devoured the dinner. We all agreed exploded turkey tasted as good as well-carved slices.

The upside of the explosion? Whenever there's a family gathering, no one lets me near the oven.

— Gail Molsbee Morris —

A Plague of Joy

Joy doesn't just happen. I have to pursue it.
~Elizabeth Myers

I t was Friday at the end of a really, really long week. Mike and I were having friends over for dinner and a glass or two of wine — definitely two.

Just before I got home, Mike texted me to say that he had to stay late at work. I was now on my own to get everything ready for the night. Already running late myself, I could feel my frustration mounting as I drove to pick up Haydn and Michael from school. I rushed them into the car and informed them that we were making a few stops before heading home, and that they needed to help me tidy the house.

Both of them started whining immediately. I turned and pointed a threatening finger at them, giving them fair warning that I was not in the mood to listen. They crossed their arms and sulked. Michael even whispered under his breath, "This sucks!" For the next hour, I dragged the boys from one place to the next. The more I needed them to hurry, the more distracted and silly they became. I told them to cut it out, but they didn't seem to listen that day. My patience was wearing thin.

Just as we finished our last errand, the boys reminded me that we needed to stop at the pet store to pick up crickets for their bearded dragon lizards. "You promised," they said. And they were right. I had. But in the frenzy of the day, I'd completely forgotten. "Fine, but we need to be fast," I said, and we raced to the pet shop.

Fifteen minutes later, we were back in the car with some new passengers: one hundred live crickets in a clear plastic bag. I pulled into the driveway with only forty-five minutes left to unpack the car, clean the house, and set the table before my guests arrived. How would I make it?

I started barking orders at the boys like a drill sergeant, but they were focused on pouring the crickets from the plastic bag into the top of their little cricket-keeper thing.

My annoyance started to soar, and I yelled at them to hurry up, but to do so carefully.

I don't really know how it happened, but the next time I looked up, one hundred crickets were jumping all over my kitchen, chirping chaotically.

I screamed and scrambled up onto a chair to get away from them. My frustration exploded, and rage suddenly gripped my senses. I could feel myself about to start yelling in a way I rarely do.

But then the most amazing thing happened.

As I watched my two sweet boys try frantically to capture the crickets, it felt like time slowed down, and I saw the situation clearly for the first time. They were running around like lunatics, screaming with laughter.

It was pure joy, and it was an amazing thing to watch.

In that split second, I realized I had two choices. I could continue feeling annoyed and angry, or I could let go and enjoy this ridiculous moment for what it was.

I chose joy.

Laughing uncontrollably, I jumped off the chair and started chasing crickets with the boys. They were everywhere! Every time we tried to put a cricket into the keeper, another one would jump out. It was like a comedy routine. We squealed with excitement and pretty much had the time of our lives. The clock was still ticking… but we didn't care.

It took us about fifteen minutes to get all of the little guys into their box. Once we were done, my boys enthusiastically helped me scramble to get ready for the dinner. It became a game to see if we could make it in time. We were all in such a fabulous mood.

Mike got home with five minutes to spare. Anticipating the cold shoulder for leaving me to deal with everything myself, he was pleasantly surprised to hear about our crazy cricket adventure. Our guests arrived. We had a fabulous dinner party, and the boys helped me tell them all about our "peculiar plague problem." For weeks after, I could still hear chirping from some crickets that had evaded capture. It always made me giggle.

That moment is a constant reminder to me that I should never let frustration keep me from enjoying life. Things go wrong, and there's nothing we can do about that. But we do have the power to decide how we're going to react to things.

Next time you feel negativity bubble up inside, just chill, take a few deep breaths, and try to think of something that makes you happy. You'll find something if you try. Wouldn't you rather laugh than lose it? Choose joy.

— Heidi Allen —

Confessions of a Lunch Maker

*I come from a family where gravy
is considered a beverage.*
~Erma Bombeck

According to my mother, my generation has it easy. She's referring to bread machines, microwave ovens, smartphones, Internet banking... the list is endless. But I can stop her cold with two words: school lunches.

When I was a kid, she made me a peanut butter and strawberry jam sandwich. On white bread. And tossed it in a brown paper bag with an apple. That was it. Simple, simple times.

My daughter uses brown paper bags to make hand puppets. Lunch bags come with insulation, pockets, zippers, water bottles, mini ice packs and a matching thermos. Peanut butter is banned in most schools, and white bread is looked upon as a nutritional wasteland. That leaves the apple. And that's precisely what my children do: leave the apple. But I keep sending the apple. No mother worth her minivan sends her child to school without fresh fruit for the teacher to see. (Tip: An apple can go back and forth for a couple of weeks before it bruises, rots and needs replacement. A banana, on the other hand, has no longevity.)

Of course, every September I hope it will be different. I approach a fresh year of lunchmaking with a fist-full of "kid-proven" recipes torn from newspapers and magazines. I vow to buy breads with flax seeds and ancient grains, certain that if I use a cookie cutter to shape them like a star or a horse, the kids won't notice the lack of fluffy white dough. But within days, the sandwiches begin returning.

It's important to me that all the food groups are represented, but I confess, as the school year progresses, each group is open to interpretation. For example, by Christmas I consider chocolate-covered raisins a fruit. By April, so are those rubbery "fruit" chews. By spring, I'm so worn out I consider cheddar popcorn both a vegetable and a dairy product.

I have one disguised vegetable trick that has yet to fail me, but it takes great commitment. The kids know it as "chocolate bread." It's actually a low-fat zucchini loaf made with applesauce. Cocoa and a half-cup of mini chocolate chips are its cover. The most important step is grating the zucchini so fine that it isn't visible to the naked eye when baked. I grate late at night when my children are sleeping.

I shared this recipe with a friend. Her children loved it, but the late-night grating wore her down. She became careless and grated while they were still up. I think it was a cry for help. She was caught, and her kids never touched "chocolate bread" again. She tried to act disappointed, but I think she was secretly glad to have her life back.

I soldier on. So, Mom, have a little sympathy. I may bank in my bathrobe, but at night as you sleep, I'm bleary-eyed in the kitchen, silently grating zucchini.

— Kim Reynolds —

6

The Wrong Bag

Every survival kit should include a sense of humor.
~Author Unknown

stumbled to the kitchen. It was way too early to be up after a long night writing. I filled the coffeepot with water and tilted the coffee bag over the filter. Nothing! I opened the bag wider and looked inside. Empty!

"Mom!" Lee called from the other room. "Mom?" I rummaged in the cabinets. There was another bag of coffee somewhere.

"Mom?" He walked into the kitchen. "Didn't you hear me calling you?"

"Yeah," I answered. "Whatever it is, just hang on a second. I'm trying to find some coffee." I checked the pantry. No coffee there either.

"This is important," Lee demanded. I paused and looked at him. "You have to make my lunch today. I'm going on a field trip to the courthouse." Oh, no! Was that today?

"Okay, I'll take care of it." I gave up the search for coffee and started looking for things to put in a bag lunch. We were out of lunchmeat so he got a PB&J sandwich minus the jelly because we were out of that too. There hadn't been time to go to the grocery store yet this week.

Ring! Ring! I snatched up the phone with one hand while searching for the Hostess cupcake hidden behind the canned veggies with the other. "Hello."

"I'm not going to be able to help decorate for Karen's bachelorette party tonight," my friend Amie said. "I have a job interview but I have all the decorations. Can you come by and get them before you take the kids to school?" Just great! As if I didn't already have enough to do. But I agreed. What else could I do?

I hung up and looked with longing at the cupcake in my hand. I'd hidden it away for a day like this, when things were crazy and I needed the comfort of chocolate. Sighing, I put it next to the sandwich I'd made for Lee. I didn't have any chips or anything to put in his lunch, so the least I could do was give him dessert.

Cody came running in. "Mom, I can't find my T-ball uniform."

"It's in the dryer." I looked over at my middle son, Rob, calmly eating his cereal. He was always so calm while the rest of us ran around like chickens with our heads cut off. I grabbed a Walmart bag from under the sink and handed it to him. "Would you grab Cody's uniform for me?"

I grabbed another Walmart bag and started packing Lee's lunch, glancing at the clock. We were running late and Cody and Lee hadn't eaten yet. I popped two waffles in the toaster; they could eat on the way. I rushed everyone out to the car and started to back up.

"Wait," Lee yelled. "I forgot my homework." I watched the minutes tick by while we waited for him to find it. He got back in and I pulled out of the driveway heading to Amie's.

"Don't forget Chelsea," Rob said from the back. Shoot! I forgot I was supposed to give the girl down the street a ride. I pulled back in and went the other way. We were really running late now. At least Amie was waiting outside with the decorations when we got to her house.

I was lost in thought, trying to figure out how I was going to do everything that needed to be done. Drop Chelsea and the older boys off at school, spend the day volunteering in Cody's classroom, pay bills at lunch, pick the boys up after school, take Cody to his T-ball game, drop the kids off at my mom's house, and decorate for Karen's party before it started at 7:00.

"Mom," Lee interrupted my thoughts. "You missed the school."

I turned around in the nearest driveway. "Sorry, guys. My mind isn't working very well today. I haven't had my coffee."

"You know coffee is a drug, don't you?" Chelsea asked. "My class went on our field trip to the courthouse yesterday and the policeman told us all about drugs."

I pulled in the parking lot. "That may be," I answered, handing Lee his lunch. "But I could sure use some."

Thankfully, the staff lounge at Cody's school had coffee made. I sipped a cup and felt my mind begin to work again.

The morning passed without incident. At lunch, I ran out to drop off some bills and order a burger from McDonald's. While waiting in the drive-thru, I noticed the bag of decorations sitting on the floor. Curious to see what naughty items Amie had picked out for the bachelorette party, I opened it. The first thing I saw was the cupcake. Oh no! I had given Lee the wrong Walmart bag. I glanced at my watch. If I hurried, I might be able to make it before they started eating.

I pulled out of line and rushed to the courthouse. As I parked, I could see Lee's teacher getting the class settled on the courthouse lawn. I grabbed Lee's lunch and ran across the street. Where was he? There! I spotted him talking to a police officer and hurried over.

"My mom does drugs," Lee was saying. "But she ran out this morning and her mind isn't working right." He held his bag up. "That's why I got this instead of my lunch."

He turned the bag upside down and dumped assorted party supplies, many shaped like… man parts… on the ground at the officer's feet. I was standing there mortified, wondering if I could just slip away, when Lee saw me.

"There's my mom right there." I hurried to scoop the stuff off the ground under the watchful eyes of Lee's teacher and the policeman. I could feel my face burning as I mumbled something about a friend's bachelorette party and not having any coffee. I glanced around to see both the teacher and the police officer trying unsuccessfully not to laugh.

Later on I was able to appreciate the humor of the situation but not right then. I was too embarrassed. But I did learn a valuable lesson that day. Always double check the bags to make sure the right things go with the right people. And keep a spare bag of coffee in the pantry.

— Kimber Krochmal —

7

A Bittersweet Victory

Accept the challenges so that you can feel
the exhilaration of victory.
~George S. Patton

I wasn't with Ron the day he spotted the Free Puppies sign. Later he claimed when he almost passed it, our car spontaneously swerved into the gravel driveway and lurched to a stop, flinging grit and tiny pebbles in all directions. That automobile reacted the same way whenever it neared Garage Sale and Yard Sale posters, too.

"You should've seen them, honey," he grinned as he recounted the story. "Those puppies kept climbing and tumbling out of their cardboard box. Each one scampering around the lawn was cuter than the next. Little fuzzy bundles of black and brown rolling around..."

"Oh, I would've loved to have seen that," I interrupted.

Ron nodded and continued. "When I crouched down and called to the pups, one in particular ran all the way across the yard, and practically jumped into my arms. That did it. I told the owner I'd be happy to take that little guy off his hands and give him a good home."

I was thrilled with his decision. The puppy was cute and cuddly. His soft fur was mostly black, with tiny patches of light brown above each eye and on all four legs. I forgot to ask what breed he was, until he grew bigger by the day. At six months old, his paws were almost as big as the palm of my hand. I later discovered he was part Gordon Setter and part "some kind of really big dog."

We agreed to let my then eleven-year-old son, Scott, name our new pup. He chose Rocky and it seemed to fit perfectly.

You know how intelligent adults sometimes do the stupidest things? We lived in a small, two-bedroom apartment on the second floor of an old complex. We both worked full-time and Scott was at school all day. Still, we thought leaving Rocky home alone all those hours during the day was a perfectly okay thing to do. Although he took to paper-training, he became bored as he grew older and searched for things to amuse himself.

The months went by and my daily phone call from Scott became the highlight of the afternoon for my co-workers. I knew every day at 3:15 my phone would ring, and Scott would recite Rocky's activities for the day. I didn't even say hello anymore.

"What did he do today?" I would sigh. The men and women in my office would stop what they were doing. A hush came over the room as they leaned my way and sat perfectly still. As I listened to Scott's account of what happened, my facial expressions would change from shock or surprise to disbelief or anger. On some days I just gasped and snorted.

"He did what?"

"Oh my gosh!"

"Are you kidding me?"

"Can you clean it up?"

"Did you tell him 'bad dog'?"

"Well, close the cabinets."

"Well, close your closet."

"Well, shut the drawers."

Rocky's days continued to be filled with mischief. He had a fondness for standard dog provisions: shoes, newspapers, magazines, tennis balls, pretty much anything else he could find. He even teethed on my lovely bentwood rocker. I wondered and worried how he could eat the things he did and not get sick. He chewed up, and evidently swallowed, chunks of our dilapidated couch, including foam stuffing, fabric, and wood. One day, he managed to dig out our wedding album and chomp on some of the photos, leaving visible bite marks.

In a way I was surprised our downstairs neighbors never complained of noise, but I assumed they worked during the day, too. Eventually, one morning I received the dreaded phone call. It was from my elderly apartment manager.

"Hello, Becky?" I immediately recognized her raspy, smoker's voice.

"Mildred! What's wrong?"

"I think you'd better come home. There's been a lot of racket going on in your apartment, and some people have complained." She coughed and hacked for a while before continuing. "I walked over that way and heard it before I got to your building. Your dog was barking like crazy and it sounded like things were falling and breaking."

"Oh my gosh. I'll get there as soon as I can."

I slammed the phone down, grabbed my purse, and dashed out of the office. "I gotta go. Rocky's in trouble."

I barely remember driving home or pulling into the parking lot. I was too preoccupied with the images floating around in my mind. What could possibly have happened? I jumped out of my car, ran into the building, and dashed up the flight of stairs. It was absolutely quiet, which I hadn't expected.

I hesitated, then silently slid my key into the lock and slowly turned it, afraid of what I might see. As I swung open the door I saw Rocky sprawled on the floor, apparently exhausted from the morning's events. Scattered all around him were pieces of my once beautiful, massive philodendron, missing so many leaves it resembled a vine. Most of the tiny nails that served as a trellis in the wall were also gone. Hopefully, they were mixed in with the many piles of potting soil and greenery.

I stepped inside the apartment and surveyed the damage. Tiptoeing between little mounds of dirt, stems and leaves, I knew my cherished plant would never be the same.

It was so terrible, it was funny, and I couldn't help laughing. That's when Rocky looked up at me with his tired, sad eyes, not even lifting his head. I'm sure he was humiliated, so I bent down to pet him and whispered soothing words.

"Poor baby, Rocky. What happened here today? Did that bad old plant attack you?"

I smiled and he began to wag his tail, slapping it against the hard floor. That's when he stood up and I noticed that not only was the floor covered with dirt, but so was he. It was in his fur. It was in his ears. It was in his nostrils. He began to shake from head to tail and dirt flew in every direction. As he walked over to his water bowl, I bent down to dig through the layers of soil and found some nails. I was fairly sure he hadn't actually swallowed any, but if he did I was sure he'd be okay. We always said he had the stomach of a goat. Nothing made that dog sick.

I should've expected something like this to happen. Often, when Rocky loped past that plant, the sheer movement caused the leaves to flutter and wave. He seemed a bit skittish and occasionally growled at it.

Dog versus defenseless plant. Although Rocky appeared to be the victor he certainly wasn't acting like it. I guess victory isn't that sweet when it's such a dirty fight!

— Becky Lewellen Povich —

Mending Fences

*The husband who doesn't tell his wife everything
probably reasons that what she doesn't
know won't hurt him.*
~Leo J. Burke

I retired to solid ground after twenty years as a captain of small boats, seventy feet or less, but there is still plenty of adventure in my life. I do a pretty good job of always telling the truth to my wife about these adventures, but I've become wise enough to pick my time and place to do so.

It had been five months since the last hurricane. I had been keeping something from Judith and it was time to come clean. I guess I will never learn. Maybe women are right: "Men never learn."

The last hurricane had flattened some sections of the wooden fence between us and our neighbors. It was actually the neighbor's fence. They are friendly neighbors; in fact I helped them put the fence up originally. It had been three days since the storm, this fence was sitting on the ground and I had a problem. I couldn't stand it being on the ground when I had all these tools lying dormant.

Now the catch here is that Judith informed me that I would only be allowed to fix the fence as soon as Rick the neighbor got off work so he could help. "It's not our fence anyway, we don't have to rush. Blah, blah, blah, blah, blah." Now this was Monday and the fence would just helplessly lie there for at least four more days if I had to wait for Rick to be available. TV was awful. I'd finished the old list and Judith had the new list out at the binders. Besides all this she was going to visit her mother and would be leaving me alone all day to look at the fence.

As soon as the car left the driveway I started counting. Through years of testing I have found that if I can count to fifty without seeing the car come back I am pretty sure she didn't forget anything and she is gone, gone, gone. I headed right for the tools.

The major problem was the sections of fence. I could dig the holes, get the old cement and broken posts out, all that stuff. But the fence sections were heavy. Even so, I had it all figured out. The sections weighed about 100 pounds and they were awkward to handle. I planned to stand them on edge and drag them little by little until they were in place.

The project was going great. I set one new post in the front yard and nailed two fence sections back in place. I'd show her a thing or two. Never mind Judith: "You're no spring chicken. You're in your seventies. Wait for Rick." I was halfway there and it wasn't even noon.

I made lunch for myself. Yes, I know some of you may be surprised but I can make lunch for myself.

At 12:15 I was at work in the backyard. I got two posts in and one fence section nailed in place. One section to go and I would be home free. It was only 2:30 p.m. I didn't expect the inspector until 4:00!

I had the last section in place and I noticed it was not level because it was sitting on a rock. When I bent down to pull out the rock a gust of wind blew the fence section in my direction. There I was trying to remove the rock and little by little the fence slowly fell over on top of me. It caught me off balance. It was like slow motion — there was nothing I could do. I didn't have time to get out of the way. There was a tree behind me that made a perfect place for the fence to wedge itself, and to add to this trifecta there were bushes at each end of the section and the fence posts at the base.

I was lying on my back, the fence on top of me. Funny but I remember it being rather comfortable and there were no white lights. That was reassuring! I couldn't get my arms up to push the fence off because it had flattened me against the ground in a spread-eagle position.

Then I started thinking to myself. Judith was going to be home any minute and find me under the fence. The more I thought about this the harder I laughed, to a point where I had to muffle the laughter because I didn't want the neighbors to hear and rat me out to Judith. I lay there peacefully for a few minutes and then I started to squirm. I guess it's something to do with a primal survival thing. Within ten minutes I had wiggled my way out.

Judith came home; the fence was up. I went through all the "What did you do that for" crap. Because of quick thinking on my part I was spared the "I told you so" lecture and certain banishment.

Months went by. Everything was fine. Until about an hour ago.

Yes, I finally told her today. I figured enough time had elapsed. I figured I must be beyond the statute of limitation for this offense.

That's why I am here on the computer. It is quieter here.

I learned a lot today. A statute of limitation does not apply if the "I told you so" lecture is combined with the "can't leave you alone for one minute" lecture. In retrospect, I suppose it's for the better. I had no idea until just an hour ago about the vast number of men who "don't listen" and are squashed by fences in this country every day. Eye opener for me! All in all I made out rather well. There was a moment I thought I would be forced to wear my shirt with the scarlet letters AH embroidered on it.

In a way I'm kind of glad I told her. I needed a reminder of how stupid we men are. We have a tendency to forget this fact. And for the life of me I can't imagine why any man would see a benefit in keeping a secret or lying after reading this. I also now firmly believe that God intentionally planned that men lose their hearing early in life to relieve them from the din.

Now you women may have something going with the "Men never learn" thing, but contrary to your belief, something must be getting through. I know that if I take her coffee in bed tomorrow morning everything I said and did prior to that moment will be forgotten and I will be clear to start anew. I can hardly wait.

— Robert Campbell —

Making a Splash

Whatever you do, wherever you go,
don't be afraid to make a splash.
~Anil Sinha

'**ve** shared my life with three Yorkshire Terriers over the years, but the quirkiest one to ever grace my world has been Sissy, my latest. She has a host of peculiar behaviors, not the least of which is her love of fish. Tuna, cod, and salmon make her prance and go crazy. But it is her agoraphobic tendencies that are the most striking. She's happy to stay home all day and she is always going in to hiding. Sometimes, I feel as though I'm living with a covert CIA operative!

Over the years, Sissy's hiding has become a game and sometimes a battle of wills. I work from home, and there are days when Sissy and I get up and have breakfast together, and I don't see her again until dinner. I've gone on plenty of search missions only to find her hidden under my bed or beneath the skirt of my upholstered sofa. And after ten years of living with Sissy, nothing really surprises me anymore. But one day, when she was still a brand-new pup in my life, she completely floored me.

Sissy and I had battened down the hatches as a raging nor'easter was pummeling our little corner of northern New Jersey. The rains had come and stayed for forty-eight hours, complete with *kabooms* of thunder and zigzags of lightning that tore through dark skies. Sissy didn't like it — not one bit. She was shaking and shivering with anxiety, and I cuddled her five-pound body close… and she let me. The covert operative had turned into Velcro!

When it seemed as though the storm had finally passed, Sissy detached from me long enough so I could finally take a shower. I gathered some clean clothes and towels. Before I flipped on the water in the tub, I decided to keep the bathroom door ajar just in case Sissy wanted to be near me again. I figured she could curl up and wait for me on the throw rug.

I soon regretted that decision as the open door created a draft, something of a wind tunnel. The vinyl shower curtain kept billowing into the tub, sticking to my wet, soapy body. With the handheld showerhead, I doused the curtain, trying to weigh it down so it would adhere to the painted steel of the tub. But the curtain kept ballooning back toward me, which made soaping up and rinsing off quite a challenge.

At one point, Sissy's nose suddenly popped around the curtain. She stood there, quivering and wide-eyed, her beige front paws on the side of the tub.

"Privacy, please. I'll be done in a minute," I told her, yanking the curtain closed.

By the time I was through and finally flipped off the water, a loud rumble of thunder and a bright flash of lightning pierced through the mini-blinds shrouding the bathroom window. I squeezed the water from my hair as a few droplets of hard rain pelted the roof. Then there was a thunderous boom. In the silence that followed, I heard a tiny splash.

What was that? Did I drop something… maybe the bar of soap? I looked, but all was clear.

As I ripped open the curtain and stepped out of the tub, something caught my eye — a splotch of beige and brown rising up from inside the toilet bowl. I did a double take, reaching for my towel and drying my eyes to get a better look. Two triangular shapes, like dorsal fins from baby sharks, rose from inside the toilet.

The pointy ears and wet face of Sissy emerged — a drowned rat with doleful eyes.

I gasped. *Yikes — what a place to hide!*

The dog was shivering. Her pitiable look seemed to telegraph, *Help! Get me outta here!*

Quickly, I reached into the bowl. Drenched, trembling Sissy jumped into my hands as if my fingers were magnets, and she were made of iron.

She licked my wrist and looked up at me with a warm, grateful gaze as I wrapped her in a dry towel and drew her close, feeling as though the storm had bonded us.

When the sun broke through the clouds a little while later, Sissy, her hair blow-dryer soft and smelling squeaky clean from her very first bath, went back to normal — *her* idea of "normal." She scampered away from me and went into seclusion. I didn't see her again for hours.

— Kathleen Gerard —

Pickled Egg Surprise

Pride goeth before destruction,
and a haughty spirit before a fall.
~Proverbs 16:18

My mother-in-law was my biggest competition when it came to cooking. Her homemade cornbread was the perfect combination of crumble and crust — mine was mostly crumble. Her baked ham embellished with pineapples and a can of Coca-Cola was succulent and sweet. Mine was bland and boring. She had that special thing that made food delectable.

My husband and I had only been married a short time when I decided to tackle his favorite snack... pickled eggs. Although I hated the rotten smell, I wanted him to be proud of me. (And I secretly wanted to show my mother-in-law that she wasn't the only one who could make them!)

Armed with a dozen eggs and a special solution, I set them on the kitchen counter.

Later that evening, my husband walked in the door and his eyes grew as big as half dollars. "You made me pickled eggs!" he shouted. "You are the best! I will let them get good and pickled for the big game this Sunday!" He was extremely happy... and so was I. Take that, Mother-in-law!

Soon it was game day and my husband was in the kitchen preparing his snacks. I heard his fork clank against the side of the jar. Then all of a sudden he asked, "Honey, didn't you peel the eggs?"

"Peel them?" I asked bewildered. "Why would I peel them?"

"You know... after you boiled them."

Boil them? At that very moment I cringed. I wanted to sink between the couch cushions and hide forever.

"Sweetheart, you did boil the eggs, didn't you?"

With a red face and a broken spirit, I remained silent. Then he came and wrapped both arms around me — laughing of course — and said, "I love you!"

— Jeannie Dotson —

Happily Ever Laughter

Challenged

You don't love someone for their looks,
or their clothes, or for their fancy cars,
but because they sing a song only you can hear.
~Author Unknown

I was twenty-six, single, and I had just bought my first home. It was my very first "grown-up" purchase. After signing the final paperwork, I decided to stop and visit some friends before heading home to pack.

My friend has never been one for formality, so when I arrived at her house I let myself in. As I came around the corner into her living room, I was a little startled to see a man I had never met sitting on the couch.

As I was introduced to Martin, I could not help but notice that his attire was horribly coordinated. I am no fashion diva by any means, but I had to wonder what this man was thinking when he left his house that morning.

As we sat in the living room engaged in lively conversation, I noticed that Martin was saying very little. My mother had always taught me that talking over people was not only impolite but very rude. So I tried to incorporate him into our conversation. No matter what I said to him, all I got was stammering and stuttering.

Upon hearing him speak, I mistakenly assumed he was mildly developmentally-challenged in some fashion. This would explain his speech difficulty and his clothing. For some reason, when people find themselves in a situation like this, they tend to talk louder and slower. I was no exception and I must have looked like a complete idiot, given what I learned later.

After a few hours I headed home. I had a lot of packing to do, and moving day was coming up fast.

A few days later, I went shopping for some window blinds for my new home. Once I got there, I realized that my standard screwdriver was not going to do the job. So, I headed over to my friend's house to see if I could borrow a cordless screwdriver or drill from her husband.

When I got there, she explained to me it was no problem to borrow the drill, but her husband had not made it home from work yet and she did not know where he kept it. After pausing for a moment, she said that Martin was in the other room and she would see if he had one.

Within a matter of moments he appeared. This time it seemed that his speech problem was far worse than the last time we had met. Also, I could not help but notice that he had made another not-so-great fashion choice. Slowly, he told me that not only did he have a cordless drill, but he would come and help me to hang my blinds… and he would drive.

My stomach twisted, not knowing what to say. Although I firmly believed that a challenged individual should be given the same chances as anyone else, I was not sure of the degree of his disability. Could he handle this task? Could he drive? Should I trust him? After all, he was a complete stranger.

I took a deep breath and agreed. I knew that if my friend was okay with this, he must be up to the challenge. Otherwise, she would have pulled me aside and told me. Hoping for the best, I got into his truck and we headed the short distance to my new home.

When we arrived, Martin pulled a toolbox from his truck and went inside. I must say I was instantly impressed. Before hanging each blind, he measured and marked, taking extreme care not to damage or mar my beautiful new windows.

As he traveled from room to room hanging the blinds, I followed him. By this time I was more than comfortable with his ability. I just felt I should try to engage him in conversation. During this time I began to notice something. Martin spoke clearly whenever his back was to me. It was only during face-to-face conversations that his speech became difficult to understand.

Then it hit me. Martin was not the least bit mentally challenged. Why then, I wondered, did he have difficulty speaking at times?

At the last window, with his back turned, he told me that he and our mutual friends were going out on Friday. He wanted to know if I would like to come along. Without a moment's hesitation I blurted out yes. I surprised even myself, as that was something I never did.

I would never have guessed in a million years that Martin would be my husband when I first met him, but four months later we were married. By the time we said "I do" the stammering and stuttering came far less often. A few months later, I confessed to Martin my first impression of him. He laughed and said he stammered and stuttered only when he looked at me because he thought I was the most beautiful woman he had ever seen and it made him nervous to be around me. My heart melted... again.

You may be wondering... what about the poor fashion choices? Martin is colorblind.

I guess it goes to show you that you cannot always go by first impressions. If I had, I would have missed out on being married to the most wonderful man on the planet for the past eight years.

— Toni-Michelle Nell —

Surviving the Honeymoon

If happiness is the goal — and it should be —
then adventures should be top priority.
~Richard Branson

"We don't have any film left," I called out to my husband Steve, who had stopped the car and was standing in the open door, the better to see down the road.

He shook his head and sputtered, too angry to speak.

I had used the last frame of film a while back to snap a shot of the road sign: "Jupiter — 12 Miles."

"But when would we ever be this close to Jupiter again?" I asked.

"When would we ever be this close to an alligator?" he countered, gesturing to the twelve-foot moving log in the middle of the road.

We were on our honeymoon, and had just spent four days in Orlando. Now we were driving toward the Everglades at midnight, testing the boundaries of our tolerance for nature and for each other.

After the alligator slithered away, Steve opened the trunk to grab a can of mosquito spray. Mosquitoes swirled in the headlight beams, but we had no idea how thick they would be at the campsite.

I heard *pfft* and then an inhuman yowl and *clank* as the can hit the asphalt.

Moments later, Steve reassured me he was okay even though he had just sprayed DEET in his eyes.

When we reached the campground, we found a kiosk still occupied by a ranger. He unrolled the screen and leaned out. "Are you aware that the 'skeeter' is the official bird of the Everglades?" Steve chortled and passed him a few dollars to pay for the campsite.

The ranger paused before offering this tidbit: "When you've had enough, there is a lodge just a mile down from here." He looked us each in the eye before retreating behind the screen.

Steve and I sighed and continued forward, though slowly.

"What an adventure we're having," I said meekly.

"All my life, I've wanted to see the Everglades in person!" Steve crowed. "It took finding the love of my life to give me a chance to come here," he continued. "Thank you for being my wife!"

Then we stopped and opened the door.

An audible buzz immediately surrounded us. We hurried to grab the tarp and the tent, and rushed to unfurl them both at the same time, struggling to coordinate our efforts as the mosquitoes began to dive-bomb, biting our lips and eyelids. We coughed as they flew into our noses and throats. Steve flailed his arms while he tried to assemble the tent, and there was a sickening crack as the main pole broke in half.

"Just unzip! It doesn't matter!" I yelled, cinching my hoodie around my face until only my nose and eyes were open. Moments later, I said, "Never mind! Go back to the car!"

"The car has been compromised!" he shouted back.

Gallantly, he held the tent high while I ducked into safety, pulling in the air mattress and sleeping bags. I fumbled with the pump while Steve jerry-rigged the tent.

Once inside, we didn't even bother with sleeping bags, but simply lay face down on the air mattress.

After a moment of silence, I heard the *hisssss*. My souvenir "Just Married" pin had punctured the mattress. My body was covered in welts from mosquito bites. The tent was ready to collapse on us. I lay quietly next to my new husband, wondering how we had gotten ourselves into this mess.

Once we settled down, we could hear the many sounds of wildlife around us. There were buzzing things and chirping things. We heard the trickle of water not far away, and a kind of sniffing sound that I didn't want to consider. Moonlight cast moving shadows on every side of the tent. And then the growling started.

It was a deep sound, like a belch that sometimes continued into a low moan. Something was walking through the grass around our tent. A twig snapped. I heard breathing outside.

I began to weep softly.

"What's wrong?" Steve whispered.

"Alligators," I answered.

Steve snorted and turned over. "I'm sorry for bringing you here," he spoke to the tent.

"No," I sniffled. "I agreed to come. I wanted to have an adventure for our honeymoon." I said these words, but what I thought about was our wedding vow: "until death do us part." I figured this might be a very short marriage. All through the night, that grunting sound kept me awake, believing a gory death was just on the other side of the flimsy nylon membrane.

In the morning, we opened our eyes to an incredible scene, like a world far beyond earth, full of strange mangrove trees and spindly white herons. Birds with brilliant plumage swooped from branch to branch. There were butterflies in jewel tones, and spider webs glistening in the summer sun.

We cinched up our hoodies and rushed to the car, which we drove out to the visitor center. A professional photographer and his wife were there to walk the wooden path far out into the swamp; they were both dressed in head-to-toe screening, just as we should have been. The ranger advised us to rid our car of mosquitoes by driving at exactly thirty miles per hour, and then opening both doors to let the wind suck them out.

But by far the best feature of the center was a large diorama of Everglades wildlife. We could push a button next to a label to hear that animal and see it light up. Steve was fascinated with this display. He pushed every button, and suddenly I heard it — the growl that had me saying the rosary at 2:00 in the morning.

Steve pulled me close to him and said, "Isn't that the animal you heard last night?"

"Yes, that's it! I guess the alligator light isn't working."

Steve pointed into the corner at a flashing toad.

"Bullfrog," he clarified.

"But… what about the shadow walking by?"

"I dunno," he shrugged. "Raccoon?"

Also not likely to eat us alive, I realized.

When I look back on our honeymoon, I remember the amusement park, the lovely dinners, and piña coladas in the Keys. But I also vividly remember that moment, standing next to Steve, when I realized we had survived an adventure together. If someone ever asks me why in the world I agreed to go to the Everglades in June, I would have to answer, "Why ever not? It was my husband's lifelong wish to see the place in person, and my lifelong wish to stay alive."

— Robin Jankiewicz —

13

The Getaway

Things do not pass for what they are,
but for what they seem. Most things
are judged by their jackets.
~Baltasar Gracián

ith three cops aiming two pistols and a shotgun at my bride, her hands shaking uncontrollably, I came to the realization that my groomsmen were right: Marriage would be tough.

Brittney and I had barely begun our lives together, and we were already targeted as Bonnie and Clyde.

Welcome to the Friday night of our honeymoon.

It all started at 5:00 P.M. on January 18, 2008, when I pulled into the GaPac Community Federal Credit Union parking lot on Alabama and James streets to deposit our wedding checks. I'd been a member there ever since I saved $20 to open an account. I knew most of the tellers, and my aunt was the manager. Every visit was cozy.

Except for this one.

After a smiling teller congratulated me for tying the knot, I strolled out of the bank and plopped into my 2003 yellow Ford Mustang decorated by a buddy of mine in white letters on both doors with "Caleb & Britt."

Then I picked up my bride of six days at Bellis Fair Mall and headed toward northbound Interstate 5. That's when I saw red and blue lights flicker in my rearview mirror.

I went through the mental checklist:

Speedometer? Fine.

Lights? On.

Windshield? No cracks.

Full and bright, the lights now filled my rearview mirror. I pulled over. My journalist instincts kicked in as I began thinking what I'd need: license, registration...

"Put your hands where I can see them!" the officer shouted.

My checklist vaporized as the officer barked: "Roll down the window. Turn off the car. Put the keys on the roof. Open the door — slowly."

I did. All of this has to be a mistake, I told myself.

"Drop to your knees. Hands on head. Crawl backwards."

"Can I ask what this is about?" I said, turning my head toward him.

"Look forward!" the officer snapped.

He then told me, in a Bruce Willis *Die Hard* sort of way, that we'd talk later.

Cuffs clicked into place, and the officer searched me: Pens. Reporter's tape recorder. Gum. Wallet. Cell phone.

Oh, no, not the inside pocket of my jacket, I thought.

Yes, the inside pocket. The officer pulled out a two-by-two-inch booklet: *Sex for Dummies.*

"Bachelor party," I said.

The officer chuckled, and I shared a nervous laugh with him.

So, we're cool, right? I thought.

Ha. No.

I noticed a second officer to my left and two more to my right. And, to my horror, three drawn guns pointed at my eighteen-year-old bride, who had been homeschooled until college, had never lived away from her parents, and still covers her eyes when the flying monkeys appear in *The Wizard of Oz.*

I needed air. Quickly. To yell. To jump high or grow green skin and break the cuffs.

But, instead, I exhaled, and as the air squeezed through my trachea, I said, "This is our honeymoon."

I would like to say it came out clearly with some bite. Truth is, though, I sounded more like Rex in *Toy Story*. I don't like confrontation.

One of the officers escorted me to the hard backseat of a squad car. Over the radio, I heard myself referred to as "suspect" three times. An officer then took my handcuffed Brittney to one of the six other squad cars that had responded.

After some time, an officer opened the door. He told me a bank had been robbed and that the suspect got away in a yellow Mustang... one decorated with white letters on both doors.

I asked him which bank had been robbed, and then told him I had just been to GaPac. The officer reached for his radio and relayed that the "suspect" had just confirmed that he had been at the GaPac Community Federal Credit Union.

"My aunt is the bank manager there," I said.

Hope! I thought. They can't honestly believe I'd rip off my aunt's bank and make a getaway in a YELLOW Mustang, right?

The officer slammed the door shut. My face drooped.

Through the squad car's front window, I watched as a handful of lawmen eased up to my Mustang's trunk with their weapons locked and loaded. They flipped the trunk open and crept back.

Surprise, I thought.

The trunk revealed one duffle, two toiletry bags, and some clothes I had bought from the Aeropostale clearance rack.

The officer opened the door to talk to me again. Before he could say anything, I asked him if he knew an officer friend of mine, whose daughters happened to be the flower girls at my wedding just days ago.

The officer's eyes said he did know him. Then he looked down at a piece of paper in his hand and read me my rights. Shut the door again.

I felt like punching myself in the face.

Finally, after several minutes, I was asked to step out of the squad car. A witness had come from the bank. I walked with an officer past several red and blue lights until he asked me to look toward a particular vehicle with tinted windows.

I stood for about a minute, observing the congested traffic around me. Oh, and the people in the cars. I thought some might nose plant in a ditch, what with their faces plastered to their windows.

Caleb Breakey was one bad dude, I thought.

For a brief time, anyway.

Apparently, "Tinted Windows" was satisfied. An officer unlocked my cuffs, reunited me with my bride, and jotted down our names and dates of birth. He then asked if we had any questions.

I couldn't resist. "Can I take some pictures for our honeymoon?" The officer said to knock myself out, so I grabbed the digital camera out of my car and had a lawman snap three quick photos.

So for all of you folks out there planning an extravagant getaway after your wedding, think twice. Just go deposit your wedding checks at your local bank and walk out.

Who knows? Your bank receipt might show — as mine did with a transaction time of 16:48:43 — that you were within thirty feet of a bank robbery that remains unresolved to this day.

Just make sure you take *Sex for Dummies* out of your inside pocket.

— Caleb Jennings Breakey —

14

Taking His Measure

*The reason they're called the opposite sex
is because every time you think you have
your wife fooled — it's just the opposite.*
~Walter Winchell

For nearly two decades I'd dallied on the dating block, so by the time I got around to saying "I do," the adjectives "blushing" and "young" had expired. I was, at best, a "new" bride. As my friends would attest, I undertook my new wifely duties like any other job I'd ever had — I was going for employee-of-the-year. During my reign as dream wife I pledged to concoct culinary pleasures the likes of which would make Julia (if she were alive) weep; I vowed to out-Martha Martha as the diva of domestic decorating, and finally I swore I'd buy my guy some new drawers — underwear that is. His briefs were the ten-year-old leftovers from the days he'd lived at home and his mother had bought them.

I paused to think about my "for better or worse" vows. Clearly this couldn't extend to underwear so I called my husband at work with that nauseating niceness of newlyweds.

"Hey sweetie, I'm going shopping today — thought I'd get us both a little something. I'm thinking thoooongs," I said in my breathy voice.

"There's two feet of snow on the ground; I don't get it — why flip-flops?"

"Hoooney, panties — you know lacey, naughty, sexy, maybe even peek-a-boo panties."

"Oh yeah, fine, good."

"Is that your calculator clicking in the background? Are you working?"

"Uh yeah, that's where you called me."

"Never mind. Anyway, you need new underwear."

"Yeah, get me some Calvin's size 32 with the extra-large pouch. Gotta run, hon, catchya later."

I jumped on the subway and headed to Saks Fifth Avenue straight to the men's underwear department.

"Where can I find Calvin Klein jockey shorts, please? I'm looking for size 32."

"Right this way."

"Calvin's got some real estate here," I said, trying to sound clever as I eyed the square footage of underwear racks rivaling the size of my New York City apartment. And then the packaging sucked me in with such magnetic force, that a tiny "Oh my" slipped out.

Headless male hunks in skin tones ranging from honey to espresso shamelessly showcased their chiseled six-packs and heaping doses of manliness. It was enough to make a new bride dizzy. But since I was in hot pursuit of the wife-of-the-year crown, I concentrated on the labels. There was the Classic, the Body Brief, the 365 Brief, the Pro Stretch, the Cotton Modal Rib Brief, and the Pro Rib Brief. Why were these starting to sound like entrees at a steak establishment? And the Micro Modal... (yuck, what could that mean?) Anything micro in a pouch couldn't be good. Poor guy. I imagined his agent calling.

"Hey great news. You landed the underwear ad for Calvin — from here on out you'll be known as Micro guy."

While I felt for Micro guy, I was more troubled by not finding the package with the extra-large pouch. The sales associate was nowhere to be found so I whipped out my cell phone and rang up the hubby.

"Hi there, listen I am at Saks and I can't find... oh wait a second, here's the guy...."

"Excuse me, I can't find the ones with the extra-large pouch."

"Rita," he yells across the aisles. "This lady is looking for the extra-large pouch."

With my ear still firmly against the phone's receiver I heard a thud. It sounded like my husband and his phone had crashed to the floor.

"Honey, honey," I said. "Oh my God, are you having a heart attack?"

He was snorting between frantic desperate dying gasps for air and I was picturing my sudden widowhood for which I would be able to use the adjective "young." Finally, with one labored raspy gulp of air, his death rattle changed to the recognizable sound of hysterical laughter. My husband was laughing at me. He was laughing so hard that it finally dawned on me.

"Heh heh, gotta love those new bride jokes," I said, with the heat rising in my cheeks. Then I smoothed my skirt, lifted my chin and stared the clerk straight in his eyes, "Sir, I'll take a week's supply of underwear… just, please, make sure they're the Micros."

— Tsgoyna Tanzman —

The Lottery

Forget the lottery. Bet on yourself instead.
~Brian Koslow

We left the Virgin Islands in 1995. We sold Valkyrie, a very sad time indeed. Many of you have heard the one about "the happiest part having a boat is when you buy it and when you sell it." Well, I must say it depends. We lived on this boat for ten years. It brought us through some pretty dangerous yet unforgettable times. We loved her.

But we decided that we had played enough. We had worked hard but had little to show for it. We were going to find a job driving a boat for someone else. We were going to grow up and go to work!

We stacked all our belongings on a four foot by four foot pallet, had it shrink wrapped, and sent to Florida's east coast. From there we had it trucked to Judith's parents' vacation home in Cape Coral, Florida.

Judith's parents were in Michigan, so we had the house to ourselves. In the evening we would sit down after dinner to watch television. When we were in the islands, we had rabbit ears on a 9-inch black and white TV with two stations available. On a windy night the boat swung around on the mooring so that the picture came and went often. Back in civilization, TV was a great new distraction. This one particular evening the news people were talking about the Florida Lottery that had reached somewhere in the $75 million area. I happen to mention to Judith, just for the sake of conversation, that maybe we should get a ticket. You wouldn't believe the next fifteen to twenty minutes. Judith went into lecture mode.

"My father was a gambler." "He lost everything." "I would never gamble." On and on and on. I listened for a while, finally had enough, and when she was between breaths I made a dash to go buy a newspaper. I mean, give me a break; this was probably the second or third lottery ticket I had ever considered buying in my life. I walked up to the local Circle K convenience store on the corner with my hands over my head repeating "Serenity now," "Serenity Now," and bought the paper. I also bought a lottery ticket. Reflecting back, I guess it was an act of defiance. We men have to fight back once in a while to resist our inevitable fate, while involved with a female, of becoming a nonentity. After completing my little walk I went back home to the TV. The lecture was over and peace had returned.

In the course of the evening, I daringly mentioned that I had bought a lottery ticket. Surprisingly the lecture did not continue, and Judith asked me about the ticket. "What numbers did you get?" "Did you play my birthday?" "Did you play your kids' birthdays?" This was from the person who had just given me a lengthy sermon on gambling.

I finally got tired of all the questions and gave Judith the ticket. She studied it for a few moments, lost interest, and haphazardly threw it on the coffee table. I thought it kind of strange that she hadn't been more careful with the ticket. I took the ticket, folded it and put it under the coaster in which I had my glass of wine. Everything was cool and quiet until the news anchor came on and said the drawing was in ten minutes.

Judith asked if I had the ticket. It was time for a little payback. I said, "You had it last. Remember you asked me for it; what did you do with it?" I love myself sometimes.

Judith looked everywhere; she was obsessed. I, of course, helped her by saying things like, "I can't believe you lost it!" At one point she actually picked up the wine glass and exposed the ticket, but she was in such a frenzy she didn't even notice it. I went to bed. I could still hear her as she watched the drawing on TV, "I think there was a six and a thirty-two."

The next morning I woke early, as usual, and went to the Circle K to get the newspaper. I asked the clerk if he would check to see if my lottery ticket won. It hadn't, as I expected. Then I had a great idea. I bought a new lottery ticket with the winning numbers from the prior night. I put the ticket under the couch knowing that Judith would find it. It was one of the most rewarding moments in my life. She still hasn't forgiven me, but there are no more lectures.

—Robert Campbell—

Put On Something Else

Clothes make the man. Naked people
have little or no influence on society.
~Mark Twain

"You gonna wear that?" is the question I have asked my husband many times over the span of our marriage. After twenty-two years of marriage I find it amazing that the man thinks a pair of clean underwear and a new tie meet the business casual dress code requirements.

Once again the other night, getting ready for an evening out I looked at him and asked, "Are you gonna wear that jacket?"

"I was planning on it. Why? What's wrong with my jacket? You told me you like this jacket."

"Yes, I told you I like the jacket back in 1980 when I met you. Now it's old, worn, faded and small on you; besides I thought we got rid of it — where did you find it?"

"I found it on the floor of my closet. I forgot it was there until today when I decided to clean out my closet rather than listen to your constant nagging one more minute."

"I only nagged you to pick up your underwear since you ran out and the pile on the floor was obstructing the television. It was a choice of doing laundry or running to the store to buy new underwear."

"Oh, that reminds me, next time you go to the store pick me up some underwear."

"You gonna wear those sneakers?"

"I was planning on it; they're my dressy sneakers. Why? What's wrong with my sneakers?"

"Well, since tonight is formal you should wear shoes. I don't remember those sneakers. Where did you get them?"

"I got them under the jacket in the closet."

"Oh."

"Do you think I should give the jacket to our son?"

"No, he won't want it."

"Why won't he want it?"

"Well, for one thing, he has taste. We can bury it tomorrow along with the sneakers. Now go put on a pair of dress shoes."

"I wear dress shoes to work."

"Yes, dear, I know, but you work from home now, remember?"

"Yeah, so now there are boxes of untouched shoes in my closet."

"You gonna wear that tie?"

"I was planning on it. It has some green in it, which matches my shirt. Why? What's wrong with my tie?"

"It has green in it because it's a Christmas tie decorated with Christmas trees."

"Well, you gave me it to wear."

"Yes, at Christmastime, not the middle of July. Put it back and pick out a different tie. Hey, where are you going with the tie?"

"I'm planning to go to the bathroom to hang myself with it before you look at the red socks I'm wearing that you gave me for Valentine's Day."

— Cindy D'Ambroso Argiento —

Perfect

The trouble with, "A place for everything and
everything in its place" is that there's always
more everything than places.
~Elayne Bundy

As a husband, you have to be really careful what you say because your wife might just take you to task—literally—based on nothing more than a simple statement like: "I'm going to golf all day Saturday; then Sunday I'll do whatever you want to do, dear."

"That's what you said," my wife reminded me, handing me a hammer.

"What I meant was we could go to lunch. Grab a crab melt at Moby Dick's out on Stearns Wharf or something. Watch tourists try to park their Hummers in those compact-car-only spots. That's always fun. Maybe someone interesting will show up—like the guy who lets the pigeons eat breadcrumbs off his head. You know he hasn't had dandruff in years? Or hair for that matter. Plus he never needs a hat because of the sunscreen effect of all that guano. Whataya say we check that out? Doesn't that sound like fun?"

"Sure," my wife said.

I smiled at my own resourcefulness.

"Right after we finish redecorating the house."

This confirms one of my many profound theories about married life. See, I believe that if a wife only had one wall and one thing to hang on it, she'd still want to rearrange it on a regular basis. It's in the genes. This differs from most guys I know who would only take down a piece of their art to put new batteries in it so the word "cerveza" would light up again.

"Why am I moving this painting that looked 'perfect' over the fireplace — your word, not mine — just a few months ago?"

"Because it's summer and this will look much nicer up there."

"You want to put a blanket over the fireplace?"

"It's not a blanket. It's a handmade Pennsylvania Dutch quilt. It's art."

"Taxidermy is art, too. Why don't we get a moose head? We wouldn't have to move it from season to season, just decorate it with different hats and funny signs and stuff."

I waited for the accolades of approval. Instead my wife handed me a curtain rod and I began my long ascent up the stepladder.

Did I mention the fact that we have cathedral ceilings? I believe these too were invented by wives, for wives. Because no guy in his right mind, who knows he is eventually going to have to repaint his "kingdom," wants ceilings that soar to the nosebleed section.

"Higher," my wife said.

"I'm already standing on the step that says do not go above this step. What if the home repair police show up and cart me off to homeowner's jail? Then where will you be? Huh?"

"Higher," she said again.

I took another step up, cursing the existence of Pennsylvania Dutch culture on the way. "Oh look, an eagle's nest," I said.

I looked down. My wife looked like an ant.

"Perfect," she yelled.

It took about fifteen minutes to get the blanket — excuse me, art quilt — perfectly straight, then another fifteen minutes to put the painting that had been over the fireplace over the couch.

"Left. No, right. No, left. No, right."

"You know," I said. "If you ever want to try a different career. You'd have a real future leading parades."

"That's funny. You should write humor."

I thought I noted a bit of sarcasm in that statement, but before I could respond, she said: "Okay, now all we need to do is take the two landscapes that were over the couch and put them in the dining room and take the watercolor that was in the dining room and put that in the guest room and then take the photos that were in the guest room and put them in the hall and then..."

Impossible as it must seem, I finally did get this all done. And, after a few minutes of agonizing scrutiny, my wife smiled and said: "Perfect."

I sighed in relief.

That's when the front door opened and my stepdaughter Christy walked in.

"What's that?" my wife asked.

Christy — the artist/troublemaker — held up her brand-new oil painting.

"Boats!" my wife exclaimed. "I love boats. It's going to look perfect over..."

"Don't say it," I begged.

"... the fireplace," she finished.

In my next life, I'm going to be the pigeon guy.

— Ernie Witham —

18

Social Secretary

Wisdom doesn't necessarily come with age.
Sometimes age just shows up all by itself.
~Tom Wilson

n my classroom, I have students as Class Council President, Vice President, and Ambassador. While I complete the morning tasks that frustrate so many teachers, the Class Council members set up the computers, run books to the library, and turn in any notes to the office and the nurse. This leaves me free to quickly handle any paperwork.

Last January, as I was completing my attendance count verification sheet, one of my fourth-grade students approached the desk. Only half listening, I heard him ask, "Mrs. Breen? May I change the calendar?"

I glanced at the small daily calendar and noted it showed the third day of the month. I replied rather impatiently, "No, the calendar is correct."

"But Mrs. Breen, today is the fourth," Jason insisted. Jason is a very reserved student. He was finally beginning to trust me with his thoughts.

"Honey, the fourth is my husband's birthday and I'd remember that. It's tomorrow. Now, have a seat please." And I returned to my work.

He insisted and I finally looked at the large classroom calendar. I jumped up from my seat and went over to the calendar as if hoping it would change as I watched it. "Oh no! Oh my stars!" burst from me as I realized he was correct.

A horrified "You-forgot-your husband's-birthday?" statement floated past me from a horrified Jason. He stood looking at me with shock screaming from every pore of his body. With a disgusted and more than a little indignant expression, Jason returned to his desk and began to work on a writing project.

As he was leaving for the afternoon, Jason placed a piece of paper on my desk, gave me a reproachful look, and said not to read it, but to give it to my husband as soon as I got home. The letter read:

Dear Mr. Breen,

I hope you have a delightful dinner tonight. Mrs. Breen COMPLETELY forgot your birthday today until I reminded her of the correct day! She promised she'd take you out for a steak dinner. Happy Birthday.

Sincerely,

Jason

Properly humbled, I shared the letter with my husband and we went out for dinner. Upon returning, my husband wrote a note back to Jason thanking him for reminding me of his special day.

I thought that was the last of this issue until one day, as I was attempting to get the classroom Valentine's Day party underway, with twenty excited fourth-graders making suggestions, the phone began to ring. Our school secretary was asking about the student who had written the "birthday note" to my husband. Confused and thrown off balance, I told her it was Jason. She requested he be sent to the office ASAP.

Upon his arrival in the office, Jason was introduced to my husband Bill, who had brought roses for me. They shook hands and Bill thanked Jason for helping me to remember his birthday, and asked him to deliver the flowers to me.

Jason walked into the classroom with that "You're-going-to-be-so-sorry" look and I knew I had been had by Bill. Jason handed me the flowers and said, "Happy Valentine's Day. Mr. Breen remembered Valentine's Day and I didn't have to tell him." After laughing and thanking him for the delivery, I mentioned that we were going out for dinner again. "That's it?!" Jason said very indignantly. "You did that for his birthday."

I surrendered and am still laughing.

—Ilah Breen—

19

Married to a Metrosexual

We cannot really love anybody
with whom we never laugh.
~Agnes Repplier

still remember vividly my first date with my husband. He showed up on my doorstep wearing a black silk suit with elegant lace-up shoes and took me to see a jazz pianist. Before that, I'd mostly dated sloppy, preppy types clad in faded Izod shirts, whose musical tastes ran to Dire Straits and Warren Zevon. So it was a bit of an adjustment to be seen with a man who openly sported a thumb ring and was known to purchase the odd facial product.

Over time, however (fifteen years to be precise), I've come to terms with the fact that I'm married to a metrosexual. But it hasn't been easy.

Take a recent incident in a sporting goods store. We were on a trip back to New Jersey from our current home in London when my husband decided to buy himself a new outfit for power yoga.

"What do you think?" he asked the proprietor, emerging from the dressing room in a pair of form-fitting yoga pants.

The small, muscular man looked away awkwardly. "I... um... I think those are meant for... the, uh... ladies."

Even my otherwise soigné husband felt sufficiently chagrined that he opted for the less well-fitting Men's Medium over said Women's Large. But not without second-guessing himself the entire next week.

"They did fit better," he kept insisting.

"Was it the panty-liner that got you?" I wanted to ask.

According to Wikipedia, "metrosexual" is "…a neologism generally applied to heterosexual men with a strong concern for their appearance, or whose lifestyle displays attributes stereotypically seen among gay men." In the self-editing spirit of Wikipedia, allow me to offer some empirical data to flesh this definition out.

First: "a strong concern for their appearance." Absolutely. At one point, back when we lived in Chicago, my husband even had a personal shopper. This man — I think his name was Oscar — would leave messages for my husband inviting him to "Men's Night" at the local Marshall Field's. He'd invariably come home with all these tight-fitting ribbed sweaters à la Will of *Will and Grace* (prompting me to question whether Oscar's interest in my husband's look was entirely commercial). And, yes, in case you're wondering, my husband has experimented with cologne (he didn't inhale).

The second defining element of the metrosexual is a taste for the finer things in life. The first time they met, my husband described the wine as "grassy" to my father (who grew up in Newark and was thus more familiar with Pabst than Pinot Noir). More recently, when we were trying to remember the name of a certain *chocolatier* in Paris, my husband told me to go into his Outlook folder and search for the "Dark Chocolate" entry. It goes without saying that we only drink espresso in our home. Indeed, we've been together so long that it didn't strike me as odd when he recently e-mailed me a video about the optimal way to froth milk. And did I mention the yoga?

Finally, the metrosexual has an avowed fondness for gadgets. The $1,200 espresso machine and matching grinder are perhaps the most visible expression of this trait in our home. But my husband is forever reading catalogs from places like Levenger's, rendering us the proud owners of (to list a few): that magical thing that holds your bagel in place while you slice it in half… that essential stand that props your newspaper up so you can read one column at a time… and that miniature razor blade that cuts newspaper clippings without having to use scissors. While emptying our suitcases after our recent forage through Target, I was not at all surprised to discover a device that doubled as an avocado scooper and slicer. Because you never know when you'll need one of those....

To be sure, there are some advantages to having a husband who isn't — in the vernacular of my adopted country — terribly "bloke-ish." For starters, I have my very own live-in fashion consultant. My husband's well-honed Euro-sensibilities mean that whatever I'm wearing is also subject to his critical eye: "You really shouldn't do high-waisted," he'll observe as I come downstairs in a pair of shorts that extends a centimeter above my navel. Or "Oh no! Eggplant is definitely not your color." And though I'm often loathe to admit it, he's invariably right. I think I'm the only woman I know who's shopped for bras with her husband. (The owner of the bra shop thought he was a pervert, but no matter....)

Second, I've also picked up some really useful skills along the way. Formerly a Mr. Coffee kind of gal, I can now tamp an espresso with the best of them. In a city like London, where a cappuccino can easily set you back five bucks, it's highly cost-effective to be able to rival the best brews on High Street. And how many people do you know who can scoop and slice an avocado in one seamless gesture?

Finally, what other guy would be willing to watch all those Merchant and Ivory films with me?

Mostly, however, I revel in the nuances that my husband's unabashed metrosexuality affords. Jung famously suggested that all men harbor an inner feminine figure in their unconscious. I like to think that my children benefit from having a dad who's more in touch than the average Joe with his inner Josephine. My son, in particular, knows that it's okay to play the violin and enjoy museums, and that you don't have to give up those interests just because you also like soccer. And in a world where we make all sorts of gender-based stereotypes — some with profound consequences for public policy — I'm proud to have a husband who defies easy labeling. Finally, how cool is it that more than a decade into our marriage — yoga pants notwithstanding — I still find myself agreeing with the gay office intern who once confided to me that my husband was "hot"?

Would you care for an espresso?

— Delia Lloyd —

20

Husband Instruction Manual

*Why does a woman work ten years to change
a man's habits and then complain
that he's not the man she married?*
~Barbra Streisand

Congratulations on the acquisition of your brand new 2010 husband. You have chosen the best that modern biology has to offer in the way of life partners. While your 2010 husband is built to last a lifetime, these care and handling instructions will help you get the most out of your man.

Laundry instructions: Although we have implemented many improvements in this year's model (e.g. — automatic toilet seat replacement, limited childcare abilities, expectoration and flatulence control), we have not yet perfected an automatic self-laundering option. Thus, you must repeatedly remind your husband to pick up his dirty clothes, sort his laundry by color, and wash appropriate-sized loads. Some owners have found it easier to simply perform these functions themselves.

Dressing instructions: Most husbands come with only two wardrobe options — work and casual. Therefore please ensure that you assist your husband in any clothing purchases in order to avoid nasty fashion surprises. As in past years, the 2010 husband has pre-set fashion preferences which may clash with your taste. To date, we have yet to perfect an acceptable "color sense" module although the deluxe accessory package does include a formalwear option for occasional use. WARNING: Constant wardrobe monitoring is strongly recommended especially on weekends. Repeated exposure to baggy sweatpants and hole-filled T-shirts may void the warranty.

Cooking instructions: If you chose the deluxe accessory package, you can count on your husband to successfully cook meals on his own for many years to come. The standard model, on the other hand, has few kitchen skills and a limited cuisine. Unless you're willing to invest the time necessary to train your husband in the culinary arts, don't expect much beyond making toast and boiling water. However, all models do come equipped with the outdoor barbecue function.

Listening instructions: Despite years of research, we have not yet been able to produce a husband who really listens. Wives are free to urge their spouses to listen and "express their feelings" but we can offer no guarantees that you will achieve any meaningful results. Through persistent effort, some customers have trained their husbands to adopt a semi-satisfying simulated listening posture.

Fitness instructions: Your 2010 husband is properly proportioned and in good shape. However, in order to retain that shape and those proportions, you must insist on a strict regimen of daily exercise and a healthy diet. Failure to keep your husband active and eating properly will often result in a sluggish spouse with a widening waistline and a sagging seat. WARNING: Do not rely on in-home exercise equipment and always ration beer, pizza, and chips carefully.

Romance instructions: Although the listening capabilities of the 2010 husband are limited, he does possess excellent eyesight. Thus, in order to activate the romance function, emphasize visual stimuli. Sophisticated conversational and emotional skills are still not available on the 2010 husband although our genetic engineers hope to have an improved product ready by the next millennium.

LIMITED WARRANTY: Our 2010 husband is guaranteed against defects in workmanship for ninety (90) days. If, for any reason, you wish to return your husband during the warranty period, we will issue a full refund but only if he is returned in his original packaging. After that, you're on your own.

— David Martin —

21

It Takes a Licking

Sleeping together is a euphemism for people,
but tantamount to marriage with cats.
~Marge Percy

My wife Julie hates cats. I use the word "hate" purposefully because she does not simply dislike, she most undoubtedly hates them. I believe what happened early in our relationship contributed to this animosity.

Julie was never fond of cats even though she grew up on a farm where there were cats, but these, she tells me, were outside cats — mousers. These cats would crowd around as she was milking the cows. Some cats would drop down from the rafters and scare her. Others would crowd around her feet hoping to trip her so she would spill some precious cream. At times, some would be bold enough to actually jump into the pail of milk, thus ruining the contents. On those occasions, Julie would then suffer the scorn of her parents who relied on the sale of the milk to make ends meet. So it is with these eyes — cats are mischievous, devilish, downright despicable and the cause of the many ills of the world — that she perceived all cats.

We both lived in the city when we met and were dating for over eight months when we were asked to Julie's sister's acreage to help put up a playground for her kids. I think it was a test to see if I was marriage material. If I could be around the potential in-laws for a day and be coerced into slave labour, then book the church, send out the invitations, and hire a preacher, the wedding was on.

We started at 9:00 a.m. The work was exhausting, as we were building a wooden jungle gym complete with rope ladders, a swinging bridge, a fort, a slide, a couple of swings, and roped monkey bars. By 8:00 p.m. most of the work was finished except for a few minor details that could be completed in an hour or two. But we were too tired to continue and decided we would complete the job the next day. So, with apprehension, Julie agreed to stay the night.

I say apprehension because her sister had a cat — a molly. This was a house cat — a beautiful marbled tabby with spectacular green eyes. It's funny how females tend to engage in competition and quickly establish their territory.

This cat loved me. She hissed at Julie.

As we sat around the supper table, this cat rubbed herself against me, sat on my lap, and purred, all the while glaring at Julie. Julie simply looked at me with disdain as I overtly showed my affection for this pristine feline.

That night Julie and I slept on a pullout couch in the middle of the living room. As I said, we were physically exhausted from the day's work, so I quickly fell into a deep sleep. And then it happened.

Around 4:00 a.m., when what one dreams and what is real become confused, my subconscious was slowly being tickled in a sensation of wakefulness. In a groggy, sleep-gravelled voice, I murmured my approval. My giddiness woke up Julie, and her clear, succinct, stark voice surprisingly woke me up to sudden awareness.

"In what world do you think I would be licking your armpit?"

I looked over to my right and there was the cat licking my armpit like a child licking ice cream. Apparently, she liked the combination of sweat and Old Spice.

"I thought you were being kinky," I said. "You know, all the fresh country air and…"

"Think again, buddy!"

My dear wife enjoys telling and retelling this story to people every time I suggest we get a cat, or when she wishes to explain to people how weird I am, or how she still married me even after this event, which is a testimony to the strength of her character.

To date, we have been married for twenty-five years. In this time, we have never owned a cat nor do I think will we ever have one. And just for the record, after all these years, my wife has never licked my armpit.

—Manley Fisher—

I Can't Believe I Did That

22

Chicken Soup
for the Soul

Too Hot for Chicken

*Sometimes the laughter in mothering is the recognition
of the ironies and absurdities. Sometimes, though,
it's just pure, unthinking delight.*
~Barbara Schapiro

t was a warm summer morning. I had just finished reading the
grocery specials in the paper. I didn't really need anything for
the next few days. Nothing stuck out as a particularly good deal
except the bonus chicken packs: chicken quarters packed in family sizes. But if I drove over to the store (I reasoned) for just one item,
wouldn't the gas cost cut into the savings?

Five minutes later I was headed to the store on my bike: helmet
on my head, old pack on my back, and five bucks in my pocket. The
temperature seemed to have gone up a little, I noticed as I pedaled the
two miles to the store. Maybe I should bike more. I locked up my bike
and went in. The cold air greeted me pleasantly as I entered the store.
I headed straight back to the meat counter. Sure enough, there was a
stack of chicken family packs just waiting for me. While the price was
fabulous, the packages were a little larger than I had imagined. What
the heck, I thought, as I grabbed a package weighing slightly over ten
pounds, and then headed for the checkout.

"Paper or plastic," the clerk asked. She gave me a whole lot of
change for so much meat and slipped the family pack into a sack, with
most of it sticking out the top.

I headed outside, pleased with my purchase and with visions of fried chicken, chicken tacos, chicken and rice, stir-fry chicken, and chicken casserole in my head. Reality set in when the air hit my face. Not warm air, but really hot air. I realized I didn't have the car, so the chicken would be riding on my back. I stuffed it into my old backpack flat side towards my back as I reasoned with myself. It's only two miles. If I concentrate I will be home in no time.

Actually the partially frozen chicken felt cold against my back but the rest of me was beginning to sweat as the hot air rushed by me. It seemed as long as I didn't stop, I would be okay. The heat wouldn't really bother me. In my head I began to count the number of stop signs left before I got home. A signal light loomed just ahead at the top of the rise. As I approached, it turned yellow so I stopped. I had less than a mile left. I felt pretty good but the sweat seemed to be pouring off me from the heat. I was sticky all over. For a moment at the signal it was quiet. Then I heard a woman start screaming. The light turned green but the cars didn't move. Maybe there had been an accident? I looked behind me even though I never heard any cars crunch.

What I saw was a small herd of people coming up the road towards to me. There was a man in a suit, a woman with a beach towel, and a few others. I heard someone yell, "I'm a nurse." I looked around again and still, no visible accident. Moving faster, this herd of folks started talking loudly in my direction.

"Are you alright? We're here to help."

Who are they talking to, I wondered?

Someone put a hand on my handlebar as if to steady my bike. Another took my hand and looked me in the eye.

"Can we help you?" they all asked. I had no idea what was wrong. Out of the corner of my eye, I saw traffic stopping and piling up. Over the heads of the people now surrounding me, I saw someone directing traffic. I was baffled!

"No!" I told this little bunch of folks. "I'm fine!" It was their turn to look puzzled.

Someone spoke up. "Well, you are bleeding all over! Why don't you get off your bike and take off your backpack?"

I got off my bike and moved toward the side of the road. Willing hands held my bike and helped me get my backpack off.

"Were you in an accident? Were you stabbed?" I was peppered with strange questions.

Who are these people and what do they want from me?

Then I looked down at my backpack, sitting now on the white concrete strip of road. There was a red ring around it! I realized my arms and legs also had blood on them. I pointed to the backpack as I started to laugh — so hard I could barely talk.

"It's my chicken," I told the startled group of people.

They opened my backpack not knowing what to expect. And they found ten pounds of now seriously thawing chicken parts, which had leaked through the paper sack, through my backpack and all over me.

I looked like an accident victim. There was chicken blood all over my arms and legs — everywhere I looked.

Suddenly, everyone was laughing out of relief. Eventually, the guy directing traffic yelled "She's OKAY!" and motioned the cars through the green light. The lady with the beach towel handed the towel to me. A couple in the crowd told me they had followed me for a quarter mile thinking I would collapse.

All of a sudden I realized how hot it was! All this for cheap chicken!

Eventually I got home, showered and started supper. As my gang gathered around the table, everyone was talking about their day. Someone piped up, "I thought we were having chicken tonight?"

I smiled, not yet ready to share my adventure. "Perhaps you just misunderstood," I said. "It's just too hot for chicken today!"

— Pamela Gilsenan —

23

Incident at Elk Lake

*I think the next best thing to solving a problem
is finding some humor in it.*
~Frank A. Clark

double-checked my reflection as I waited for my date to arrive on that bright Sunday afternoon in May 1989. I'd worked hard to put together just the right outfit: a pretty scarf, crisp white blouse, neatly ironed capris, and new leather flats. At eighteen years old, I was still self-conscious about my fashion sense, but what I saw in the mirror reassured me.

My date arrived and held open the passenger door of his sports car. Our plan was to go for a drive in the country just north of Victoria, British Columbia, and then to find a little restaurant to have afternoon tea. We chatted comfortably as we cruised down the Pat Bay Highway.

"Look," I said, as I spied the sign for Elk/Beaver Lake Regional Park. Neither of us had ever been to the park, and we decided on impulse to check it out. The beach was packed thanks to the beautiful weather, but we managed to find a parking place. A pleasant trail took us away from the noise, first through a forest, then briefly past a residential area, and finally alongside a series of small ponds. We'd been walking for about twenty minutes when, for the sake of my new shoes, I suggested it was time to head back. Instead of simply turning around, however, we decided that we would explore the faint path that led through the field on our right, in the hope that it would let us make a circuit around the far side of the ponds.

To our frustration, the "path" petered out quickly. But we could see water through the bushes in front of us, and we were certain that if we could just get through a few waist-high weeds and brambles, we'd be at the pond. From there, it would be an easy stroll around the shoreline.

The brush was considerably denser than we realized, but the deeper we got, the more determined we were to keep going. We were convinced that the way forward had to be easier than the way back. A good twenty minutes later, we finally reached the water's edge, only to be greeted by an even denser thicket on our left and an unstable bank on our right. To test it, we took a few tentative steps along the shore — and were instantly ankle-deep in oozing muck.

Wiser people probably would have retreated at this point, but we were young and didn't know the meaning of the word "defeat." There were bulrushes in the pond in front of us, but through them we could see freshly mown grass on the far side. It was less than a stone's throw away. We conferred briefly and came up with a plan: All we had to do was leap from one mini-bulrush-island to the next mini-bulrush-island, and in a few hops we'd be across.

There was one problem with this strategy: The bulrush "islands" weren't islands at all — they were floating clumps of vegetation. The first hop put us in slime up to our thighs. A few more awkward leaps, and we were both submerged to our waists.

By now, we were too invested to turn back. We gritted our teeth and pushed on. After several more minutes, we reached the edge of the bulrushes — only to discover that twenty feet of the muddiest water imaginable still separated us from the far shore.

Our moment of reckoning had arrived. We could go back the way we'd come — guaranteeing us another miserable half-hour — or we could commit ourselves fully and dog-paddle across.

We dog-paddled.

If everything we'd suffered so far wasn't bad enough, we had an audience that afternoon: Three men were training their dogs to retrieve decoys from the pond. Later, we learned that the pond was — and still is — an official Retriever training area. Imagine how those men's mouths hung open as two fully dressed young people swam out of the rushes past their dogs and climbed up onto the bank beside them.

My lovely outfit was now covered in brown slime — we were both dripping from the neck down — and we still had to make our way back to the parking lot. We passed a number of people on the trail that afternoon, and not one of them had the nerve to ask us what had happened.

Finally, we reached the parking lot, and my date graciously asked if I wouldn't mind changing into one of the pairs of paper coveralls he just happened to have in his trunk, before getting into his sports car. I took the folded pair he handed me and set out for the women's restroom. But for some incomprehensible reason (given how crowded the beach was that afternoon), the women's restroom was locked, which meant that I had to find a spot in the bushes to wriggle out of my clothes. And if that wasn't bad enough, there was one final humiliation. My date hadn't handed me just any pair of coveralls. The ones he'd given me had been used as part of an astronaut costume the previous Halloween. I had to walk the entire length of the parking lot in a white paper suit that said NASA down the side.

My date and I had only been seeing each other for a few months at this point, and our misadventure at Elk Lake could have been the end of our brief relationship. It wasn't. In spite of the space suit he made me wear, I fell in love with my fellow dog-paddler that afternoon. I can still remember the precise moment it happened — as I was swimming through the slime beside him. *This is the one,* I thought. He had an appetite for adventure and a great sense of humour. We climbed into his car that afternoon, and we both laughed until we were in tears.

I married Bern the following summer, at the tender age of nineteen. It's been twenty-eight years since our impromptu swim in a Retriever pond, but five kids, three grandchildren, and many adventures later, we're still laughing.

— Rachel Dunstan Muller —

24

The Scam

*It's important to our friends to believe that we are
unreservedly frank with them, and important
to the friendship that we are not.*
~Mignon McLaughlin, The Neurotic's Notebook

The dinner party was set for Saturday night. I was busy all
week preparing the menu, shopping, cleaning, and cooking.
There would only be four of us at this dinner but you'd have
thought that I was preparing for royalty. The reason? Our very
good friends were coming to dinner and we wanted everything to be
perfect. What better way to show people you love them than with the
food on your table?

We do love our friends very much, but they have one habit that
drives us crazy. They think they are coffee connoisseurs, and they
don't hesitate to inform you of that fact. Over and over and over again.
They talk about this new bean and that new growing area, coffee cups
versus mugs, black versus cream and sugar, various brands of coffee
makers, etc., etc., etc. You get the idea. And we tolerate it. But just
because you tolerate your friends' behavior doesn't mean you can't try
to fool them. My husband Frank and I were planning to pull off the
scam of the century.

Our friends arrived on time and we had some wine and appetizers out on the patio. Then it was time to move inside for dinner. The
table looked beautiful and, if I do say so myself, the food didn't taste
bad either. We finished dinner and soon it was time for coffee and

dessert. I excused myself from the table to go into the kitchen and make the coffee.

Now it began. Frank knew what he had to do. He had to keep our friends occupied so that they wouldn't come into the kitchen. If they did, the whole thing would be ruined. And he did a great job; I could hear lots of talking and laughing going on in the dining room.

I was nervous. Would our scam work? Frank and I can be pretty devious when we work together, but our friends were coffee experts and Frank and I were not. We liked good coffee and drank it every day but, according to our friends, we just didn't really understand all of the finer points and techniques that go into making a really good cup of coffee. They always offered to bring and make the coffee when they came to our house for a meal. I could have been insulted by their offer, but instead I decided to put their taste buds to the test.

I made lots of noise while preparing the coffee. I hoped that our friends would think that all the noise meant better coffee. I turned on the coffee bean grinder that I had bought especially for this scam. Boy, does it make a lot of noise! Of course, they wouldn't be able to tell that I had put rice in the grinder rather than coffee beans. The noise level would be the same. Then I put a fresh coffee filter in the coffeemaker, added the filtered water, and very, very carefully counted out the number of scoops of coffee I needed for twelve cups. Twelve cups of instant coffee, that is! From a jar. No beans to be seen.

Now you have to understand that as far as our friends were concerned, to drink instant coffee is a terrible, horrible sin. They would never, ever do it. It would be like talking back to your mother, or worse! They would rather drink nothing than drink instant. They said it tasted terrible. They said they always knew when they were served instant coffee. No one could fool them. And they were always talking about this bean or that bean from this country or that country. Frank and I were sick of it. Tonight, we would test their knowledge. Their special coffee this evening would be made from "instant" beans!

Time to serve. I took a deep breath and entered the dining room carrying the china cups and saucers, and a silver coffee urn on a silver tray. Presentation is everything. They didn't take cream, sweetener or sugar. Nothing would hide the flavor of the beans. I set the tray down on the table and poured coffee for everyone in grand style. They sniffed, they swirled, they sipped, and then they sighed. Yummy, they said. Absolutely delicious. Could they have a second cup? And then maybe just a little more?

Of course.

They complimented me over and over again and said that finally I had learned how to make really good coffee. They said it was obvious that the beans I had chosen had made all the difference. I thanked them and tried not to look at Frank. They asked which beans I used. I told them that it was a secret blend of various beans that a friend had suggested and I wasn't able to divulge the exact combination.

After they left, Frank and I had another cup of my fabulous "secret blend" coffee and just laughed and laughed. Both Frank and I had done our parts and we had pulled off the scam of the century. Our coffee connoisseur friends never guessed that they were drinking instant coffee. And we never, ever told them — it remains our little secret. To this day they still talk about the delicious coffee that I made for them a few years ago. When I get up enough nerve, I am thinking of trying the experiment again, but this time I think I will make... instant decaf!

— Barbara LoMonaco —

25

Chicken Soup for the Soul

The Art of Parenting

Don't worry that children never listen to you;
worry that they are always watching you.
~Robert Fulghum

N o one teaches us the art of parenting. Why aren't classes required? Why aren't we required to pass some kind of test to get a license to be parents? Certainly I wasn't prepared for this most important of all jobs.

After four children, though, I felt like I had a handle on it.

Or I did, until our nine-year-old son Robbie needed to complete a cultural arts requirement to earn an arrow point for Cub Scouts.

To appreciate the enormity of this, one needs to understand our family. We are not cultural arts people. My husband and three older children breathe sports. Football. Baseball. Soccer. Planning a cultural arts excursion for my crew took creativity and a large dose of courage.

After I presented Robbie with several possibilities, he decided to visit the local museum.

I loaded our four children in the car, placing the one-year-old in his car seat and strapping the other children in seatbelts.

"Remember," I told Robbie, "in order for me to sign off on this, you need to look at every exhibit. No slacking."

"Do we all have to go?" our daughter whined.

"Yes," I answered in my best mother-of-the-year voice. "This is supposed to be a family activity."

We arrived at the museum, and I congratulated myself on arranging this field trip, a nice alternative to the many sporting events we normally attended. I paid the entrance fees and walked in with four children in tow.

My heart dropped to my stomach, which was already doing an uneasy roll, as I gazed around the room.

I had neglected to find out what the museum was currently displaying: nudes. Of all kinds. In every shape and size. Oil nudes. Watercolor nudes. Clay nudes. Porcelain nudes. Bronze nudes.

One painting of a woman, with an improbable third breast placed in the center of the belly, caught Robbie's attention.

"Mom, is that her belly button?" Robbie whispered.

I could only shake my head helplessly.

True to my edict, we gazed at every exhibit.

An hour and forty-five minutes later, we trooped back to the car, where we repeated the process of car seats and seatbelts.

At home, I put the baby down for a nap, gave everyone a snack, and turned to Robbie. "Bring me your Cub Scout book and I'll sign off on the requirement."

Later that night, I recounted the adventure to my husband. "Nudes," I said. "Hundreds of nudes. Fat nudes. Skinny nudes. And we looked at all of them. Every single one."

"You're a good mother," he said. Wisely, he turned what sounded like laughter into a cough, but I caught the twinkle in his eyes.

I threw a pillow at him but decided he was right. I was a good mother.

Parenting. Definitely an art, not a science.

— Jane M. Choate —

26

The Moonlit Kayak

*There's nothing more addictive or incredible in life
than reinventing yourself and allowing yourself
to be different every day.*
~Thalia

A few months ago, I met a handsome doctor on a business trip. He was visiting Miami and wanted a tropical, outdoorsy date. I am a chunky, short redhead who considers shopping at a bargain store to be exercise. If I'm feeling exceptionally motivated, I park far away from the entrance.

"You have to do something exciting. Get out of your comfort zone. He wants a tropical outdoors adventure. *Bienvenido a Miami, baby!*" my sister said when asked for advice.

"How about going to Pollo Tropical for dinner? We can sit on the patio with a bowl of *tostones*," I replied. "In this heat, I think that is tropical enough."

Ignoring me, she went on. "Go camping or play beach volleyball or hiking or… kayaking! That's it! Kayaking! My co-worker just went full-moon kayaking and says it was very romantic. I can get you the information." Sis reached for her phone.

"Let's see — outdoors, exercise, water, mosquitoes, alligators — it is so *not* going to happen," I declared with certainty.

The next day, my sister and I were wandering in a gigantic mall trying to locate a sporty outfit that would make me look like I kayaked all the time. Apparently, I also needed (pretty) waterproof shoes. Isn't *pretty waterproof* shoes an oxymoron?

I picked up Dr. Jack at his hotel. I was wearing some kind of elastic black sport shirt with cranberry-colored shorts. On my feet were ridiculously expensive, pink plastic Mary Janes that my sister and I found at the Crocs store. *Fifty dollars for plastic shoes. This guy better be an awesome date,* I thought.

The drive out to the bay was wonderful. My companion was charming. The conversation flowed with ease. We arrived at Oleta River State Park and found a parking spot near the full-moon kayaking hut. I placed car keys, iPhone, and a lipstick in Ziploc bags inside a small, plastic purse. Of course, I needed lipstick! I *was* on a date after all. We got paddles and life vests, and watched a kayaking safety demonstration. The guide explained the correct way to get in and out of a kayak and how to paddle. The taller you are, he told us, the greater the chance of tipping.

Jack is 6'5". I was starting to lose my cool composure.

About fifty kayaks were bumping into each other as we slowly left the mangroves and paddled toward Biscayne Bay. Every time someone gently hit us, I thought my heart would dive into the water. Orange paddles seemed to miss my face by inches. Alligators probably lurked just below us.

Once in open water, the ride became smooth. I loosened the death grip on my paddle. This was when I first looked around. The moon was breathtaking. Its reflection on the bay reminded me of a poem in Spanish that I heard in high school. The breeze was warm and made my red curls dance around my face. The lights on the tall buildings in the distance twinkled like faraway stars. And a lovely man was sharing a yellow kayak with *me*. Guides everywhere watched over our group. I stopped worrying about tipping over, or being an alligator's Happy Meal, or getting paddled in the face. I was alive and blessed. I was doing something totally uncharacteristic, and I loved every minute of it.

We arrived at a beach with a campfire. Dr. Jack pulled me out of the kayak, smiled and kissed me. It was a fairy tale and, like Cinderella, I was wearing awesome (albeit plastic) shoes. Leaving our kayak and life vests on shore with the others, we sat on the wet sand. Jack and

I kissed, sipped wine, munched on s'mores, and listened to a guitar-playing guide sing "Margaritaville" and "Brown-Eyed Girl" under the light of the full moon. We stayed until the end, and there were only a few kayaks left. Someone took ours, so we grabbed another.

I ended up with a diminutive life vest. I was only able to hook the bottom part of the vest — the one that belonged around my waist — under my breasts. Forget about latching the top. Who needed it to fit anyway? I was not going swimming.

While gliding over the water with the satisfaction that I was now an accomplished outdoors athlete, Jack got cute and rocked the kayak. Someone screamed. Swallowing water, I realized I was the one making the Banshee-like noise. Slow motion. Thoughts crossed my mind. The small life vest could not hold my weight since I was definitely not floating. I was grateful for the Lasik surgery that I had that allowed my eyes to open underwater. I was regretful for the Lasik that made me clearly see the darkness, algae, and muck. I kicked my feet. I felt my fifty-dollar Crocs slipping. I felt for the purse I attached to the life vest. Car keys, lipstick, and my loyal Siri were still with me. I sent God a "please let the Ziploc bags work so there is no water damage" prayer. I spotted Jack at a surprising distance, holding on to the back of our kayak and calling my name. One of the tour guides was with him, her kayak parallel to ours.

The sound of me coughing out murky water made them look my way. Slowly, I reached the kayaks. We were alone. It was very dark. I was scared. The jig was up. Words came out at once. "I will not be able to get back in this thing. I am a wimp. I have never been kayaking in my life. I have never done anything remotely athletic at all. My shoes are new and slipping off my feet. I bought them yesterday with the outfit so I could look cute and sporty. If I lose the shoes, my sister will make fun of me forever!"

The guide smiled. She was totally calm. What was wrong with her? Couldn't she see this was a crisis? "Hand me the shoes." Her voice was a sweet lullaby. I handed them over. "They are pretty. I will not lose them, I promise." She placed them inside her own one-person kayak. "Hold onto the side of your kayak, and I will pull you up from the top latch of your vest. I will have you sitting in the kayak in minutes."

She reached for the vest's top latch and grabbed a handful of my breasts.

"Your life vest is too small!" She was surprised. The lullaby voice and Zen-like peace were gone.

Panic. More words. "Someone took our kayak and our life vests. We had to take one left behind. This vest obviously belongs to a girl who does not eat and has no breasts. I could not hook it over mine because I *love* donuts."

She was calm again. "No worries. Let's try this. Pull yourself up while your friend and I steady the kayak. Once you are halfway, I will grab the bottom latch and get you in."

I pulled so hard that the Incredible Hulk had nothing on me.

And yet, I was still in the water.

I am never leaving Biscayne Bay. I should arrange for my mail to be delivered and call my pet sitter.

Jack chuckled and swam behind me. "I will push you up."

I was mortified. Jack was grunting loudly near my left ear from the effort of trying to lift me out of the water. He had one hand on my butt, the other, who knows where. *I am going to die of embarrassment.* When there was movement because my date was, undoubtedly, Ironman, the guide instructed me to quickly lift my right leg over the kayak and push. It was not easy or pretty. My grunts were now harmonizing with Jack's. It worked. Between the pushing, grunting and pulling, I was straddling the front of the kayak.

I am a beached whale in cranberry-colored shorts, I thought.

It was over. I breathed. I was safe.

"You have to let go of the kayak and get inside the seat." *Oh, God, it is not over.*

"Why can't I just stay hugging the kayak? I love it so much," I asked in a Minnie Mouse squeak. Both Jack and the guide patiently convinced me to let go of my new love. After earthquake-like movements, I was, once again, sitting in a kayak.

Jack got in like the flutter of a butterfly's wing.

We slowly started on our way back. "You know, Jack, if you had wanted to grab me, all you had to do was ask." We laughed. I relaxed. The three of us fell into pleasant conversation.

On dry land, I hugged and thanked our guide, and was reunited with my pink Crocs. Jack and I—dripping water, holding hands, laughing, and listening to the squishy sounds of our shoes—walked back to the car.

In life, people stay away from experiences that might end up in the disasters we build inside our heads. Sometimes we are right—what we fear most, actually happens. We take a risk and end up falling out of a kayak into a dark bay. Isn't that just fantastic?

—Marta A. Oppenheimer—

The Most Expensive Bike Ever

Never do anything that you wouldn't
want to explain to the paramedics.
~Author Unknown

t all started when our family went Christmas shopping and my husband, Jerry, decided he wanted a bicycle. While he was contemplating the best model for him, my son's heart was drawn to a black freestyle bike. He begged and pleaded but I stoically ignored him and left with Jerry's bike in tow.

A few days later I had the opportunity to go Christmas shopping on my own and was able to pick up Eli's dream bike. After all, it was a good price, and that would take care of the "special" present for Eli. When I got home I left the bike in the back of the van so I could hide it after the boys went to sleep. Jerry had been up since 3 AM and was exhausted so he headed for bed. Soon after, I sent the boys on their way. When I was sure they were asleep, I brought the bike in to hide until Christmas. I thought it would fit behind the bed in the spare room but quickly saw that that idea was not going to work, so I headed for the attic.

The door going into the attic locks automatically, so my main worry was that the door would close behind me and I'd be stuck in the attic overnight. If only.

I entered the attic and looked around, finding the perfect spot to hide the bike. As I rolled the bike over to its new home, the floor gave way beneath me. I was hanging in mid-air! You see, our attic floor is covered in plywood except for one spot that has three short planks. One of the planks had been moved and wasn't situated on the rafters properly. When I stepped on it, it flipped up like a teeter-totter, whacking me in the shin and dropping me through the ceiling of the garage.

As I dangled there listening to unknown things crashing to the ground beneath me, my first thought was, "Oh no! I hope the boys don't hear that and come out and see the bike!"

No worries. Everyone — yes, everyone — slept right through it all.

I reached down and grabbed my shin, only to pull my hand away when I felt all the blood through my jeans. Of course, my hand was now covered in blood which I wiped off on my already blood-soaked jeans. After all, I didn't want to get it on the bike. Somehow I managed to extricate myself from my dangling position and find some footing in the attic.

I examined my shin and saw that most of the blood had been soaked up by my blue jeans. The rest of the blood had reached the top of my sock and had pretty much stopped there. I decided my leg could wait while I finished hiding the bike. Part of my reasoning was that the real pain might kick in and I wouldn't be able to finish the job. The other part of my reasoning was that by taking care of it now I could avoid having to climb the stairs again (I'm almost fifty and am very good at escaping anything remotely like exercise).

After hiding the bike behind empty boxes I went downstairs. Curiosity overcame pain and I headed for the garage to survey the damage. I noticed it was rather dimly lit in there. Then I realized we were missing one of the florescent lighting boxes which had always hung on the ceiling right in the general vicinity of the now gaping hole. It occurred to me that the falling box was the delayed crashing sound I'd heard after puncturing the ceiling. I'd knocked the box off, it had dangled by the wires for a moment before coming crashing down — on Jerry's car! His prized possession!

I panicked! The car was covered in glass shards so I couldn't get a good look at the damage. I knew that if I brushed the glass off the car it would scratch it, so I went inside and got the vacuum cleaner. I gingerly took the vacuum and sucked up the glass, trying to pull it off the car vertically. Once all the glass was off, I took a look at the car in the dim light and saw that the side mirror was badly scratched and there was a two-inch scratch on the door next to it. Later, in full light, I noticed the windshield had scratches all over it and there was a small dent in the door as well. The original price of the bike combined with the cost in sheetrock, lighting, and car repairs had now become astronomical.

After finishing things up in the garage I finally took a good look at my leg. After washing the blood off, I saw that I had a scratch about the size of the one on Jerry's car. It didn't seem to be very deep. Next to it, however, was a small gouge that seemed to be the source of all the blood. On examination I realized that it could probably take one stitch, but I was determined not to add an emergency room fee to the cost of this bike. I butterflied the edges of the cut together, covered it with a huge bandage and Neosporin, and got into bed.

Before falling asleep I started thinking about the big bruise I was going to have on my upper thigh in the morning. I thought, "It's probably not a good thing to just lie down while this bruise forms. Couldn't it form some clot that will migrate to my brain and kill me?" I tossed and turned most of the night from pain and worry about blood clots and telling Jerry about his car.

Around 5 AM I woke up, turned over and was startled by flashing lights around me. I thought that possibly the neighbors across the street were driving out of their driveway and shining their lights through our windows. Then I woke up enough to realize that we have room darkening curtains and nothing ever shines in that brightly. I turned over the other way and saw more flashing lights! Now I was more panicked than I was over Jerry's car. "The blood clot has reached my brain and I'm dying! This can't be! Surely this is not IT!" But every time I moved I saw flashes of light before my eyes. I stopped moving. I lay there and thought about the cost of the funeral added to the cost of the bike.

Jerry woke up and I told him, "I fell through the ceiling in the garage last night." He chuckled, stopped short and said, "What?" I repeated, "I was hiding Eli's bike in the attic and I fell through the ceiling into the garage." He quit chuckling and said, "You're not kidding!" I related the evening's events to him and to his credit he didn't even ask how damaged the car was. I ended my story with the statement of my imminent death from a brain clot that was causing blinding flashes of light. It was a mystery to both of us.

I decided to get up and let the clot do its work. As I sat up I was hit with more blinding flashes. I also noticed that my pajamas were sticking to my body. As I pulled on one of my sleeves a flash of light emanated from the static electricity in my pajamas! I leaped out of bed with the realization that I wasn't dying! I told Jerry, "Look!" and proceeded to pull my clothes away from my skin up and down my body. Sparks were flying everywhere and in the pitch-blackness of the room, they were blinding.

At least I was going to live to pay the bills.

— Barbara Nicks —

Ooh La La

Mistakes are the usual bridge between
inexperience and wisdom.
~Phyllis Theroux

My principal came by my room that morning while I was still hanging a few last-minute posters on my walls, and the minute she walked in to wish me luck, I felt extremely unprepared. As she walked out of my classroom, I looked at the clock and realized that in fifteen minutes the first class of my teaching career was about to walk in my door. Freaking out just a little bit, I looked down at what I was wearing and immediately hated it. My outfit consisted of a plain white top with black pants and heels. As a person who loves fashion, I felt plain, but I figured I should be conservative on the first day, since I wanted my high school students to take me seriously.

It hit me that I would only be about six or seven years older than them and I freaked out even more. I reminded myself that I had been preparing for weeks; not only that, I had been preparing for years. I graduated from TCU with not only my bachelor's degree in Secondary Social Studies Education but I also graduated with my master's degree in Secondary Education. It was time and I was ready. So why were my hands shaking and my forehead drenched in sweat?

The day went by in a blur. With my freshman classes, I think they were just as nervous as I was. It was their first day in high school and sensing their apprehension eased my own. My sophomores, on the other hand, were all excited to see each other after the summer break and seemed very curious about who this new teacher was. Since the students all seemed to like my activities well enough that first day, it made the rest of our time together enjoyable.

My entire first year went by in a blur. By spring break, I was ready for summer. My first year of teaching was exhausting and consisted of a number of triumphs and some failures. I experienced happy moments with my students and instances where I wanted to cry. However, I never cried in front of them. I was determined to stand strong in front of these high school kids.

One time I wanted to cry from embarrassment because of a video I had shown in class. It had been one of those mornings, and I needed something for my first and fifth period World Geography students to keep them at the same pace as my other classes. We were studying Western Europe and I had traveled to Paris a few summers before, so I went into our school library's video closet and checked out a Globe Trekker episode on Paris. As I watched the video, I composed questions for the students to answer. The students watched the portion of the video that I had planned, and answered the questions I had prepared, but I had miscalculated and we still had fifteen minutes left in class. I figured I would just let them keep watching the video.

It was a Globe Trekker episode for goodness sake — how bad could it be? Well... it turned out to be a little inappropriate when the guide in the video visited the Moulin Rouge. I began to feel uneasy but I reminded myself that Globe Trekker episodes air on network television and teachers across the country use the videos in their Geography classes. Nevertheless, I moved a little closer to the computer... just in case. Sure enough, for a good three seconds there was a shot of a topless Moulin Rouge dancer. I swear it was the longest three seconds of my life.

It was one of those moments when your brain goes faster than your body. I knew I needed to turn off the video and turn it off fast, but my hands fumbled as some of the students, mostly boys, laughed and told me to leave it on. It was a good thing the room was dark or they would have seen my face turn as red as the skirt on the Moulin

Rouge dancer!

I thought for sure this was going to be the end of my teaching career. There I was, a new teacher, and my students saw a topless girl dancing on a big screen! Yes, a big screen. My first year took place pre-Smart Board when I hooked my personal laptop up to a projector to play videos.

For the rest of the day, I had students walking into my classroom saying things like "I heard we get to watch a cool video today, Ms. Townsend," and "I can't wait to see this video I have been hearing about all day!" I could not stop thinking about what had happened, replaying the class period over and over in my mind. Of course, I did not show that video the rest of the day despite the complaints that first period was able to see it and the rest of my classes were not. I thought I would never recover from the embarrassment.

Looking back on that day, I laugh about it. I learned my lesson. I no longer show a video in my classroom that I have not watched all the way through. I told few people at the time because I was so embarrassed and afraid for my job! The teachers I did share this with thought it was hilarious and recounted their own classroom mistakes and the lessons they learned. Now I can file this away as a valuable lesson to share with new teachers.

— Adrienne Townsend —

Adventure for Two

An adventure is only an inconvenience
rightly considered. An inconvenience is
only an adventure wrongly considered.
~G.K. Chesterton

y boyfriend Mike and I decided, after only three months of dating, that we wanted to spend our upcoming semester abroad together. It was a complicated decision and I was criticized by many of my friends for compromising the "real" purpose of studying abroad (apparently experiencing new things can only be done properly alone). However, by the time we were boarding our plane for Valparaíso, Chile, we were confident we had made the right choice and relieved that, after all our goodbyes to family and friends, we wouldn't have to say goodbye to each other.

One of the greatest benefits of our decision was that it gave us lots of opportunities to travel to exotic places together, something most couples our age never get to do. A few months into our trip, we planned a weeklong excursion to the Atacama Desert in the northern part of Chile. Though we knew we would spend most of our time in San Pedro (the tourist hub in the middle of the desert that offers accessibility to the most popular attractions), we wanted to cover a lot of ground and not have to depend on bus schedules, so we decided to rent a car and leave ourselves free to follow a map and explore wherever we pleased.

Mike and I spent a couple days of our trip traveling around the

I Can't Believe I Did That | 95

northernmost region of Chile and then decided to devote an afternoon and a good part of a night to making the 500-mile and 14-hour trip to San Pedro. We passed through the last town we would hit before San Pedro just as darkness set in. Now there was nothing left (not even pit stops or gas stations) but miles and miles of unfamiliar desert in the dark. We had heard the roads in the north weren't safe, and even that there were highway robbers in some areas, so we started to wonder if our late-night driving was such a good idea.

About half an hour after we had crossed into Región II (the region of Chile where San Pedro is) a large silver pick-up truck started tailing us aggressively, and then cut in front of us abruptly and recklessly. As soon as it was ahead of us it hit its brakes, forcing us to slam on our own. "What the hell?" Mike said out loud. My first thought was that it was a drunk driver, and it was obvious to both of us that we were better off avoiding the truck, so Mike passed back in front and sped off.

Immediately, however, the silver truck accelerated behind us and once it was tailing us again the passenger pulled out a flashlight and started shining it at our mirrors, flicking it around like he wanted us to pull over. Our next guess was that the truck wanted help, but we agreed it would be insane to pull over in the middle of the desert at what was now almost 1 a.m. for a complete stranger. However, despite all our obvious attempts to escape, the truck kept following us until it passed us again and slowed down ahead of us, still flicking the flashlight in our direction. Now every time Mike tried to pass the truck it would swerve to the middle of the road and block his attempts. It seemed it had trapped us.

I suddenly became very nervous. "DO NOT STOP FOR THEM," I pleaded, worried that Mike would give up. But we still couldn't get past. My heart rate sped up as I wracked my brain for an escape plan. Suddenly, Mike slammed on the brakes. "What are you doing?!" I yelled at him, panicked. The truck stopped too, just feet from us, and a tall Chilean man in a black jacket stepped out of the passenger side. I wondered what Mike was thinking, but I looked at his concentrated face and decided I trusted whatever plan he had. When the man was halfway toward us, Mike suddenly hit the gas and drove between the man and the truck. The truck slammed on the gas too and tried to block us, but Mike swerved around it.

We sped off in a confusion of headlights and screeching wheels. I watched in the rearview mirror as the truck slowed and allowed its passenger to scramble back in, but once he had, the truck sped up to follow us again. Luckily, we had a head start and we were going as fast as we could. I congratulated Mike on his stealthy escape but he was deeply concentrating and seemed convinced that we were far from safe. He put me in charge of looking backwards and keeping track of the headlights behind us, alerting him if any of them seemed to be moving particularly fast. But at the speed we were going I felt sure we had lost the truck quickly.

Just then a new thought occurred to me: what if it was customs? We had passed through what Mike thought was a weigh station when we entered Región II, but no one seemed to be there, and there were no indications that we should stop, so we had driven right through. What if it was a customs checkpoint and not a truck stop? I proposed this theory to Mike but he was unconvinced, mostly because of how recklessly the truck had been driving, and the fact that it was completely unmarked (in a country where outward appearance and formality are taken very seriously).

Mike continued to speed, since all signs indicated that our pursuers had bad intentions, and in the process we completely guzzled our gas. We realized this just as we were heading up into the mountains of the desert. Slowly, we registered the gravity of our situation: we were alone in the desert mountains, about to run out of gas, in the middle of the night, potentially with highway robbers following us.

Mike started driving especially slowly to conserve gas since all the driving was uphill. The gas tank arrow was down past empty, and I could tell that Mike had become the panicked one. I assured him that I had driven with the arrow past empty for a week without a problem, and he seemed relieved, but I silently reminded myself that the driving I did was infrequent and never up a steep mountain. We continued inching our way up and with such concentration that I felt as though we were pushing the car on with our minds, willing it around every turn. At each corner we would pray we had found the top and were heading down, but instead we encountered more and more hill.

Just as we started to hear a sucking, bubbly noise that sounded like an indication of a completely drained tank, the peak of the mountain came into sight. We willed the car on as it crawled to it and, miraculously, began its descent. I had never been so relieved. We coasted down the rest of the mountain, braking as little as possible to conserve momentum, and rolled into a gas station at the bottom. Hallelujah. We survived our first (and hopefully last) desert car chase.

The next day, we related our story to several people in San Pedro, including a police officer, and everyone told us we must have been chased by highway robbers.

A few days later, on the way back to where we started our road trip, we passed through the mysterious truck stop again, and this time we were asked to stop and hand in our documentation. It was customs after all. As the woman behind the counter was stamping and signing things, Mike turned to me with an embarrassed but amused smile and mumbled, "Look behind you." I turned around, and there, in the parking lot sat the unmistakable silver truck.

Now we can only imagine how suspicious our very deliberate getaway must have looked, and we were extremely relieved that the woman behind the counter didn't have us arrested for evading Chilean authorities! But in this moment of relief, just like in the moments of panic, fear, exhilaration, and delight that had preceded it during our trip, I was reassured that Mike and I had made the right choice in going abroad together. Having someone you love along for the ride, I decided, makes any adventure much better.

— Emily Oot —

30

A Day at the Beach

It is one of the blessings of old friends that
you can afford to be stupid with them.
~Ralph Waldo Emerson

had always heard people say it was very hard for three people to be close friends—you know, the odd number problem. Two people can be close and so can four but three people... not so much. Obviously my two friends and I forgot to read the memo. We met in a class in high school and clicked from that very first day. We shared clothes, make-up, shoes, and most importantly, we shared our lives, hopes, and secrets. We were close.

We graduated, went to college, married, had kids, and stayed close as ever. Then two of us moved from Los Angeles to a beach town on the central coast of California, leaving our other friend behind. You have to make an effort to stay close when you don't live in the same city but we three made a pact before we moved that we would get together at least once a month. And we did just that. We would alternate—one time we would go to Los Angeles for the day and the next time our friend would come and spend the day with us. That worked.

The years flew by and now we three best girl friends had children in high school and college and it was even easier for us to get together. No young children at home to worry about. We still shared everything and we were looking forward to our friend coming to our central coast town one warm August day to spend some time at the beach with us. Rather than fix a picnic lunch we splurged and order lunches from a gourmet deli here in town. And we even decided to include a bottle of our favorite wine.

The day was perfect. Warm but not too hot, with a soft breeze blowing. We three spread out our blankets on the sand and got ready to eat. Eating has always been very important to us and we have shared some of our deepest secrets over meals. The lunch was delicious—why is it that things that you don't have to prepare yourself always taste better? And we enjoyed some of the wine too!

We had been sitting, eating, sipping, talking, sharing, and laughing for a few hours when we decided that, before we had our dessert, it would be really nice to stretch our legs and take a walk down the beach. This was the perfect beach to walk along as it was about a mile long and it had a nice wide sandy path to follow. When it got too warm we could just walk along in the water to cool off. Could things get any better?

Since it was a weekday, there were some people on the beach but it wasn't crowded. We walked for a while and the beachgoers thinned out to practically nothing. But way, way down the beach we saw a big group of people. They were far enough away from us that they looked like tiny ants. We thought we could walk to them, then turn around and walk back and have dessert. That would be enough exercise for us.

How could three friends talk as much as we did? How did we find so many things to talk about? We never seemed to run out of things to say. We were walking and talking and getting closer to that big group down the beach. We could tell now that some of them were playing in the water, some were playing beach volleyball, some were walking around, and some were relaxing on the sand. We were so engrossed in our conversation that we practically walked right through the volleyball court before we stopped short. And stop short we did.

Something was wrong with this picture. OMG! These people didn't have any clothes on. Nothing. They were naked! We were in the middle of a nude beach! Okay, a few of them had hats on and one guy had on a pair of high-top tennis shoes but... that was it.

"Hello girls. Want to join in our volleyball game?"

Are you kidding me? We didn't know what to do. How to react.

What to say. And excuse me but... where do you look? The three of us just stood there with our mouths open and our eyes popping out of our heads. We probably stood there for no longer than five seconds taking it all in but it felt like we stood there for hours. And then, at exactly the same time, we all reacted in a way that three adult women should when they find themselves among a group of naked people. We turned and ran like rabbits. No one said a word. We just ran. We hightailed it back down that beach so fast you would have thought we were running in a race — and we needed to win. After a few minutes I tripped and fell in the sand. That's also when we started laughing. Actually we got hysterical. You know the kind of laughter I'm talking about. The I-can't-catch-my-breath-because-I'm-laughing-too-hard kind. No wonder those people were way, way down the beach. Duh. They weren't wearing anything!

We finally made our way back to our beach blankets and were so glad to be back among people... who had bathing suits on. And we laughed. We ate dessert and we laughed. We finished our bottle of wine and we laughed harder. How had all three of us been so naive as to not realize why those people were so far down the beach, away from the usual beachgoers? Why couldn't we have walked in the other direction and looked at the seals and pelicans instead? Of course, if we had gone in the other direction, we would have missed out on a wonderful story to share with our families and friends. And we're still laughing about it today.

— Barbara LoMonaco —

31

Nowhere to Go

*Running is an unnatural act, except from
enemies and to the bathroom.*
~Author Unknown

It was a beautiful Sunday afternoon in early September. The marathon was only a month away and I was in the midst of a grueling training regimen. On this particular day I was scheduled for a fourteen-mile run, the longest I would have all week. So before I left, as always, I did some light stretching, ate a small snack, and of course, drank plenty of fluids. Soon enough I had my sneakers tied, headphones covering my ears, and was out the door.

The conditions were ideal for running — temperature in the mid-60s, clear blue skies, and a gentle breeze. With autumn knocking on summer's door I wondered if there would be many more days with such wonderful weather. I headed west towards the city center, seven miles one way, seven miles back. I reached the downtown high-rises with my body relaxed, my lungs breathing in a perfect rhythm and my legs feeling as strong as ever. But then, suddenly, out of nowhere, just as I reached the halfway point, I had to go.

It comes as no surprise, when running for hours at a time, that one would have to relieve oneself at some point. Normally it's not much of a problem, especially if you were lucky enough to be born a male, as I was. You simply jog off to the side of the road, find a concealed area, usually some bushes, and proceed to conduct your business. But on this day it was different. I was in the middle of one of the largest cities on the West Coast. There were no bushes or shrubs, only open sidewalks and exposed brick buildings. And on top of that there were people everywhere, strolling the city streets, enjoying the sunny day. I'd run myself into quite the predicament.

I headed back towards my apartment and with every step the feeling in my body became more intense. I began eyeballing side streets and alleyways, but with little luck. There always seemed to be a person walking around, or a slow-moving car in the near vicinity. Damn this beautiful day, I told myself. If it would only start raining, that would clear the streets and give me some privacy. But the sun continued to shine and the people laughed and smiled, as if they somehow knew what I was going through and were in on the joke.

I came upon a fast-food restaurant and knew that they would have a bathroom inside. On the men's room door there was a sign that read, "Restroom Key at Front Counter." I patiently waited in the short line. When the people in front of me were finally done ordering I very nicely asked the cashier for the bathroom key. "The bathroom is for customers only," she said. "If you want to use it, then you will have to purchase something."

I tried my best to explain my situation. "I'm out training for the upcoming marathon," I pleaded. "I don't have any money on me, but if you give me a break, I promise to come back later and buy something."

"Sorry, paying customers only."

I wanted nothing more than to scream, but was afraid that it might make it worse. What was the world coming to? Is there nowhere to go to the bathroom? I continued east. My muscles felt fine, but the faster I ran, the worse it got, so I had little choice but to keep a moderate pace. Everything around me seemed to be a reminder of the situation I was in. There was a woman watering her flowers with a garden hose. And a man washing his pickup truck. Then I saw a dog lift his leg on a fire hydrant and almost lost it. It was probably the only moment in my entire life when I actually wished that I were an animal.

Finally I felt like I couldn't hold it any longer. I saw some bushes in front of a house and considered taking my chances. But then I looked around, and if it wasn't just my luck, there was a police department directly across the street. I weighed my options. On the one hand I really had to go, but on the other, how would I ever explain being arrested for such a foolish thing?

In the end I decided to hightail it home. I was only a couple of miles away, and ran faster than I had ever run before. I probably set a personal record that day in the two-mile, and when I finally arrived at my apartment I could have been the happiest man on Earth. I frantically searched my pocket for the door key and then fumbled around trying to insert it into the slot. I slammed the door behind me and sprinted through the living room. At last I reached the bathroom, and of course, it was locked. My roommate was taking a shower.

—J.M. Penfold—

Doggone Funny

The Great Table Caper

Fun fact: In most U.S. cities, to protect both people and dogs, "leash laws" require that dogs in public be on a leash that is less than six feet long.

Early one fine spring morning, Tyler (a large Golden Retriever), Zoe (a large red Doberman) and I (a woman of a certain age) headed out for a walk. Our destination was the lake in the neighborhood. First, though, we visited the local coffee shop so I could get a cup of tea to drink as we walked.

I tied Tyler and Zoe, who were very sweet and obedient dogs, to the base of a metal table that was in a cordoned-off area for the restaurant next door. When the restaurant was closed, I often tied them to a table. As usual, I turned to look at them before going in and said, "Be good. I'll be right out."

It was a Saturday morning, and very few people were about or in the coffee shop. After getting my tea, I went over to the condiment station to doctor it with some sweetness. My back was to the door. While stirring in the sugar, I had slipped into a bit of absentmindedness. All of a sudden, a man's voice boomed from behind me, bringing me out of my reverie. "Someone own those dogs out there?" he called out.

Leaving my tea, I sprang to the door. Outside, mayhem reigned. Tyler, Zoe and the table were gone. Tables and chairs were knocked over. The black straps that cordoned off the area along with their metal stands were on the ground. I ran to the middle of the street. Tyler, the table, and Zoe — in that order — were running away as if the devil himself was chasing them. The metal table bounced, making a loud noise, which caused Tyler to run faster.

I ran after them, yelling, "Tyler, stop! Stop, Tyler, stop!" I could see that Tyler was the instigator since he was in the lead. He looked back at me, then at the table, and then back to me. His eyes said, "Mom, I can't. There's a table chasing me!" He kept running.

Zoe looked back at me, and her eyes said, "Mom, he's gone crazy; I don't know what to do." She was definitely at his mercy, and Tyler was at the mercy (in his mind) of the table.

I continued to run after them and yell at Tyler to stop. He'd look back at me, wanting to obey, but then he'd look at the table that kept chasing him and continue running. He'd swerve toward a parked car, causing the table to swing out, and I'd pray, "Please don't hit a car." Thankfully, he'd correct his course to the middle of the road and somehow avoid hitting any cars with the table.

I was not in shape to be running full tilt, and I had no idea how long the "table chase" was going to last. It appeared as if the threesome was headed toward our home, but there were six or so blocks still to go with a couple of parking lots, woods, and busier streets along the way. And poor Zoe, she had no choice but to run. I think she had her senses about her and would have stopped if she could, but as Tyler was in the lead, she was an unwilling accomplice. When I called out, she'd turn her head to look back at me, and with her eyes would say, "He's gone mad. Help me."

A few blocks into the run, with me huffing and puffing, it occurred to me: I could be mad and frustrated, or I could laugh. I chose to laugh, which made the running even more aerobic. But the absurdity of a woman of a certain age running after a dog who thinks he's being chased by a bouncing table was too much.

Soon, I was winded and could feel my heart beating fast. Then another thought came, "Oh, my God! I'm going to die of a heart attack chasing these dumb dogs and a table. What a stupid way to die. I hope my family will get a good laugh out of it."

The dogs crossed a grassy median that sent the table bouncing and swinging even more. The trio was headed to a parking lot with several cars in it. Tyler came close to a new red truck, and I thought, "I'm going to be buying a bumper today." Luckily, he veered away from it just in time.

Out of the corner of my eye, I noticed an employee standing in front of a Michael's craft store. He looked at the dogs, looked at me, and then did a double take. Then he took off after the dogs, running diagonally to them, and stopping them just as they were about to cross a busy road and careen into another parking lot filled with more cars.

I slowed down to catch my breath as I saw he had the dogs under control. Then a new thought sprang to mind: How the heck was I going to get the metal table back to the restaurant while controlling two large dogs? Should I leave the table? Tie the dogs to something stationary at the coffee shop and come back for the table? Could I even carry it after running so fast? Or should I take Zoe and Tyler home and bring my car for the table?

By the time I walked up to David (my hero) and the dogs, he had untangled them. The table was up on one of his shoulders. I thanked him while he passed Zoe and Tyler's leashes to me and marched off to the restaurant like it was an everyday occurrence to rescue a damsel in distress from renegade dogs and a fiercesome table. He was a godsend.

By the time Tyler, Zoe, and I got back to the coffee shop, David had just finished reestablishing order to the outside dining area. It looked as if nothing had ever happened. I can't remember ever being so grateful for a stranger's help, and I profusely thanked my Good Samaritan.

But it didn't seem enough. I wanted to show him my gratitude with more than just words; I wanted to give him something that was heartfelt. Cooking is something I do from the heart, and my apple pie is a favorite among friends and family.

So, I went home and made David an apple pie. It was still hot when I took it to the store just before he got off work. Months later, I was in Michael's and saw David. I repeated my thanks for his help, which he kindly brushed off. However, he thanked me for the apple pie, saying it was the best he had ever eaten.

By the way, from that point on, Tyler and Zoe were always tied to a stationary object, such as a lamppost, when we went to the coffee shop.

— Ann Denise Karson —

I Saved a Dog

Mix a little foolishness with your serious plans.
It is lovely to be silly at the right moment.
~Horace

I save dogs quite frequently. It's a deep-seated instinct in me. A forlorn, lost, four-legged hairball running down the street is all it takes to set me off. I go into a frenzy. *MUST. SAVE. DOG.* My senses tingle; my synapses fire. My heart pounds and my breathing becomes raspy. Everything blurs and I become intensely and profoundly focused.

He must be scared. She must be hungry. He needs me. She might get hurt.

I become a determined woman on a mission… a mission to save the dog.

And, usually, I am quite successful. Most of the time, I save the dog and the day. Two weeks ago, I saved Cookie. I was driving down the street when I noticed a brown blur in my peripheral vision. My heightened instincts kicked in. I assessed the situation: *Yes, it's a lost dog and — gasp — it's barreling for the major intersection ahead!*

Immediately, I switched into Superhero Doggy Saver mode and started weaving in and out of traffic. The dog was slipping from sight, so I had to take fast action. I screeched my car to a stop, halted traffic, and ran at lightning speed toward the runaway dog.

I pushed a skateboarding kid out of the way. "Hey, old lady!" he shouted at me. But it was okay because he didn't know I was a superhero at work. I flew farther down the street. Just before the dog met with certain death from an oncoming car, I scooped him up.

I am sure I heard cheers and hurrahs. Horns were honking. My girls said, "Oh, my gosh, Mom! You almost killed us!" To which I responded with Super Hero Honesty, "I'm so sorry! I forgot you were in the car."

Cookie had a tag, and we called the number. We returned Cookie to her grateful owner and counted it as another successful mission. Just another day in Superhero Doggy Saver land.

But my family thinks I might be a tad obsessed. They've wondered if there is a therapy group for people like me. DRA… Doggy Rescue Anonymous. But I can't help it. When I think of a lost dog's fear and helplessness and innocence, it affects me in a way I can't describe. It's an emotional trigger. Even watching rescue videos on Facebook evokes it. When my girls walk in and see me at my computer with the tissue box, they sigh and say, "Mom's watching dog-rescue videos again."

But even if I do go a little overboard, there's no denying that I have saved a lot of dogs. Owners thank me, and at the end of the day, tears turn to joy. It's a wonderful, glorious, worthwhile thing that I do.

Last week I sprang into action once again. I looked out our front window and saw a beautiful German Shepherd sniffing around in our front yard. Wow. Now, lost dogs were even coming right to me. My savior reputation was getting around. I put on my imaginary cape and went outside to save the day.

The dog had no tag. I had never seen it before. *How would I ever find its owner? How long had it gone without food and water?* I was overcome with worry and concern for the poor dog. I switched into rescue mode.

I grabbed a leash and took the lost dog around to our back yard. I cordoned off our four dogs despite their protests. I got bedding and supplies. I enlisted my daughters to put their best art skills to work. We made lots of flyers and posters.

FOUND FEMALE GERMAN SHEPHERD

We diligently drove all around town, plastering up the dog's picture.

A couple of days later, we received a call. It was the dog's owner! The dog's name was Lilly. The owner sounded so frantic, so worried. He said he had just moved to a new neighborhood, and Lilly had wandered out the front door. He had only looked away for a minute, and he couldn't understand how she could have disappeared so quickly.

He had just bathed her, so her collar with her identification had been removed. He had been looking for her non-stop, without sleep, ever since. Needless to say, he was ecstatic we had found Lilly. He was overflowing with gratitude.

He said he was ready to get in his car and come get her. "Where do you live?" he asked.

"We live on Oak Street!" I said, eager to hear how far the dog had traveled.

The voice on the other end hesitated a beat. "Oak Street?" he echoed.

"Why, yes! Where do you live?" I asked enthusiastically.

"Oak Street," he said, flatly. "I'm your new neighbor. I live right next door…"

MUST. SAVE. DOG.

—Julie Theel—

34

Masked Bandits

In the game of life it's a good idea to have a few early
losses, which relieves you of the pressure of trying
to maintain an undefeated season.
~Bill Vaughan

My dad prided himself on the large, bountiful gardens that he oversaw every summer. He beamed over the juicy tomatoes, crisp radishes, and refreshing watermelons that he produced; however, he was most pleased with his sweet corn.

Yet there was one minor problem with Dad's garden: it was located right next to a wooded ravine with a stream — prime raccoon country. And any gardener worth his salt knows how much raccoons love sweet corn.

And so it went that summer. Upon inspecting his beloved garden every morning, Dad would find telltale raccoon tracks in the soft, tilled dirt. Then he would discover bent-over corn stalks containing empty shanks where ears of sweet corn used to be.

At first, my dad tried a friend's recommendation. Dad ran an extension cord from his workshop down to the garden, and plugged it into my portable radio. Figuring that the all-night musical onslaught would scare the ring-tailed bandits away, Dad smugly went to bed that night.

However, the next morning's inspection revealed that the raccoons had ravaged his sweet corn again. Dad joked to his friend that not only did the masked marauders still get his sweet corn, but they even changed the radio station!

Thus, Dad must've figured that the next best thing to protect his sweet corn would be a live, human guard — namely, me — and my faithful canine companion, Queeny. A mixed-breed mutt that we had rescued from the local dog pound, Queeny was my best friend. We did everything together, so this would just be another adventure. Besides, her eyes, ears, and nose would be indispensable in detecting any raccoons.

So in my youthful ignorance, I allowed my dad to talk me into sleeping out by the garden with Queeny.

There I was — ever vigilant — atop a small hill that overlooked the garden. I was lying on the ground in a cheap sleeping bag meant more for a Friday night sleepover than a hot, mosquito-infested night in July. Next to me lay my trusty ol' Daisy BB gun. At the end of my sleeping bag lay my faithful Queeny. Refusing to sleep, she was poised to pounce on anything. I also had a couple of pieces of cold pizza that Mom had wrapped in aluminum foil next to my sleeping bag.

Under a full moon and a starry sky, this impromptu guard station began its watch. Queeny and I waited… and waited… and waited.

Eventually, I dozed off.

Suddenly, Queeny barked.

In my sleeping bag, I sat upright.

Queeny bolted for the garden.

I unzipped my sleeping bag and leapt up.

Queeny disappeared into the corn stalks.

I grabbed my BB gun, cocked it, and ran after her.

Queeny chased something into the wooded ravine.

I lost sight of her.

"Queeny! Come here, girl!" I shouted.

Within seconds, she was back by my side, running excited circles around my shins. "Nice job, girl!" Queeny and I turned about, and traipsed back through the corn stalks.

"By God, Queeny," I boasted, "no raccoon is going to get any sweet corn on our watch."

Queeny and I departed the garden and marched back up the little hill. At the top, I sat down upon my sleeping bag. There, I lay down my BB gun, and scratched Queeny behind the ears. Then I looked about.

My pizza was gone.

—John M. Scanlan—

35

Bringing Up the Rear

When it comes to skiing, there's a difference between
what you think it's going to be like, what it's really like,
and what you tell your friends it was like.
~Author Unknown

For sixteen years my family and I shared our lives with an amazing Beagle named Brandy. I say amazing because although he astonished us, horrified us, humbled us, delighted us, inspired us, and at times downright exasperated us, he never once ceased to be a little devil-may-care rake. His was the spirit of the swashbuckler, never to be bowed or broken. We could not help admiring it. His escapades became legend both in our city neighborhood and in the fields and streams around our cottage. One of Brandy's adventures the second winter he was part of our family is indelibly etched in my mind.

It began one beautiful day in early March, that time of year when the snow crust was as hard as pavement and sun-glazed to the slipperiness of an eel's back. Skiing conditions, both downhill and cross-country, were in the treacherous to suicidal range. Undaunted by the precarious footing, my friend Christiana and I set out to walk our dogs — Brandy and Christiana's Boxer named Ross.

We headed through the woods and across a meadow glistening with snow diamonds and framed by spruce and pines iced in ivory under a perfect sapphire sky. The sun warmed our faces, awakening pleasant thoughts of spring, but also glazing the snow's hard surface with a treacherous liquid sheen. Several times Christiana and I caught each other's sleeves to prevent falling. Even the dogs were finding it difficult to remain on their four paws.

At the far end of the meadow the land dipped downward into a long, sweeping slope of virginal white that terminated in a cluster of alders and dogwood. When we reached a vantage point, all four of us paused to view the panorama.

Suddenly I saw Bran's ears prick into that alarming stance that indicated "the game" as Dr. Watson would say, "was afoot." Following his line of vision, I saw a rotund lady in a pink ski suit perched atop the hill about fifty yards away. On her feet was a pair of cross-country skis.

"What can she be thinking?" Christiana, a veteran skier of the Austrian Alps said as she, too, caught the object of Bran's interest. "Cross-country skis... on this slippery crust... on a hill?"

As we watched, the lady plunged her poles into the crust and then squatted to adjust her boots. Her pink bottom hung between her widely spread skis.

And then disaster struck. A howl went up from the smallest member of our company. Before I realized what was happening, Brandy was off, charging toward that pastel bundle as if someone had just yelled, "charge!" or he'd discovered the Energizer Bunny slowing down within his reach.

There was a scream, a frantic scratching. The lady, still in squat position, plunged down the slope, pink rear end bouncing over each natural mogul with an accompanying shriek.

Christiana, Ross, and I half-slid, half-staggered down the slope toward the crumpled mound that had finally come to an abrupt halt in the thicket at the bottom. Brandy had vanished into the bush.

"Are you all right?" Christiana, a nurse, was instantly at her side.

"Yes, yes... I think so." Slipping and sliding on the skis still miraculously attached to her boots, the woman hung suspended between my friend and a dogwood like the personification of that well-rounded cartoon creation in Michelin tire commercials. "But who owns that miserable little dog?"

Christiana and I exchanged glances. "We have no idea. He's been following my Boxer through the woods all morning," my quick-thinking friend replied.

We helped the woman unclamp her skis and assisted her to her car parked on the road below the meadow. That was that… we could but hope… as Brandy stuck his head out between two small pines.

But it wasn't. Not by a long shot. The following morning when Christiana returned to work in the hospital, a colleague told her of an unusual case she'd treated the previous day.

"This lady had bruises and lacerations all over her bottom," she reported. "She tried to tell me it was the result of some kind of weird skiing accident involving a dog. Now I ask you, do I look gullible enough to swallow a crazy story like that!"

— Gail MacMillan —

Lead Me Not...

*Fun fact: The Americans with Disabilities Act,
passed in 1990, says that disabled people and their
assistance dogs must have access to public places.*

was not surprised to see a woman with an old Golden Retriever, her guide dog, asking a couple for directions to one of the smaller restaurants. The Scarborough Town Center in Toronto is such a large shopping plaza that it is easy, even for a sighted person, to become confused. When the couple didn't know where the restaurant was, the blind woman left.

Forty minutes later, after a totally unsuccessful bathing-suit shopping expedition, I passed the restaurant. The same woman was plodding along several stores ahead of me. I knew that she had walked right by her intended destination, probably not for the first time.

I rushed to catch up to her. "Excuse me," I called, "but are you still looking for Moxie's Grill?"

When she said "yes," I put my arm out and suggested that she take it.

"You walked by the front door a few minutes ago," I said. "You are going to have to teach your dog to read," I added jokingly.

"He knows exactly where it is. I meet my friends there every couple of days," she said matter-of-factly. "He's just pissed off because I won't take him for a ride on the escalator."

— Joei Carlton Hossack —

The Battle for the Sheep Pillow

Siblings are the people we practice on, the people who
teach us about fairness and cooperation and kindness
and caring, quite often the hard way.
~Pamela Dugdale

Sometimes, my two dogs do things that remind me of the two
sisters, Sue and Diane, I used to hang around with when I
was a kid. At least once a week, the sisters would fight over
something one of them had... and the other one wanted.

For example, one Easter Sunday, Sue came over to show my family
her new Easter outfit. As we were admiring it, Diane stormed into the
house, ran over to Sue, reached up underneath her dress and yanked
her slip—a frilly half-petticoat—down to her ankles.

"Give me back my slip!" Diane shouted.

"No!" Sue shot back. "I need it for this dress!"

A tug-of-war, accompanied by ripping sounds, then ensued.

Well, last Christmas, my Rottweilers, Raven and Willow, made
me believe that after fifty years, Sue and Diane had actually returned
in canine form.

It all began one day when I was Christmas shopping and happened to see a fluffy dog pillow in the shape of a sheep. It was on sale,
so I thought I'd buy it for Raven. My other dog, Willow, already had
a stuffed bunny she carried around all the time, so I figured Raven

deserved the sheep.

Well, my gift to Raven was a big hit... with both dogs. Willow decided she wanted that sheep pillow, and she was going to stop at nothing to get it.

Thus began endless days of sheep tug-of-war, Rottweiler style, which included growling in a variety of octaves and decibels. Because Raven sounded like a cross between Godzilla and a rabid wolf when she growled, she usually won the battle. Then she would take the sheep to a far corner of the room and plunk down on top of it to conceal it.

But Willow would wait, lurking behind the recliner or under the kitchen table, until an opportunity arose, such as when Raven would leave the room to get a drink of water. Then Willow would swoop in like a vulture that had been eyeing a fresh carcass and snatch the sheep. When Raven returned to her spot and saw the sheep missing, she'd run and jump on Willow, and the fighting would begin again.

I began to feel as if I had a front-row seat at a World Wrestling Federation match.

There was only one solution to the problem. I had to buy another sheep pillow and give it to Willow. But as luck would have it, when I returned to the store, all of the sheep pillows were gone.

So I did the only other thing I could think of to resolve the problem and restore peace in the house: I took the sheep pillow away from Raven and hid it in the basement.

Although I felt certain I'd been sneaky about hiding the sheep, Raven seemed to instinctively know I was guilty of sheep-napping. She developed a creepy habit of standing and staring at me — a evil-looking, "I want to drain your jugular vein" kind of stare. When I was watching TV, there she'd be, standing next to it and staring at me. When I was trying to read, she'd be peering out from behind the end table, her eyes boring into me. She didn't blink, she didn't move, she just stared, sometimes for more than twenty minutes at a time. It was like the Vulcan mind meld, where she was attempting to merge her thoughts with mine. And those thoughts were saying, "Give me back my sheep pillow... or else!"

About a week ago, I was in a department store and happened to spot a colorful display of pillows in the shapes of animals. I searched through them, hoping to find a sheep to give to Willow, so both dogs would have one, and I would be able to live in a calm, quiet house once again. There was no sheep, so I bought a hippopotamus, thinking Willow wouldn't know the difference.

The first thing Willow did when I gave her the hippo was rip out its eyes and spit them onto the rug.

Her message was clear: She wasn't all that fond of the hippo pillow.

Meanwhile, Raven continued to stare at me. When I woke up one morning and opened my eyes to see two dark Rottweiler eyes glaring into mine, that did it. I decided I'd rather put up with the dogs fighting than risk waking up without my jugular vein. I went down to the basement and brought the sheep pillow back upstairs.

Almost instantly, the dogs transformed into Hulk Hogan and The Rock, using their best headlocks and scissor holds on each other as they battled for the prize. They crashed into the end table near the sofa. I'd just set down a cup of tea, and it splashed everywhere. And Raven's growling got worse, kind of like a buzz saw on turbo speed.

Yesterday, just as I was on the verge of taking the sheep pillow for a long walk in the woods and "accidentally" dropping it into the brook, Raven suddenly decided she didn't want it anymore. When Willow grabbed it away from her, she didn't make any attempt to resist. Even Willow seemed stunned by the abrupt change of attitude. She brought the pillow over to Raven to taunt her with it, which, in the past, always had incited a battle. Raven only yawned and looked away.

As it turned out, the reason why Raven lost interest in the sheep pillow was because she decided she'd rather have the hippo. She picked it up and carried it to the corner, then fell asleep on it. I figured maybe she felt sorry for it because it had no eyeballs.

And the moment Raven woke up, Willow pounced on her because she wanted her hippo back.

Here we go again.

— Sally A. Breslin —

38

A Hot Dog

*Genius is the ability to put into effect
what is on your mind.*
~F. Scott Fitzgerald

"**D**akota, you're freaking me out." It was the kind of hot and muggy night that made your toes sweat. I lay in bed trying to beat the heat and get some sleep, but no air conditioner could keep up with the stifling weather. It didn't help that my 120-pound Akita was sitting in my bedroom doorway, just staring at me.

"Seriously, Dakota go lie down. It's late," I ordered.

That's when the "wooing" started. Akitas, especially my Dakota, communicate by "wooing" instead of barking. Barking is reserved for warning strangers to stay away and chasing squirrels.

"Wooo-wooo," he said.

"Dakota, it's hot and I'm trying to sleep. Please, go lie down," I whined.

He woo'd again, before walking to the side of my bed, laying his big head on the edge, and letting out a sharp huff.

I rolled over, turning my back on my mangy mutt. "Go to bed."

Dakota then put his two large paws on the bed and hoisted himself up, until he was breathing on my head. His hot breath on the back of my neck was not helping.

"Fine." I threw off my sheet. "Do you want to go outside?"

I marched to the back door, yanking it open with more force

than needed. "Go!"

Dakota sat down and woo'd at me. Apparently, that was not what he wanted. I slammed the door.

"Are you hungry? Do you need water?" I asked.

I checked his water and food bowls. Both were full, but I emptied his water bowl and refilled it with fresh water. I sat it in front of him.

"Woooo," he replied, not touching the water.

I threw my hands up in frustration. "What do you want?"

Dakota turned and headed back to the hallway. I followed. Getting to the hallway, Dakota started pawing at a large, white, box fan. I turned it on. He then lay down, releasing a big sigh, as if to say, "It's about time."

— Jennifer McMurrain —

39

Wonder Dog

The dog was created specially for children.
He is the god of frolic.
~Henry Ward Beecher

His name suggested a dog much larger, but Brutus weighed in at thirteen pounds and stood one foot high, full-grown. A curly, black, cocka-pomma-peeka-poo, he puffed out his little barrel chest and swaggered around the house like a big dog. He loved hanging out with us kids and we loved including him in everything we did.

We lived just north of Seattle and snow was a rarity. A foot of snow was cause for a celebration. School was cancelled, and the road to our house became a giant hill for slipping and sliding. Brutus knew something was up when all four of us started pulling on our coats, boots, mittens and stocking caps. Naturally, he wanted to go with us. He immediately started his "we're going for a walk" prance by the front door.

"No, Brutus," said my sister, shaking her head. "You're too little."

"Yeah," said brother number one, "the snow's taller than you are!"

Brother number two frowned. "I'm little, too," he said with trembling lips. "Brutus can go. He can follow the trail like I do."

"But you've got snow gear," said my practical sister. "Brutus would get all wet."

I looked from Brutus, eagerly standing by the door wiggling all over, to my little brother, struggling to fight back tears. "What if we made Brutus a snowsuit?"

I went to the kitchen and got a Wonder Bread bag. "This should fit him."

Brother number one got the scissors and we fashioned a covering for the dog by cutting out leg and tail holes in the bread sack. We pulled it on his trembling body. He looked ridiculous but I don't think he cared.

"He's a Wonder Dog!" said brother number two excitedly. "Now he can go with us!"

Mother took pictures of us tramping out in the snow, Brutus in his Wonder Bread bag scurrying along behind. But it wasn't long before we realized we'd forgotten something important. Brutus had been inside all day, and after only fifty yards or so, he hunched over to poop. We suddenly realized we had forgotten to leave the business end open.

We all screamed, "NO! NO! NO!" and chased after him to remove the sack. Of course he ran, staying just out of our grasp, thinking we were playing. We floundered in the snow until total exhaustion set in, when we literally collapsed upon the front porch steps. Brutus then took care of his business, while we all moaned from our seats on the stoop, still trying to catch our breath. Mother came out the front door, laughing so hard she was crying.

"Here," she said, holding out the scissors. "You cut the bag off him, and I'll run him a bath."

"Why me?" I asked incredulously.

"Because you're the oldest, and you should have known better."

"Why didn't you stop me?"

Mom laughed. "I honestly didn't think of it either, but you're the brilliant one who came up with this great idea."

Brutus was running in circles in the snow, trying to figure out what the bulge was trailing along behind him weighing him down. Seeing him dragging his poop behind him put us into fits of laughter. Mother called him, and he came to her for help. Together, we held him still and cut the bag off him. Brutus loved his bath time, and ran around the house dragging his towel along with him until he was dry. We'd had almost as much fun as if we'd been out sledding… almost.

—Jan Bono—

Cold Crime

The greatest crimes are caused by surfeit, not by want.
~Aristotle

For months we put up with our dog's raids upon the refrigerator. With no one at home during the day, Tubbs would help himself to whatever he fancied: hot dogs, sticks of butter, lamb chops. He managed to wedge his nose between the refrigerator door and the rubber gasket. After prying it open and looting the shelves, he left the door ajar, a telltale sign.

Not that we needed any clues. All we had to do was follow the trail of greasy wrappers and Styrofoam containers. They usually led to Tubbs, hiding under the kitchen table, a guilty look on his face — or was it indigestion?

A shelter puppy, he was of dubious ancestry. They claimed he was part Husky, part Lab. I believe he was a descendent of The Great Houdini's dog, except instead of getting out of tight situations, he gets into them.

The local handyman who came to fix the refrigerator door scratched his head upon hearing my story. "One of my customers had a cat who turned on the TV," he said. "He'd lie on top to keep warm." Nonetheless, he'd never heard of a dog breaking into a refrigerator.

After examining the door, he said we had structural damage from Tubbs's repeated attacks. And as the model was fourteen years old, he advised me to junk it. "The new models have heavier doors," he said. "He'll never get in."

Thus my husband and I found ourselves in a gigantic appliance center with aisles of gleaming refrigerators in designer colors. Some were so big they had walk-in freezers. One had a TV screen built into the door. When the salesman asked what we had in mind, I said we wanted a refrigerator door so heavy it required two hands to open. Then I told him about Tubbs's amazing ability.

"That's a new one to me," he said.

"It's a rare talent," I said, and one we could live without.

After testing dozens of refrigerators, we found an appropriate model. The door was so tight it would discourage an orangutan.

Back home we set about emptying the contents of the old refrigerator. Some items were so ancient, we classified them as UFOs: unidentified frozen objects.

Still, it was a sad moment when the delivery men hauled the old fridge to the curb, putting a gleaming new model in its place. Soon we were ooh-ing and aah-ing over the new appliance. It offered everything: ice on demand, spacious no-defrost freezer and best of all, a door that closed with a thunk.

I'd love to say we lived happily ever after, but I'd be lying. The following morning we left the house, secure in the knowledge that our groceries were safe. Upon arriving home, however, we found chaos. The dog had managed to break into the refrigerator, stealing a pound of thinly-sliced Virginia ham and a half pound of provolone. A mangled and punctured canister of Parmesan cheese lay under the kitchen table. Tubbs had done it again!

There's a saying: "The best solutions are the simplest." Before outfitting the fridge with a combination lock, I got another idea. It happened while my brother and his family were visiting. The day they left, I watched him secure the suitcases atop their station wagon. He used long bungee cords. The proverbial light bulb went off in my head.

Now before we leave the house we have a checklist: coffee pot unplugged, answering machine on, industrial strength bungee cords circling the refrigerator.

It's a small price to pay compared to the spoiled food and ruined meal plans of the past. In the meantime, I'm waiting for Tubbs to discover he can gnaw through the bungee cords. Until then, what's for dinner?

—Sharon Love Cook—

Tim Russell
Is in Hiding

Yesterday I was a dog. Today I'm a dog.
Tomorrow I'll probably still be a dog. Sigh!
There's so little hope for advancement.
~Charles M. Schulz

The phone rang. I did not know it was for the dog so I answered it.

"Hello?"

"Mrs. Russell?"

"No." Usually only telemarketers called and asked for Mrs. Russell; my name is Farmer.

"Is this the residence of Tim Russell?"

"Tim Russell is my dog." I spoke the truth. Our secondary phone line was listed under our Jack Russell's name so we could avoid paying the phone company's unlisted fee.

"Your dog?" The rude person did not identify herself.

"Yes."

"I see. You named your dog Tim Russell?" she laughed suspiciously.

"Yes." I was aggravated.

"May I speak to him?"

She must be kidding, I thought, "Sure."

How was I to know she was not a telemarketer?

"Timber!" I yelled and laid the phone on the floor. Timber ran

Doggone Funny | 131

over and loudly snarfelled the receiver, expecting it to be a treat. I resisted the urge to command him to speak. Leaving the phone on the floor, I continued with my e-mails. Tim went back to his nap when he discovered the phone was not food. Eventually a tone emanated from the receiver so I hung it up. Whoever it was did not call back.

Originally I thought it was a brilliant move to list our secondary phone line under the dog's name. I got a kick out of handing it off to him when unwanted callers asked for "Tim Russell." Lesson one was never underestimate the absurdity of this world. Someday I may learn that others are more practiced at absurdity than I am.

Tim Russell is now in hiding. It is not a good idea to let your dog talk on the phone. A month after the last doggie phone chat, he received a bill from a local hospital. I laughed and then shredded the bill. Surely reality would triumph.

The next bill came from a collection agency. I wondered if I should respond. I wondered if my dog's credit rating would be ruined if I did not. I wondered if I could get credit cards in his name and run up the bills. With credit, could he get a mortgage for a luxury doghouse? I wondered if a dog owner is responsible for the dog's credit because the owner is the dog's legal guardian or if it was because the dog was under eighteen. I was confused. Admittedly, I was amused the dog was getting a bill.

Out of politeness and naïveté, I called the collection agency to explain that the only hospital my dog had visited was Dr. Dan's Vet Clinic and that we did not owe him anything.

Lesson two was never call a collection agency out of politeness. I was in tears of frustration trying to explain that Tim was a dog. How many different ways can one state a simple, uncomplicated truth? He is a dog. He barks. He chews on bones. He chases cats. He even eats dog food. During the whole conversation, Timber sat and watched me intently, no doubt wondering why I kept repeating his name into the phone. I did not let him talk!

Evidently I did not do a good enough job explaining as we continued to get billed for some other Tim Russell's unpaid hospital visit.

Vainly trying to be a good citizen, I called the hospital and explained the problem. I pleaded for them to get the collection agency off my back. The billing clerk was very understanding. She even got a good chuckle from the mistake. She said she would gladly correct it.

Collection agencies are the Pit Bulls of the money world. We continued to get threats and collection notices. I disconnected the phone number listed under the dog's name but the notices continued. I wrote nasty letters to the collection agency. That did not help.

As a last-ditch attempt to stop the collection agency harassment, I sent them a picture of Tim, a copy of his AKC registration and a copy of his latest vet bill marked PAID. I suggested that they call the vet if they had any further questions. Perhaps if they called Doctor Dan, he could more clearly explain that my Jack Russell Terrier is a dog and that it was unlikely he had been treated at the local hospital.

Finally, we moved. The move was totally unrelated to Tim Russell's $165 hospital bill. However, I did not request Tim Russell's mail be forwarded. Our new phone is not in his name.

I have not heard from the collection agency since. My only fear is that they will put out an arrest warrant for Tim. No doubt they will send a canine unit.

—Jane Marie Allen Farmer—

Chapter 5

My Crazy Family

Matt, Mitts and Magic

Never ever doubt magic. The purest honest thoughts come from children. Ask any child if they believe in magic, and they will tell you the truth.
~Scott Dixon

My husband Matt doesn't believe in magic. So when my mother sent an Elf on the Shelf to our family four years ago, Matt wasn't exactly thrilled. Our son Luke was four years old at the time, and he named our elf Waffles.

Waffles wasn't the type of elf to get into too much trouble. The mere fact that he flew to the North Pole every night to report on Luke and his younger brother Evan and returned in the morning was enough to dazzle their young imaginations. Every Elf on the Shelf comes with rules, and Waffles was no exception. For instance, Waffles does not speak, but can be spoken to. But the most important rule is that Waffles will lose his magic if he is touched by human hands.

This year, Luke and Evan learned that Daddy didn't believe in Christmas magic. They were okay with that, but reminded him that Santa has elves and brings presents, so they would continue to believe. But it bothered me that Matt was so open and decisive about magic not existing. Christmas is such a magical time for me, and I wanted my children to grow up feeling the same way. Over the past year, Matt and I had had several heated arguments regarding faith and science, and what our kids should or shouldn't be exposed to. I didn't know to what extent Matt would tell the children about his beliefs, or whether he'd try to convince them to feel the same way.

I continued showing my belief in magic. One morning, Waffles had pinned himself to our bulletin board in the kitchen. Luke moved a pinned page to get a better look when the tack fell out, and Waffles dropped to the floor. We stood, mouths agape. I worried the jig was up, but Luke didn't miss a beat.

"We have to move him somewhere else," he said. "Somewhere safer."

"Okay," I said, my brain whirring. I needed a way to pick up Waffles that wouldn't break the most important rule. I grabbed the oven mitts and scooped Waffles up in my hands. With the care one would give transporting a Fabergé egg, I delicately placed Waffles on a higher perch on the mantel. Matt watched me with I'm-married-to-a-crazy-lady eyes, thinking the whole thing silly. I, on the other hand, felt I had averted a Christmas disaster.

The next morning, Waffles sat on top of a light in our chandelier above the dining-room table. We only used the table for company, and the boys knew to never go in there, so Waffles chose a safe enough place. That evening, I sat down at the kitchen table with my children. Matt grabbed the food from the stove to transition to the table.

"I smell smoke," Evan said.

Immediately, I looked at the stove and sniffed the air. "I smell something, too." From my seat, I had a clear view into the dining room. The lights were on and had been on for a while.

"It's Waffles!" I froze in my chair as smoke billowed from Waffles.

My husband stepped toward the dining room and froze for a split second. He backtracked to the stove and grabbed oven mitts.

My heart pounded as my husband ran to Waffles, mitted up, and freed him from the scorching light bulb. He ran the elf patient, who was still smoking with one leg dangling by a thread, through the kitchen to the back deck.

Our hero returned and saw the fear in Luke's eyes.

"It's okay, Luke." He hugged our son. "The cold air should cool him off."

We sat in silence, looking at each other. I couldn't hold it in any longer: I burst out laughing. Evan followed, and then Luke. Matt laughed and shook his head. "Waffles needs to be more careful," he said.

After the kids went to bed, I retrieved Waffles from the back deck. His right leg fell off completely, and his left hung on by mere threads. His bottom was inverted, taking the shape of the light bulb. Burnt red fabric covered the top of the light bulb.

Waffles recovered on ice in our freezer for two nights until he was stable enough to go back to the North Pole. His surgery was a success, and he made a full recovery. After insurance, his medical expenses only cost $29.99 out of pocket.

Our relatives and friends followed the Waffles saga on social media. Many added their prayers for Waffles to pull through, along with their jokes and personal elf experiences. While we still laugh at the ordeal and say it seems like something out of a television show or movie, there is one part of the incident that struck me: the oven mitts.

Let me be clear. Waffles may have been smoking, but he was not up in flames. He could have easily been picked up by his head and moved outside or under the faucet. The mitts were not retrieved for safety. Matt, the grown man who adamantly claims magic is not real, wore those mitts in order to save the elfin magic.

It may seem a small gesture, but it meant the world to me. Matt made the decision that it didn't matter what he believed. Magic brought such joy to our children's lives that it would have been wrong to take it away from them so young. And the fact that a Christmas elf gave that gift to our family is, in itself, magical.

— Mary Shotwell —

43

The Zamboni

My other car is a Zamboni.
~Hockey Saying

By the middle of December the small pond in back of our home was starting to freeze, the first fragile layers of thin ice crusting on its surface. As soon as we saw those, my brother and I kept a constant vigil. We walked down to the water's edge each day after school, putting progressively more and more weight onto the ice until one of us — the braver, usually my brother — was able to tiptoe out a few feet, one arm grabbing tightly to a rope. Once there, he would jump up and down, pounding his boots into the ice, testing it.

"It's a few inches, at least," he turned to me and said a week after the vigil had started. "Come out."

I let the rope down and picked up my hockey stick, holding it horizontally so I formed a giant "T." Should I go through, the stick would hopefully bar me from going completely under. Inching onto the ice, I stood next to my brother and then both of us jumped up and down, shuffling closer to the middle of the pond. The ice creaked beneath us and we stopped, waiting to go through, hockey sticks ready. But the ice was quiet, easily four to six inches thick.

"Tomorrow," I announced. "It'll be perfect tomorrow."

Rain can do one of two things to a backyard hockey rink. It can either make it the sweetest, smoothest surface you have ever glided across, or it can turn it into those bone-jarring rumble strips on the side of major highways. Bam-bam-bam-bam-bam-bam. More often it is the latter, especially early in the season when the weather shifts between freezing and melting during an afternoon. On Saturday morning we discovered that was what had happened to our ice. Millions of ice pebbles scarred the surface. Undeterred, we strapped on skates, threw down a puck and tried to make the most of it.

Shortly after christening this year's season, my brother skated over to me. "Th-th-th-th-th-is... s-s-s-s-s-t-t-t-t-inks," he said, bouncing to a rest beside me.

"Yes, it does," I agreed. "Let's go see Dad."

Our father has a gift for figuring out solutions to such problems, rigging up impossibly complex contraptions that sputter and smoke and break numerous environmental laws. Creating the perfect ice rink was one of his favorite projects. One year, we ran a series of hoses onto the ice to flood a new inch of water on top of the bad one. The hoses froze, the ice clumped in awkward waves, and the rink was useless until it melted and refroze a week later. Another year, we took an axe to a corner of the pond and chopped through to the liquid beneath. We then set a sump pump into it with a hose running out to the middle of the pond. The theory again was to flood the old surface and create "glass" to skate on. At the rate the pump worked, it would have taken us the entire winter. As it was, after a few hours, the hose froze, the ice clumped in awkward waves, and the rink was useless until it melted and refroze a week later. This year, however, he tried something totally different. Revolutionary.

The homemade, portable Zamboni machine.

Taking an old feed trough from the back yard, my father instructed us, once we dragged it down to the ice, to fill it with wood — twigs, branches, logs, anything. He then tied a rope to a hole at one end of it and with the help of some lighter fluid and a match, set the whole contraption alight. My brother and I stared, perplexed. Half the enjoyment for my father, I think, came in explaining how his contraptions were supposed to work.

"Once the fire really gets going, the metal will get really hot," he said. "Hot enough to melt ice. Then we just drag it around and it will act like an iron, smoothing down the rough spots." As always, my brother and I smiled. His plan did sound good.

Half an hour later, a suitable time as any, my father picked up the free end of the rope, latched it over his shoulder, turned about and leaned forward.

The Zamboni didn't move.

He tried again.

It still didn't budge.

"It's too heavy," he announced. "We need to take some of the wood out."

My brother and I looked at each other and then at the wood. It was on fire, right?

Dad grunted. "Fine. I'll do it." Deftly pinching unlit pieces, he emptied half the wood out and picked up the rope again. By now, hours had passed since we first stepped onto the ice.

"Here we go," he said and hefted once more.

The Zamboni jerked to life. Dad set forth across the pond.

More so than any image I carry with me from a decade of skating on ponds with friends and family, I can picture perfectly Dad trudging away from the two of us, his thick mountain-man jacket on, a ratty pair of blue jeans, tan boots and a red Folgers Coffee hat on his head. Behind him, like some poor, mistreated pet, stumbled the gray trough, tiny embers shooting over its lip onto the ice.

He walked slowly, so as to give the Zamboni extra time to do its ironing. After about twenty yards, still moving forward, he said to us over his shoulder, "Well?"

I'd like to say that there before us was blazed a path of glassy ice, as neatly done as any giant machine in a professional rink... and that over the next few hours he patiently walked line after line, like mowing a lawn, until the entire pond was the sweetest, most perfect surface ever created in a back yard. I'd like to say that. Sadly, it was impossible to tell where exactly the Zamboni had traveled. The bumps and grooves caused by the rain were still there, though they might have glistened a bit more, as if sweating.

"Well?" he said again.

"Nothing," I answered.

For many people this might have been the sign to end the project — drag the trough off the ice, put the fire out, and wait for the pond to melt and refreeze in a week. That was what my brother and I thought. But not our father. As we scooted off the ice and returned to the kitchen for hot chocolate, he kept going, patiently walking line after line. He stayed out there for another hour, perhaps two, while we watched occasionally through the sliding glass door. Eventually, as afternoon turned into early evening and the temperature got colder and no one was checking up on him anymore, he dumped the trough into the snow on the bank and clambered through the back yard into the basement. The pond would have to wait for warmer weather.

There's a lesson in the Zamboni about fatherhood, I think: that it is not about being perfect in your actions but perfect in your intent. Love is not smooth as glass, but bumpy as pebbled ice with ridges, and holes, and places to fall down. Sometimes no one will be watching you walk line after line, but they'll remember that you were out there and they'll smile, the sweetest, smoothest, warmest smile you've ever seen.

Perhaps the Zamboni really did work.

— Michael Sullivan —

Men in Training

Boys will be boys, and so will a lot of middle-aged men.
~Frank McKinney "Kin" Hubbard

Three generations of boys were sitting on the floor on Christmas morning — the grandfather, the father and the toddler. The toddler had just opened the last gift under the tree. It was an amazing train set, the kind of train set the grandfather and father had only dreamed about as little boys. The toddler was so excited. The grandfather and the father were even more excited, judging by the gleam in their eyes. The train cars were ready to roll so all that was needed was to put the track together the way you wanted it. Simple you say. Not even close!

The various configurations that you could assemble filled a twenty-page booklet. Did you want a simple oval? Are you kidding me? A figure eight? How boring. How about an up and down and over and around and through? Now that sounded much better to the older boys. The toddler would have been pleased with the simple oval but his playmates wouldn't hear of it.

Out came all of the parts. No one bothered to look at the instructions — oh, no... why would anyone bother to follow directions? The grandfather and the father proceeded to try to put the pieces of the track together. How frustrating. Nothing seemed to fit right. Part A really didn't go with part B. And part C was nowhere to be found. After much grumbling and mumbling and a few pointed "I told you so's" the track was put together and ready to use. The toddler was so excited. Finally he would be able to play with his gift.

Well, not exactly. The grandfather and the father explained to the toddler that, being the loving and concerned people they were, they wanted to test it out to be sure everything worked correctly. How thoughtful of them. And so there they sat, grandfather and father, having a play date on the living room floor. The only things missing were the engineer hats.

The train made its own sounds, and thank goodness for that. At least the grandmother and the mother didn't have to listen to two grown men making choo-choo and chug-a-chug-a-chug-a-chug noises. Unfortunately the only sound the train didn't come equipped with was the whistle, but the two big boys more than made up for that. Each time the train went around a curve or started up a hill, or down a hill, the grandfather and the father made lovely and quite realistic train whistle sounds complete with arm movements. Whoo-whoo. Can't you just hear and picture that? They took turns driving the train and actually got along quite well except for the time the father thought it should be his turn to make the whistle sounds and the grandfather was sure it was his turn. The toddler had to step in and settle the dispute.

What's a toddler to do when his grandfather and his father won't let him play with his very own toy? What are a toddler's grandmother and mother to do while they watch this whole scene? They tried to console the toddler and distract him with his other new toys. They tried to explain to him how nice it was that the grandfather and the father cared so much about him and were taking all this time to work on the train so it would be perfect for him.

The toddler was smarter than that. He knew exactly what was happening. The grandfather and the father had taken his toy and wouldn't share. But finally, after what seemed like hours, they invited the toddler to come over and sit cross-legged with them on the floor, next to the train. They even let the toddler drive HIS train... up and down and over and around and through. And they let him make the whistle sound... but not all the time. The grandmother and the mother watched this all happening and decided that for the next Christmas, identical toys needed to be bought for all three boys… the grandfather, the father and the toddler. No sharing necessary. Boys will be boys.

— Barbara LoMonaco —

45

Body Language

Speak the truth, but leave immediately after.
~Slovenian Proverb

"Is that when I get my peanut?" asked my two-year-old daughter. We were talking about what her life would be like when she was four like her big brother and how she would be able to do all the big-kid things that he did.

"What are you talking about?" I asked.

"My peanut. Do I get my peanut when I'm four?"

Oh.

Maybe Freud was right.

My disappointed daughter listened to my explanation about the difference between boys and girls, and how she would not grow a peanut like her brother's by the time she was four. Then, presaging the day she would become a doctor, she proceeded to interview random men on the street in our town, asking them, "Do you have a peanut?" Luckily, none of them knew what a peanut was either!

Her patient assessments resumed when she was about four. I had, of course, worked hard to indoctrinate my children on the danger of smoking, and in fact one of their grandfathers had already contracted cancer from smoking. So I shouldn't have been surprised when my budding doctor approached a man on the street one day, and loudly announced, "That man is stupid and he's going to die." I can only hope that was the last straw for him and he decided right then and there to quit.

My son's medical education was limited to one, most important lesson. We all know that the best way to have a conversation with your son is to have him sitting in the back seat of the car right behind you where you can't see him except with the eyes in the back of your head. So that was when my seven-year-old felt comfortable asking me, "How do you make a baby?"

It was a little earlier than I had expected to have the conversation but I forged ahead and told him: "When a man and a woman love each other and get married, the man puts a seed inside the woman to grow a baby." You could practically hear the violins playing.

But that wasn't enough and he pressed on, so I had to expand a bit on the methodology. When he demanded a full explanation because he couldn't understand how this could possibly happen, unless the woman swallowed the seed like a pill, I was forced to divulge all the gory details. There was a long incredulous pause, and then I heard a tremulous little voice in the back seat saying, "So how do you adopt?"

— Amy Newmark —

46

The Ugly Elf Tradition

You will do foolish things,
but do them with enthusiasm.
~Colette

ad never could resist an auction. The fast-talking auction-
eer. Chattering bidders. A raised finger here and there.
Excitement in the air. Best of all, mystery items. Who knew
what kind of bargains one might get in a plain cardboard
box?

Besides, it was almost Christmas, and Dad always put off his gift
shopping until the last minute. This year, perhaps he could do his gift
buying by bidding on those mystery boxes. And so he did.

The bidding moved fast and furious. Next thing we knew, Dad
had snagged one of those promising, mysterious packages. It was a
good-sized box, and we all felt excited when Dad cut it open.

What did we find? The most ugly Christmas ornament ever
designed by a human being — a nasty little hard-plastic elf. It was red
and green, traditional festive seasonal colors, but that elf frowned out
at the world with pure hate. We'd never seen a belligerent Christmas
ornament before.

Worst of all, the box held dozens and dozens of hateful, nasty
little elves. Now what?

Determined to turn this disaster into a victory, Dad insisted on
using those dreadful elves. Every gift we gave that year — to friends,
neighbors, the milkman, letter carrier and trash collectors — included

an elf tied cheerfully to the gift package, fastened firmly so nobody could pretend to lose theirs. To the best of my recollection, no one thanked us for the ugly elves. No one pretended to like them or called them cute.

And, of course, since there was an almost endless supply of nasty elves, we put a bunch on our own Christmas tree, too.

Those elves were sturdy. No matter how often I tried dropping them on hard floors, they never broke or even cracked. They were just about indestructible.

My very first Christmas tree in my own home had elves on it. Mom insisted, and Dad agreed. I'm sure my brother was forced to take his share, too.

And the ugly elf tradition persists. My daughter, in her own home with her own family, has to decorate her tree with an ugly elf or two or three. The things go on forever. Most likely, my kids' kids will be hanging nasty little ugly elves on their holiday trees some day.

By now, it's a solid family tradition, and we all have to do our part. Nobody gets a free pass. Nobody gets to skip the ugly elves. Being indestructible, the elves will be part of our Christmas celebration forever. Mine hang at the very back of the tree where I don't have to see them.

Did Dad learn his lesson about mystery auction items? Nope. Next, he bid on an English racing bike as a gift for me, and he won. The bike never did work right, but it looked great under the tree where it blocked our view of a couple of those ugly elves.

— Karen M. Leet —

47

Last Laugh

Mirth is God's medicine.
Everybody ought to bathe in it.
~Henry Ward Beecher

My father's funeral could have been a sitcom. There wasn't much to laugh about in the last few years of Dad's life. On Christmas Eve 1996, my mother had a stroke. It left her partially paralyzed and unable to talk clearly. Dad spent the next four years caring for her, despite his own battle with prostate cancer.

In November 1999, they moved to a nursing home, where Dad died in mid-February 2000. The final few weeks were especially difficult. He had grown up in an orphanage and the last place he wanted to be was an institution — or, more precisely, an institution was absolutely not the last place he wanted to be. He was an independent man, but he was no longer able to get around on his own, even to use the bathroom. And he was in so much pain that his moans often brought tears to the nurses' eyes.

He died during a snowstorm on a Sunday night. The memorial service was Thursday, the only bright day in a week of stormy weather.

He had left no instructions for a memorial service and he hadn't been to church for years. But he had been raised a Catholic and at one time considered entering the priesthood. So we asked the local parish priest to conduct the service, even though he knew Dad solely through our brief descriptions. We had no way of knowing that he would accidentally provide us with one of our most cherished memories.

My sister Sandra, who travels widely, has a knack for relaxing anywhere and a certain lack of inhibition. At one point, before anyone had arrived at the funeral home but the two of us and my son-in-law, who had driven us, she decided she was exhausted. So she lay down on the floor. Bill, one of the funeral directors walked into the room — and almost fainted when he saw what looked like a body lying at the front of the room.

That gave us a small chuckle, but there was more in store. The organist was the mother of the funeral-home owner, a nice woman whom I'd met before. We'd picked a couple of songs for the service, and asked her to finish with "On the Street Where You Live." Both our parents loved show tunes. During our teens, if Dad came home with a few drinks in him, he often asked Mum or me to play his favorites on the piano, including "On the Street Where You Live." That, we decided, should be the very last song.

We dug out Mum's sheet music so Mrs. Anderson could practice before the service. Then, at the last minute, she asked us to pick a few more songs, explaining that sometimes services went on just a little longer than anticipated and that she didn't want to run out of music. So we made our choices, again emphasizing that "On the Street Where You Live" should be the last one.

People were starting to arrive. Dan, my husband, wheeled Mum in. She looked very nice, dressed in a red woolen jacket, hair freshly done, wearing a touch of make-up. This was the biggest social event she'd been at in years, and although she sometimes wept silently, she spent a lot of time looking around to see who was there, occasionally waving with her good hand.

One of the last to arrive was Dan's Uncle Andy. He and my parents had been friends as teenagers. He was a bit eccentric, to put it politely. He had lived alone most of his life and frequently wandered around unshaven, wearing appallingly stained or worn clothes. But he had gone all out for the funeral. His hair was neatly cut and combed, he was clean-shaven, and he was wearing an orangey-red denim leisure suit straight out of the 1970s.

Sandra and I rolled our eyes at each other, but said nothing. Mum gave him a big grin and held his hand for a few moments.

The music began. We were still greeting people when "On the Street Where You Live" started. Just as we realized what was playing, the funeral director came over to explain. "My mother is in the early stages of Alzheimer's. She can't drive any more, can't live alone, but she's a talented musician and I hate to take this away from her."

"Oh," one of us said. Sandra and I exchanged quick looks, silently communicating, "I'm okay with this if you're okay." We both knew that if it had been Dad, he would have been falling over himself to be nice to Mrs. Anderson. So we soothed Richard, telling him everything would be just fine.

As we took our places at the front of the chapel, we both noticed that Mrs. Anderson had taken off her shoes and was pounding the pedals in her stocking feet. The priest slipped behind the lectern. Conversation ebbed. Mrs. Anderson kept playing.

And playing.

Father Paul looked at us. I looked away. Sandra raised her eyebrow. Father Paul looked at Mrs. Anderson. Everyone looked at Mrs. Anderson. Finally, the priest went over, put his hand on her shoulder, whispered something in her ear. She nodded, but kept on playing until the song was over.

We had met Father Paul two days earlier and knew that he was a former mailman who had come to the priesthood somewhat later in life. A small man with protruding front teeth and short hair that stood on end, he looked a bit like Alvin the chipmunk trying to be a punk star.

The vestments, of course, didn't belong to a punk star image — the chasuble was creamy colored, flecked with darker threads, as though it had been spun from wheat. But he was wearing dark running shoes, possibly to make a quick getaway after the funeral.

And then he called our father Harold.

Dad's name was Frank. He had a great laugh and a great sense of humor. Puns, slapstick, political satire, all might provoke a chuckle or a roar. He was also deeply amused by children, animals, and the ridiculousness of everyday life.

When the priest called him Harold, Sandra and I studiously avoided looking at each other. Somewhere in a back row, one of my friends poked another and whispered, "Cheryl's going to have a fit." She was right, but not for the reasons she thought. Sandra and I were trying not to burst into a fit of laughter.

When we were teenagers, Bill Cosby was one of the family's favourite comedians. Sandra had started calling Dad "old weird Harold" after one of the characters in Bill Cosby's comedy routines. When the priest mistakenly used the name, we both thought of that. And smiled, knowing that somewhere out in the universe, Dad was smiling with us.

— Cheryl MacDonald —

48

Number Two

You can learn many things from children.
How much patience you have, for instance.
~Franklin P. Jones

Our fixer-upper was in need of repair to various parts of its concrete construction. With each cement job, my husband Larry would smooth out a nice, even finish. We would walk away with pride.

We would return later to admire our work, only to find a "Z" etched into the cement. One of our many children had become a Zorro fan and was leaving Z's everywhere possible. We would question the children as to who had left their mark, but, as any true Zorro knows, anonymity is of utmost importance.

One day after smoothing out a new step in front of the bathroom, Larry pleaded with me to guard the step while he went after more supplies. He then asked that the children not etch any Z's in the new step. When he left I set up a chair and grabbed a book to pass the time while I kept watch.

But I was called away from my post — probably to break up a wrestling match turned rough. And when I returned there was something new in the cement. Not a Z; a 2.

I wanted to make sure that I wouldn't mess up the step, so I called Larry's cell phone to ask him what tool to use to make the cement perfectly smooth again. The conversation went something like this:

Me: Hi, babe. Sorry to interrupt your shopping, but I need to know how to fix the cement. One of the kids made a number two in it.

Him: WHAT? Why would they do such a thing?

Me: Oh, you know how kids are... So how do I go about fixing it?

Him: I just don't understand kids sometimes. What on earth were they thinking?

Me: Listen, babe, it's no big deal. I can just smooth it out.

Him: SMOOTH IT OUT? You can't just smooth it out. That's disgusting! Why didn't they just use the toilet for the number two? The bathroom is right there!

I don't know why it took me so long to catch the obvious miscommunication, but when I did, I couldn't contain the laughter. It must have been contagious because he began to chuckle too.

Finally I was able to compose myself and explain that it was a numeral two that someone had drawn in the cement.

To this day, this is not only our funniest adventures in miscommunication, it is our favorite home renovation story.

— Carrie M. Leach —

49

The Gift of Love

The greatest gift that you can give anyone
is your pure love.
~Debasish Mridha

eenagers. Some say it's hard to live with them. I say it's sad to live without them. That is where my heart was the Christmas our son Chris was nineteen and our daughter Melissa was seventeen. I was overwhelmed by the reality that in just a few short years, they would both be off pursuing their own lives. I decided I wanted to tell them how much I loved them in a way they would never forget.

I came up with a plan. Being a good kindergarten teacher, I chose to use the five senses as my way of accomplishing this important assignment. It would require a separate gift for each sense for them to open on Christmas morning.

For the sense of sight, I gave each of them a framed photo of the three of us. This was no easy task since I was usually behind the camera. I did manage to find one nice one of us in our front yard, so that would have to do.

The sense of taste was accomplished through the compiling of a recipe book for each of them containing some of their favorite dishes I had made over the years. I really had to think through some of these recipes since I don't usually measure everything as I cook.

When it came to the sense of smell, I bought each of them a small bottle of my favorite perfume. I figured if they were missing me, they could smell the cologne, and it would bring me closer to them.

A CD called *The Line Between the Two* by Mark Harris containing the song "Find Your Wings" was how I wrapped up their sense of hearing. This song said everything I wanted them to know. I gave them roots, and now I wanted to give them wings!

This just left the sense of touch. For this one, I had to get a little more creative. I decided to make each of them a fleece blanket. On the blanket I hand-appliquéd a cutout of my hand with a red heart in the palm. The idea was that when they wrapped the blanket around themselves, my hand would be over their heart. I know it sounds a little cheesy, but I was all in by that point.

Christmas morning finally came. I was so excited to give them their special gifts of love. I saved these special gifts until the end. When it was time, I explained how much I wanted them to always know my love, and I was using these five gifts to convey that message.

I had them open the CD first so we could all listen to the song together. They proceeded through the rest of the gifts, saving the blanket for last. As they opened the blanket, they looked at each other, and then looked at me with tears in their eyes. Our daughter Melissa asked finally, "Mom, are you dying?"

Well, I didn't see that coming!

—Janell Michael—

50

The Ballot Box

The ballot box is the surest arbiter
of disputes among free men.
~James Buchanan

y fourteen-year-old son, Steven, thought Britney Spears would be a good name for the new kitten. She didn't really look like a Britney Spears or even act like a Britney Spears. In fact, she couldn't dance or sing, but Steven liked the idea of Britney Spears living in his house. Unfortunately, my husband, Sam, didn't like it.

"Come up with something better," I said.

"Cleo," Sam said, "short for Cleopatra."

"She doesn't look like a Cleopatra," said seventeen-year-old Jeff, who normally couldn't be bothered with family decisions but had taken a sudden interest in naming the cat. "I think she looks like a Kenshin."

"He's not naming the cat after a Japanese cartoon character," said Steven, referring to Jeff's interest in Japanese animation. "That's a dumb name. I'm not naming my cat a dumb name."

"Britney Spears isn't dumb?" asked Jeff, not waiting for an answer.

"It isn't as dumb as Kenshin, the cartoon guy who can't talk English unless he has subtitles," Steve battled back. "You're not naming my cat after a dumb cartoon guy who carries a cartoon sword."

"Look at her face," said Jeff. "She even has markings like Kenshin. See the stripe? That's like Kenshin's scar."

"I don't like it," I said, backing up Steven.

"So, you have a better idea?" asked Sam.

"Of course, I do. I think we should name her Trouble. She has been a pest since we brought her home." I was thinking of how little work I'd gotten done since this kitten, who likes to watch computer screens while being stretched across my chest, entered our life. I was thinking about how she hadn't been declawed yet and how she climbed up my furniture. I was thinking of how miserable she'd been making our older, more set-in-their-way cats, who were simply putting up with her until they were hungry enough to eat her. I was thinking about her level of energy and her inability to find a place to sleep.

"Trouble is a dumb name," the men all said at once.

Thus, the dilemma of naming the new kitten began. But with every dilemma comes a solution. We decided to let everyone who came to see the new kitten vote on a name. We would put Britney Spears, Kenshin, Cleopatra, and Trouble on a ballot. We would even leave a space for a write-in vote. The name with the most votes would win. I set the deadline at 5 p.m. Sunday.

The voters started arriving. First, Steven invited everyone he knew in the neighborhood and from school to vote. Mothers and fathers of his friends came in to meet the new kitten and vote.

"Her name is going to be Britney Spears," he said confidently, as each vote entered our ballot box that looked strikingly like a Reebok box. Then Jeff started arriving home after school and after work and after karate class with a different girl or girls.

"This is Megan," I'd get, as his newest female interest would squeal, "Oh what a cute kitten, Jeffrey."

"Doesn't she look like a Kenshin?" he'd ask.

"Kenshin?" she'd ask, as he pushed a ballot in front of her and guided her hand toward the right hole and helped her fill in the circle with the arrow pointing toward it. I was amazed at how many Megans my son knew. And Crystals. And Stephanies. And Melissas. And Jennifers. And Andreas.

Thanksgiving was a tumult. No one was watching the ballot box, but when I asked my husband if his relatives all voted, he smirked and said, "Looks like it's going to be Cleopatra. By the way, that was great STUFFING," Sam added.

On Sunday, we watched the clock. At five o'clock, we took the box and began to open it at the kitchen table. A few minutes later Steven arrived. "I have one more friend who wanted to vote," he said waving another ballot.

"Sorry," I said. "Five o'clock deadline and it's ten minutes after!"

"That's not fair," Steven said, "it's only a few minutes late. Every vote should count. In a fair election, every vote should count."

We sat around the kitchen table a long time. We held the ballots up to the light to make sure we were reading each vote correctly. We argued about whether it was confusing with the circles being so close together. We argued about legibility and intent. We argued if one ballot was for Kenshin or if it was a coffee stain. Another ballot had two votes and we decided to throw that ballot out, even though my husband insisted it was chocolate syrup and not a vote for Britney Spears. We argued if we should count the mail-in votes from Grandma and Cousin Bob even though they hadn't met the cat. We thought it would be too close to call, but one name got three more votes. We counted the votes again. The vote came out similar, but not the same. We counted the votes a third time and fourth time until we were convinced we were close enough to have a name. Unfortunately, Steven has voiced a formal protest and said he is taking it to the Supreme Court, so the count is still not official, even though it's been certified by the veterinarian. Her name is Cleopatra, Queen of Denial.

— Felice Prager —

51

Almost Perfect

*The only thing faster than the speed of thought
is the speed of forgetfulness. Good thing we have
other people to help us remember.*
~Vera Nazarian,
The Perpetual Calendar of Inspiration

Our fourth child arrived in November 1984 — a sweet, healthy girl with dark, fuzzy hair and big, blue eyes. I was very glad she arrived in November because Christmas would soon be upon us, and I needed every day left to organize and prepare.

That year, more preparations were required than usual, as eight additional people were joining us for the holidays — my parents, an aunt and uncle, their daughter, her little boy, and their newly married son and his wife.

Our families had always been close. With our homes a few streets apart, we were together a great deal and shared many good times. So, although there'd be a few more people that year, they were all special to me, and I was excited to have them join us.

Snow was falling in huge, quarter-sized flakes as the crowd arrived on Christmas Eve day. Parcels galore were carried in, and our kids checked every tag as they crammed them under the tree. Extra shaking and sniffing took place when their names were on the tags.

"Okay, everyone is assigned a room, so find the door with your name on it and make yourself at home." I did my best to direct everyone, with my new daughter tucked tightly under one arm. "And when you're settled in, come down for hot chocolate or tobogganing in the back yard."

Squeals of excitement ricocheted from the walls, and the celebration was suddenly in full swing.

At supper, the table was surrounded by rosy-cheeked kids smelling like the great outdoors. The men chatted as the women reviewed the traditional menu for Christmas dinner.

"Do you have all the vegetables, dear?" my mom asked sweetly. "And were you able to get the jellied salad started so I can finish it tonight?"

"It's all done, Mom," I answered.

"What about buns? Did you find those nice soft ones?"

"Yup—fresh as I could get."

"And the turkey is defrosting in the garage?" asked my aunt. "We'll stuff that right after dinner."

Complete silence hung in the air as my face turned red. "Ahhh… the turkey is still in the freezer. I forgot it needed to thaw."

Both my aunt and my mom gave a soft gasp. "Oh, dear." Mom sounded calm, but her brow was furrowed. "How are we going to manage that?"

"Good grief!" my aunt added. "You always defrost the turkey a day ahead." She didn't sound quite as calm. "It's impossible to stuff now."

Years later, I realized I could have just cooked that turkey from frozen, but at the time, dealing with "new baby brain," I panicked.

"My microwave isn't working," I said. "I don't know what to do!" The ladies stared at my stricken face, obviously thinking the same thing.

My husband overheard our laments and pitched in. "We have a microwave at the office. I'll take the guys there, and we can enjoy a sauna while it defrosts."

The plan was brilliant! Within minutes, the men were all loaded in the car, with my newlywed cousin securing the twenty-five-pound turkey on his lap. While they were gone, we cleaned up dinner, corralled the antsy children to listen to *The Night Before Christmas*, tucked them in their beds, and then continued preparations for the next day.

Nervously, we watched the clock. The men finally returned, entering the kitchen carrying a greasy bag, with faces reflecting something akin to fear.

"What happened?" I asked.

"Well," my husband said, "I forgot that the microwave was just a tiny one. The turkey was double the size of the oven, so we crushed it as best we could and squeezed it into the opening. It took every muscle we had to do it, and... you may not like the results." He opened the bag and pulled out an object that had no resemblance to the bird they left with. "By the time we got it crushed and into the microwave, it was squished up against the sides and top, filling the whole space."

"Got a little fried," my cousin said with a grin.

I looked at the squashed, leathery turkey and could only imagine what had taken place inside that office. Perhaps muscles had been used, but by the look of it, I suspected the heel of a shoe had been involved. "Well," I said, "we can go to bed now, since stuffing it is out of the question."

We dropped into our beds, and it felt like we had just fallen asleep when we awoke to a horrific noise. Squinting at the clock revealed it was 4:00 a.m.! The noises were getting louder, so I left my warm covers to investigate and discovered our six-year-old son had found the tool set that was waiting for him under the tree. He'd opened it and was trying out the hammer and saw, in the dark, on what I could only hope was not our furniture.

Soon, the whole house was awake. With sleepy shouts of "Merry Christmas!" everyone staggered down the stairs. I fed the baby while we watched the kids open the rest of their presents. In spite of the chaos, something niggled at the back of my mind. There was something I was forgetting, but I couldn't put my finger on it. Knowing it would eventually come to me, I let it go and enjoyed the morning.

After the torn paper and candy wrappers were cleaned up, the men were snoring where they sat, so we ladies finished preparations for the Christmas dinner, making sure everything would be perfect. It was nice to have the extra help as we worked together in the kitchen. I reviewed the menu. The veggies were cooked, the gravy was made, homemade cranberries awaited in a fancy dish, the buns were cut and buttered, the jellied salad turned out perfectly, and Mom had prepared a beautiful cabbage salad. I found and cooked some stove-top stuffing to make up for the traditional stuffing, and even the mutilated, overcooked turkey didn't look too bad sitting on an elegant platter.

It was all there. We'd done it! The dinner bell rang, and the hungry herd charged to their places at the table. I hadn't figured out what had been bothering me earlier, but the joy of the day quickly replaced any worries. I smiled at my family sitting on either side. Nothing could possibly spoil this.

The aroma of deliciousness filled the room, and we could almost taste that turkey as we joined hands for prayer.

After giving a heartfelt grace, my husband declared, "Well, it's been quite an adventure, but everything looks amazing. Let's eat!"

We started to load up our plates when our nine-year-old daughter leaned over and asked, "Has anyone seen the potatoes?"

Well, it was almost perfect!

— Heather Rodin —

Holiday Hiccups

52

Home Invasion

Many of our fears are tissue-paper-thin,
and a single courageous step would
carry us clear through them.
~Brendan Francis

t was Christmas Eve. Or Christmas Day, technically. The glaring backlight of my phone reminded me how late it was as it guided me into my house. I quietly closed the back door behind me and snuck up the stairs, wincing at every groan of the floorboards. My parents knew I was going to be out with friends late, but I still didn't want to wake them. I made it to my room and crawled into bed, exhausted. I fell asleep quickly.

The next thing I heard were hoarse, terrified whispers from my sister across the hall.

"Oh my god, oh my god, oh my god..." I heard my sister Erika say slowly and quietly.

What was happening? I guessed it was around 4:30 a.m. I was still waking up, but I could hear the terror in her voice. She repeated her words over and over again, speeding up and getting louder. I had no idea what was going on.

"Oh my god, oh my god, oh my GOD..."

I was still groggy and confused. Was she dreaming? Sleepwalking?

"Who are you?" I heard her say.

I woke up instantly. I knew then what had happened: our house had been infiltrated. The possibility of expensive items waiting under the tree must have been appealing to burglars, and no one would expect a robbery on Christmas Day. The perfect crime.

I don't know how much time had passed since I woke up. Erika was still sobbing, calling out to the figure standing feet from her. I felt a rush of aggressive bravery. My sister was in danger. Maybe my parents were too — I had no idea if the intruders had made it into their bedroom or not. But me — I was alive, and I was the only one who could help her. The only one who could save my family.

How could I defend her? What weapons did I have? I had no idea, and no plan at all. In my bed, I needed to go for two items quickly: my glasses and my light. I'd be blind without either. I only needed one swift move to get to both. Once the light was on, I would have only seconds before her attacker realized I was awake and coming. Seconds to find a weapon and charge into Erika's room. Seconds to survive. I flipped over in my bed and reached to my nightstand.

But I didn't make it to the light, or to my glasses. To the weapon, or to Erika. Instead, I froze in horror, because in front of me stood a blurry and dark figure, feet from my bed.

They were in my room too.

The panic kept me frozen for seconds that seemed like hours. I could still hear Erika, but my room seemed so still, so quiet. It was just me and the man in my room. I didn't move, and neither did he. It was horrifying.

"WHO ARE YOU?" Erika screeched.

Suddenly, the blood rushed through my entire body, unlocking my joints and pushing me forward. I struggled with the light, turning it on while I searched for my glasses. I tried to hide a terrified sob while I fumbled around on my nightstand. What was I going to do? What was he waiting for?

My palm smashed into my glasses. Shaking, sweating, and crying, in what I assumed would be my last moments, I jabbed my glasses onto my face and looked up at my attacker.

Before me stood a cardboard cutout of teen heartthrob Edward

Cullen. The singer Justin Bieber was in Erika's room. They were Christmas presents from our parents.

— Monika LaPlante —

53

O Wholly Overwhelming Night

A child is a curly dimpled lunatic.
~Ralph Waldo Emerson

The Christmas Eve children's service overflowed with little ones, laughter, and anticipation. Kids squirmed in holiday dresses or once-a-year ties in the crowded pews. To entertain the families squeezed into every possible seat, piano students pounded "Silent Night" or "The First Noel" on the choir director's piano. When their turns ended, they rushed back to their smiling parents and grandparents.

My little family missed most of this. We decided to forgo getting seats at the children's service in favor of a shorter wait time beforehand. Our younger daughter, two-and-a-half-year-old Mary Claire, has been nicknamed "Our Lady of Perpetual Motion." She needed room to roam so we were off standing at the back of the church anyway.

We strolled into church just before Father Jim began his procession. Twinkling lights and Christmas hymns greeted us. I spied an opening near the low baptismal font. It provided some breathing room, perfect for a toddler on the move. A few minutes later, my husband came in from parking the car and we stood together, holding hands, for the opening prayers.

When Father Jim called the children forward for the Christmas story, the real magic began. Each Christmas Eve, he creates a giant flannel storyboard on his vestments and robes. The little ones place felt pieces of the story — cutout sheep, shepherds, baby Jesus — on his vestments. By the end, Father Jim is covered with fabric, the children enjoy the story, and the congregation giggles at the show.

Our older daughter, a kindergartner, grinned with excitement. She was in charge this year, and took her role seriously. Throughout December she had "practiced" reenacting the Christmas story with our toy nativity set. She'd perched her little sister on her lap and told the story — with a few fractured carols sprinkled in — over and over. It always ended with a rousing rendition of "Happy Birthday" to Jesus.

I watched nervously as our girls walked hand-in-hand down the long center aisle for the children's message. Kids poured out of every pew, clamoring for a seat on the altar steps. We were on high alert, afraid Mary Claire might make a run for it. We didn't need to be. Our daughters sat sweetly side by side in their fancy holiday dresses and hung on every word. My eyes were damp when Father Jim finished and the girls ran back toward us. I hugged them tightly. What a special Christmas this was becoming!

Yet as the service continued, Mary Claire's patience wore thin. She hadn't napped enough that day. My husband sent me "the look." He thought it was time to go. I waved him off. I was high on Christmas spirit and didn't want the joy to end.

"Look at Father Jim," I whispered quietly into Mary Claire's ear. "He is saying prayers for Baby Jesus!" She watched for a moment. I pointed toward the lights on the Christmas tree. "Aren't they pretty? Look at all the colors!"

The distractions worked. Soon her hot baby breath whispered questions into my ear. Pleased with my solution, I caught my husband's eye and smiled. "See!" my confident smile said. "We're good. I've got this!" In my smugness, I wasn't paying attention when a few moments later, another question came.

"Mama, who's that?" she whispered, while her chubby finger pointed toward the large stained-glass window on our left.

"That's Jesus," I answered.

"What's he doing?" she hesitantly asked.

And then I did it. Unthinkingly, and with complete disregard for the not-even-three-year-old sensibility, I answered, "That is when he dies."

A quiet moment settled over the church. Then she erupted.

"He DIES?" she shrieked. "Baby Jesus DIES? HE WAS JUST BORN!"

My mind raced to catch up as she shouted louder and clearer than I thought was possible.

"Noooo!" she sobbed. Every person around us turned to look while I frantically tried to undo what I'd done. "Of course he was just born! Today is Jesus's birthday! Yay! Hurray for Baby Jesus!"

It was too late. She sobbed with all the grief a child can muster. Tears slid down her flushed round cheeks faster than I could wipe them. Despite the understanding smile and stifled chuckle of the grandmother nearby, I knew it was time to go. I looked toward my husband, who already had our five-year-old bundled up and the activity bags packed. I had never been more grateful to him as we made our quick exit.

At home, with presents under the tree and carols in the background, we returned our little family's attention to the celebration of the season. Bedtime stories and cookies for Santa restored the magic. With the kids tucked into their beds, my husband and I laughed and laughed over the evening's events and the unpredictability of children.

— Katie O'Connell —

54

It's the Thought that Counts

A person without a sense of humor is like a wagon
without springs — jolted by every pebble in the road.
~Henry Ward Beecher

By 11:30, a second UPS driver sprinted to our porch clutching yet another box. It was looking like UPS had relocated their local distribution facility to my driveway. With just a few days left until Christmas, I began to sense Barbara's and my "no-gift agreement" was off.

Back in November, my fiancée and I had decided that new granite kitchen countertops and appliances would be our Christmas gifts to one another. I went along with the plan. After all, lugging fifteen-pound granite samples into our house for several days was considerably less painful than strolling zombie-like through the women's department at Macy's in search of the girlie things she would delight in receiving for Christmas. I was off the hook.

How could she be so incredibly thoughtful every Christmas? How could I be so predictably clueless when it came to buying a few nice gifts for the woman I love? How naive was I to think I could avoid perfume counters and jewelry cases this year? I hoped these daily deliveries were for Barbara's kids or grandchildren, but somehow, I knew some of those boxes would be for me.

At 3:35, a FedEx truck delivered yet another reminder that I was probably getting more than a slab of gold-flecked granite and a dual-fuel oven in my stocking. The stark realization that I might be the only one opening presents on Christmas morning caused a sudden rush of blood to my face. At fifty-eight, I hadn't experienced a hot flash. Until now.

The pressure was on and I needed to produce a couple of tasteful gifts with about ninety-six hours to get it done. I immediately thought of the online pajama company I had heard about on the radio earlier that morning.

"Guaranteed Christmas delivery," echoed through my brain. These ads were directed at men like me. I was familiar with their line of PJs and knew I could find just the right set for Barbara to slip into while I opened the gifts that now lined the front hallway of our home.

I browsed and browsed. Then I pointed and clicked some more. "Sugarplum flannel." Nice, but flannel isn't too sexy. "Sweet snow-flake thermal pajamas." Even I know this is not the best choice for a menopausal woman. "Red Seduction Chemise." Nice! But would Barb question my motivation for such a selection? The search continued.

Then they caught my eye. "Oh-So-Soft Lavender Pin Dot Nursing Pajamas." Barbara is a Registered Nurse and loves all things lavender. How clever was I? I'd managed to find a personal gift with time to spare. All I needed was a couple of stocking stuffers and I'd be golden.

Christmas morning arrived with all the festive touches. Lighted tree, fireplace aglow. Warm cinnamon buns rested on a glistening new granite kitchen countertop. And a set of pajamas just waiting to be opened sat under the Christmas tree.

Without ever acknowledging that both parties broke the no-gift rule, we began to unwrap our presents. Baking supplies for me. Lindt chocolates and a final unwrapped gift for her. "TO: Barbie, FROM: Mikey," the tag read.

"Oh! I love the color," she exclaimed with joyful enthusiasm. "And so soft." It looked like the PJs were a hit. Barb pulled them from the tissue-lined box and held them up to be sure they would fit. "Perfect fit," she assured me.

Barbara's twenty-eight-year-old daughter Shannon was visiting and seemed to approve as well.

"Are those buttons on the shoulders?" she asked her mom. Even though I hadn't recalled seeing shoulder buttons from the Internet pictures, I thought they added a nice touch.

"What kind of pajamas did you say these were?" Shannon asked me. "Nurse's pajamas," I replied. "See? The top looks like hospital scrubs. They're pajamas for a nurse."

As if on cue, both Barbara and Shannon laughed about as loudly as I'd ever heard. Before they explained, it dawned on me why they were so amused.

"See? The buttons allow these flaps to…" Yes, I got it. Those weren't hospital scrubs. I bought nursing pajamas for a woman who, as far as I knew, would never need them again.

But Barbara loved them and wore them to bed later that Christmas night. And not once did she question my motivation for giving her a shoulder-buttoned pajama top for nursing mothers!

— Mike Morin —

55

The Ghost of Turkeys Past

Just because something is traditional
is no reason to do it, of course.
~Lemony Snicket, The Blank Book

For years, our family Christmas feast has consisted of a standing rib roast with all the trimmings, paired with an abundance of side dishes and desserts. But it wasn't always that way. Before the Christmas of 1970, we served a big roast turkey on both Thanksgiving and Christmas. Only the desserts changed — from pumpkin pie in November to mincemeat pie and Grandma's special butter rum cake in December.

The tradition changed that fateful Christmas in 1970 when the turkey was set out to brine. Grandma had always done this. Mom did this. So, I followed the tradition and did it. The sink was filled with cold, salted water and the bird was placed in it to soak.

The bird for that Christmas was a beauty — huge, almost thirty pounds. My father had paid a fortune to a local turkey farm to get us the biggest, best bird possible. It would be a true feast for all. The cookies, pies, cakes, and puddings had all been made. The candied yams were ready for the oven and the cranberry sauce was chilling in the refrigerator. All that was left was to brine the turkey a few hours, then pat it dry and refrigerate it while I made the stuffing to get it ready for an early morning oven. Due to its huge size, it needed to be rotated in the brine because it was too large to actually soak the whole bird at one time. The brine only came halfway up the body of the bird as it soaked, breast down in the sink.

I was just about to go in and turn the bird in the brine when a scream from the kitchen changed my plans entirely. My three girls came running out shrieking that the bird's ghost was there and the monster was going to get them! Their father and I ran into the kitchen to see that the "dead bird" soaking in the sink was hopping all over the place and splashing water everywhere.

My husband approached the bouncing bird with caution and made a grab for it. It slipped from his hands, as heavy as it was, and bounced onto the floor where it continued to do a jig across the tile.

The girls continued to scream while our two Collies started barking and jumping at the naked, dancing bird. I managed to push the dogs and now hysterical children back into the living room and held them at the doorway while their father continued to try to control the giant bird. Finally, it hit a corner between the sink and refrigerator and got wedged in. It continued to bounce up and down, breast side down, until finally something started poking through the back of the bird.

A smear of black appeared through a small hole near the spine of the fowl. Then a set of whiskers and a paw appeared. Our little cat Johnny had actually climbed into the open cavity of the bird and was happily chewing his way out. His little black and white head popped out through the hole in the back of the giant bird and he looked straight at us as he continued to gnaw off another chunk of raw turkey.

Of course, we could have removed the cat, washed the bird out (which was now stuffed with cat hair) and salvaged the dinner plans with none of the guests the wiser, but somehow, none of us wanted to eat turkey after that. I called my dad and told him what had happened. He made an emergency run to the local butcher and came over with two large standing rib roasts, enough to feed the crowd.

Thus began the new family tradition that my children now follow in their own homes with their own families. Johnny is long gone, but to this day, everyone who is still around to laugh about it remembers the day the turkey jumped out of the sink. And to this day, we still have turkey on Thanksgiving, but we always have roast beef on Christmas.

— Joyce Laird —

Having Mercy

Dogs act exactly the way we would act
if we had no shame.
~Cynthia Heimel

y father and stepmother, Polly, had owned many Boxers, each with a distinct personality. Their latest Boxer, Mercy, joined the family a couple of months before Christmas. Dad and Polly watched her carefully when they set up the tree and started putting wrapped gifts under it. Some of their previous dogs had been drawn to the tree and the gifts, but not Mercy. She seemed oblivious, even when they placed edible gifts under the tree, including a big, wrapped box of dog biscuits.

A few nights before Christmas Polly woke up while it was still dark and silent, as she often did. As she passed the living room door she glanced in, and what she saw made her stop cold. They'd been robbed. The area under the Christmas tree had been stacked high with colorful gifts. Now every last present was gone. Suddenly Polly was struck by a much worse thought.

Why hadn't Mercy barked? Where was she? Had the thieves taken her, too?

She checked Mercy's bed and found it empty. Mercy was nowhere to be found. In a panic, Polly was about to wake Dad, when she noticed a piece of red ribbon on the living room floor. A few feet away, there was a scrap of wrapping paper and a little further on, some glitter. It all seemed to form a trail, leading to the back door.

For a moment, Polly stood at that door, hesitating.

Should she open it? What if the thief was still there?

Finally she flipped the light switch and cautiously opened the door to the back yard. And there was the perp.

Mercy lay under her favorite tree, surrounded by packages that were chewed, gnawed, pawed and emptied. Mercy had silently carried one package after another, through the house and the doggy door, to where she could pillage in private.

Anything that was edible was gone, including chocolates, cookies, fancy breads, candy canes, and four pounds of Milk-Bones. Beautifully wrapped boxes now had gaping holes and were damp with dog saliva. And Mercy was in the middle of the mess, looking guilty, sorry… and a little sick.

Fortunately, nature took its course and Mercy didn't need to have her stomach pumped. In the morning, Dad and Polly cleaned up the mess and salvaged what little they could.

"Who needs presents?" laughed Dad, happy that Mercy survived her midnight snack.

For Polly, the loss of the presents wasn't the worst problem. It was identifying who'd sent what.

"How do I send out thank-you notes?" she fretted. "Mercy destroyed all the tags."

In the end, Mercy herself provided the answer. The day after Christmas, Polly returned to her easy chair to find Mercy looking guilty as she licked the now-empty plate where a donut had been. Polly quickly snapped a picture of the shame-faced pooch, and sent a copy with each "thank you for the ??" note, along with the story. Polly was a little embarrassed, but we all got a good laugh and Mercy… well she obtained mercy.

— Teresa Ambord —

57

Ho Ho Ho, Ouch!

If you carry your childhood with you,
you never become older.
~Tom Stoppard

A s Christmas was approaching, my husband and I decided that a perfect gift for our then three-year-old son would be a battery-operated motorcycle similar to the real one my husband rode in his free time. We knew our son would love it. After searching in what seemed like every store in our area for just the right replica, we finally found it. The purchase was made and it was stored in our bedroom closet.

We talked about our purchase during the weeks leading up to Christmas, anticipating the joy it would bring to our son. But, being parents new to this toy assembly job, we never anticipated the amount of time that it would require to put the motorcycle together. We thought that Christmas Eve would be the perfect time to start the job. We always go to a family Christmas Eve celebration so this meant that it was already 9 PM, after our son was fast asleep, before we could even get the box out of the closet and begin the assembly. Big mistake!

Once the box was opened, it was apparent that this "simple vehicle" was not so simple. It came with multiple screws, plastic pieces, stickers, pages and pages of vague instructions and a miniature Allen wrench… all the things needed to put the motorcycle together. Both my husband and I worked on it, and it took almost three hours.

After careful inspection of a job well done I decided that the best way to test the new vehicle was to take a ride on it. The instructions indicated that it would hold up to one hundred pounds. The thought never crossed my mind that they actually meant it. I mean look at all the other things the instructions mentioned that were not necessary — like the four extra screws! I hopped on. It was a great ride. I drove through the living room and around the dining table. I was having a ball until, well until we heard the sound… the sound of plastic cracking! I jumped off only to find that I had cracked the entire frame. My husband was furious and had that "what have you done" look on his face. I was hurt, offended and then panicked. It was 11:45 PM on Christmas Eve and I had just broken my son's main gift. What was I going to do?

I immediately called the store where we bought the motorcycle. They always stayed open until midnight on Christmas Eve, thank goodness for us, and they had another motorcycle in stock. They said I'd have to hurry as they were closing in fifteen minutes. My husband, who was not speaking to me by this time, drove to the store and got the new motorcycle. By the time he returned home he was a little calmer but still thought I was a crazy woman and couldn't understand why I had to try riding the thing in the first place.

We began again. Unfortunately, it didn't go any faster the second time around, but we did manage to use more of the screws this time. At 3:00 AM the new motorcycle was built. Much to my husband's relief, this time I decided that I would not try and ride it. I would let my son test it out in the morning. I got into bed tired, relieved and depressed. Depressed to learn the truth… I was too big for children's toys and motorcycles.

Christmas morning came in less than four hours. My son was so excited about his new motorcycle — it was just like his dad's. And Dad was pretty pleased too.

My son is now thirteen and his real motorcycle is in our garage… right next to Dad's. I can't say the child in me has gone away but I have learned that there are some things better left for the boys.

Now my husband and son go for their long motorcycle rides together. My son tries to talk me into going with them. I make eye contact with my husband and remember why this is "their" thing. I had my day on the bike in the living room and that was all I needed.

— D'ette Corona —

58

Wild Kingdom

Heav'n has no Rage, like Love to Hatred turn'd,
Nor Hell a Fury, like a Squirrel scorn'd.
~"Chippy" Congreve

was eight years old and I would remember that Christmas forever. It all started when my father made the announcement at dinner that we were not going to do our typical "tree night." We always did the same thing. We would go out to dinner, drive around a bit to enjoy the holiday lights, and then wind up at the same tree lot. We made a big deal out of choosing just the right tree, and then drove home with our prize tied on top of our car. We would spend the rest of the evening setting it up and decorating it. I would get to stay up as late as I wanted, but typically wound up asleep on the couch, leaving my parents to finish the decorating.

Mom and I had already made dozens of cookies with red and green ribbons through them that we would hang on the tree. As the boxes were slowly unpacked there was a bowl of popcorn to munch on while listening to Mom telling the same, familiar stories of Christmases past that were attached to each ornament.

But this year, my father said we were going to cut down our own tree. I wasn't too happy about this. Dad was definitely not the outdoor type. But, he said, business friends of both my parents had recently bought some land that had a lot of Douglas fir trees on it and they offered to let us choose one for Christmas. We could drive out to their ranch early in the morning, enjoy a nice visit and brunch with them, cut our own tree and be home by late afternoon to set it up. It would be fun.

It took some cajoling to get me to go along with it. I didn't like change. I preferred the comfort of our rituals. However, when Dad told me they had horses, I changed my mind. Like a lot of kids, I was horse crazy.

So it was all set. The day came and the trip was long, but the ranch was beautiful and there were a lot of fir trees. They had to drag me away from the horses to actually help choose one, but finally it was done and Dad and his friend cut it down and tied it to the top of the car.

I had to admit that it was a beautiful tree. It was much deeper green and very thick. It was much prettier than the trees on the lots. The ritual at home went as it always had. Dad set up the tree in the stand and attached the lights. Mom told stories as she unwrapped the ornaments. We munched popcorn and hung the ornaments, cookies and tinsel, while the music of familiar carols filled the air.

I don't know what time I fell asleep on the couch, but I do remember it was 3 a.m. according to the clock by my bed when I woke up to hear my parents yelling, a cat screeching, a dog barking and what sounded like a train rumbling and bumping from the living room and down the hall between our bedrooms.

The bumping and banging was the Christmas tree. Our dog Lassie was completely entangled like she had on a harness in the light strings and was now charging up the hall back toward the living room hauling the tree behind her. A terrified squirrel was about two feet ahead of the raging dog, only to be met by Mom's cat, Mr. Mitty, who dove off the top of the drapes at the terrified animal.

Mom pushed me back into my room and dashed after Dad to help. Of course, I came out and watched from the hall. Dad managed to grab Lassie but she was so tangled in the light strings the best he could do was carry her back into the hall where he and Mom pushed her into the bathroom, tree and all, and shut the door. Lassie, however, was not going to go silently and a volley of barking came from behind the door.

Mitty had the terrified squirrel cornered on the mantel, which was now devoid of all holiday decorations. The squirrel was ready to fight. Dad tried to move between the cat and the little beast, just as Mitty took a leap. He missed the squirrel but landed on Dad's back with all four paws — claws out. Dad screamed, fell over a chair and the cat took off for parts unknown. Now it was just Mom, Dad and one very upset gray squirrel. Evidently, that tree had been his or her home and the branches were so thick that the little creature simply hid away in them until the decorating was done and the lights went out. Then it ventured out, only to be met by a Collie and a Tomcat. It probably jumped back into the tree for safety, but both the other animals had already seen it and jumped into the tree too.

Dad motioned to Mom to open the back door. She slipped past him, opened the door and then she hurried back. Dad picked up a magazine and swung it at the squirrel and started yelling. Mom picked up a throw pillow and did the same. Not to be left out, I ran into the living room yelling and waving my arms. We went through the house like hunters beating the bushes for game until the squirrel took the best path of retreat and dashed out the back door and up a tall elm tree to safety.

It was now around 3:30 in the morning and we all stood looking at a house in total ruin. Instead of getting mad, Dad started laughing, Mom joined in and we all went into the kitchen. Mom made some hot cocoa and we sat at the kitchen table reliving the event and laughing even harder — -until Lassie started to howl.

Dad got up to go take care of the poor dog and see if anything at all could be salvaged from the ruins. Mom hustled me off to bed.

Mom and Dad spent the wee hours of Christmas morning putting everything back into place the best they could, and when I got up, although short a few ornaments, and all of the cookies (Lassie ate them), the tree looked perfect to me. The presents were there and all was right with the world — except Mom and Dad were not quite as chipper as they were on other Christmas mornings.

It was our first and last venture into cutting down our own tree. However, it did create a memory that lasted through generations.

—Joyce Laird—

59

Striking Chaos

Three phrases that sum up Christmas are: Peace on
Earth, Goodwill to Men, and Batteries Not Included.
~Author Unknown

y husband and I pushed our shopping cart through the department store aisles, each colourful display trumpeting festive cheer.

"Think we'll find anything as good as the singing clock under our tree this year?" I asked.

"We can always add it to Santa's list," Paul said. He wasn't really listening, too transfixed by the array of holiday chocolates and candies.

The singing clock was one of those items popular for about ten minutes in the late 1990s. The clock was supposed to chime a different bird song every hour.

My mother had clipped a magazine ad and ordered the clock for my father, who had recently entered a care home.

Paul and I had been sharing a Sunday dinner with her when she showed us the ad.

"You know how Dad loves all feathered and furred creatures, so I'm sure he'll enjoy the sound of birds in his room," Mom said, confidently nodding her head and pushing second helpings on anyone within range. "The ones advertised on TV sound incredibly life-like."

She should have ordered from the TV ad because the makers of this clock from her magazine had apparently never listened to a real bird! I was there when the package finally arrived in the mail with only a day to spare before Christmas. Together we tore open the box and slipped in a handful of batteries, ready to be transported to a tranquil summer garden in the Canadian Prairies.

Our garden vision quickly wilted. Oh, the birds did "sing" on the hour all right, but instead of melodious chirps and tweets, the clock's mechanical noises were closer to a loud pinball machine than a meadowlark. One birdcall sounded like a machine gun's rapid fire.

"Mom, you can't give this to Dad!" I shrieked. "He'll think he's under enemy attack!" At first I figured she was crying when her head tilted downward as we sat side by side at the kitchen table. But no, I soon realized, she couldn't answer because she was laughing too hard.

"But I don't have time to shop for a new gift!" she said through her giggles.

Another unusual detail about the clock was its face. Except for two obvious bird species, the robin and the blue jay, we couldn't identify any other drawings. And all the names were printed in Latin.

If, when referring to songbirds, you use words like Turdis Chrysolaus or Zosterops Japonica, then you shouldn't be reading this story. You should be filling out your application to Mensa.

"Look through the packaging," Mom said. "Maybe there's an English translation."

After a thorough search no translation could be found, although I did find instructions, and here they are, exactly as written:

ADJUST THE HANDS MUST BE CLOCKWISE TO AVOID STRIKING CHAOS. IF STRIKING CHAOS, RESET CLOCK ACCORDING UP-ON. FROM PM 10:00 TO AM 5:00 SILENCE WITHOUT ANY VOICE. IF BIRD'STWITTER SOUND MODULATING, CHANGE NEW BATTIES.

I really tried, but this time it was me who simply couldn't continue reading aloud. Along with my mom I was laughing so hard I was crying.

Of course the clock never made it to Dad's care home, so on Christmas Day he received much of the chocolate Paul had purchased. Instead, Mom kept the clock for herself and retrieved it from the closet every time friends and relatives came for a visit. Each guest was treated to a demo, followed by waves of laughter from young and old alike. The $29.95 plus shipping was the best Christmas money Mom ever spent.

I hope to receive that clock myself one Christmas. It sure would be more fun than another fruitcake!

—Shannon Kernaghan—

How I Spent My Christmas Vacation

*By and large, mothers are the only workers
who do not have regular time off.
They are the great vacationless class.*
~Anne Morrow Lindbergh

Day One: Here's a parenting tip for the New Year; never ground your children from the Nintendo and the Xbox the day before Christmas vacation begins! However, I managed to keep four boys busy decorating cookies. The over-use of cinnamon dots left our snowmen looking rather bloody, but the boys seemed to enjoy that.

Day Two: I thought it would be fun to spend the afternoon singing Christmas carols, but if I hear "Jingle Bells, Santa Smells" one more time, I'm going to scream! I took our oldest son out to buy presents for his brothers. He is really thoughtful. Too thoughtful. Two hours too thoughtful. I've never spent two hours in the Dollar Store before today. I never will again.

Day Three: My husband isn't speaking to me. He took our seven-year-old Christmas shopping. Many hours later they're back. Having bested his brother's shopping time, our younger son was quite pleased with himself. My husband, however, was not. "Have you ever spent

THREE hours at the Dollar Store, trying to get a kid to spend his allowance on his brothers?" All I said was, "Why do you think I sent you?" Now it's colder in here than it is outside.

Day Four: Since the current temperature is a whopping five degrees, it would be nice if there was snow on the ground. All we have is ice. Unable to bear the whining about the Nintendo, I bundled up the children and sent them out to play on the ice. They played happily for ten minutes. Unfortunately they discovered the painful difference between ice balls and snowballs. Hot cocoa soothed fragile nerves—until we ran out of marshmallows.

Day Five: It's Christmas Eve. Eight hours with the in-laws, sixteen people for dinner and children who've discovered Grandma's ceramic reindeer holds M&M's. Around midnight, snow began to fall and silence descended as well. I filled the stockings to the soft strains of "Silent Night" and enjoyed the fragile peace.

Day Six: Christmas morning, 4 AM. "Mom! Mom! It's Christmas! Santa came, he came!" Through the dim glow of the clock, I gaze blearily into the big, blue eyes of a wide-awake boy. "If you don't get back in bed this instant, Santa is going to make a return trip to give you a lump of coal," I growled. "It is NOT Christmas morning when you can see the moon and the streetlights are on." I kept the stocking and the child trudged back to bed. At this point I wasn't even sure he was mine.

Day Six officially: Christmas morning, 6 AM. Ho Ho Ho! The blue-eyed boy came back. He really does belong to me.

Day Seven: The kids played happily. The Nintendo/Xbox ban has been lifted. Now I am the one that is whining. My pleas to the grandparents for restraint had once again fallen on deaf ears. Now, it's been left to me to figure out where to put all this stuff. I waded through colorful debris and stepped on G.I. Joe's pistol. I think it's permanently embedded between my toes.

Day Eight: We are out of batteries already! Fights broke out over whose turn it is to play Nintendo. You'd think a forty-three-year-old man would be better at sharing.

Day Nine: The rain fell, the ice melted, the children whined and I cried.

Day Ten: I called the daycare on the corner to ask about their rates. "Oh are you going back to work?" the owner asked. "No," I replied, "I'm going crazy." She hung up on me.

Day 11: I staggered home from the mall where I exchanged one remote control car, which never "remotely" worked, one set of jammies labeled too lame to be worn by a twelve-year-old and one set of dishes so hideous that they prove beyond all doubt, I am NOT my grandmother's favorite. My husband greeted me at the door, waving the Visa bill. I turned to run, but could still hear him bellow, "Can you explain this one-way ticket to Hawaii?"

Day 12: When I was a child, Christmas vacation seemed to last a couple of seconds, but now I understand why Mom would cross each day of vacation off the calendar in bright red marker. Four lunches are packed and ready to go. Four backpacks wait by the front door. I realized I might have been rushing things when my oldest child refused to get out of bed. I checked the clock. It was 5 AM. The streetlights still shone and the moon was faintly visible in the dusky sky. I sat down in the living room and smiled as I sipped my coffee. I'll let the children sleep a little bit longer while I enjoy the first day of MY Christmas vacation.

— Cindy Hval —

61

Cops and Mummers

Tradition does not mean that the living are dead,
it means that the dead are living.
~Harold Macmillan

C hristmas traditions can vary depending upon where you live. On the west coast of Newfoundland, traditions are pretty much the same as anywhere else, with one minor exception. There's this thing called "Mummering" that up until the time I was ten years old, I'd never even heard of. My Irish mother grew up with this strange tradition in a small village on the east coast of Newfoundland. But I remember the night I discovered mummering had begun to spread to the west coast of the island.

Mummering consisted of adults dressing in costumes on Christmas night, covering their faces and going from door to door visiting neighbours. At each house they were welcomed to enjoy a drink of Christmas cheer, play a few tunes, perhaps dance a few jigs, and have the people who lived there try and guess who they were. I'm sure it was great fun for the adults! However, to me, a ten-year-old with a vivid imagination, an encounter with adults completely disguised at Christmastime was an experience I'd never forget!

That year, our family of nine had shared the usual warm family traditions, from finding the perfect Christmas tree, to mother's annual reading of *The Night Before Christmas*, to finally waking up on Christmas morning and discovering Santa had once again surprised us with presents. Although we didn't usually get all of the things we wanted, there were seven of us children and Santa was a busy man, so we were happy with whatever we got. After all there were millions of children in the world so how could everyone get exactly what they asked for anyway?

Mom and Dad always spent Christmas Eve and Christmas Day at home with us, but after supper in the evening on Christmas Day they took a little time for themselves, visiting friends to play cards and perhaps enjoy a few seasonal spirits. My oldest sister, who would have been sixteen at the time, usually remained at home to babysit.

But that year, my sister wanted to visit her friends, so Mom and Dad left my other sister, who was two years older than me, in charge. We spent the evening playing with our games and things from Santa, but around 9:30 my sister tried to make us go to bed. The younger ones listened to her and went off to their beds, but my brother and I decided to defy her and stay up. After all, she was only two years older than me!

It was around ten o'clock when I heard a car door slamming outside our house. Since we lived at the end of a quiet lane on the outskirts of town, there was very little traffic on that dirt road, especially in wintertime. As it was much too late for Christmas visitors, I stood at the living room window, wiping frost off the pane, straining to see who could possibly be coming to our house at that hour.

It wasn't until the two very tall figures reached the stairs leading up to our front door that I was finally able to clearly see who was coming. Fear sent shivers down my spine as I jumped back from the window. In a voice choked with fear I said, "There's a mummy and a zombie coming up the steps."

Laughing, my sister pushed past me to look out the window. Her face turned completely ashen, and she fled the room as fast as her feet could carry her, hiding under the bed in our bedroom. So much for her being in charge of things! Meanwhile, my little brother ran into the kitchen, grabbed the bread knife off the sideboard and hid behind a big chair in the living room, carefully staying out of sight.

Thump, thump, clump, the footsteps drew ever nearer, while I stood there alone, frozen with fear, unable to run. The telephone was on a little table right next to the front door, the fairly thin directory beneath it. Grabbing the phone and directory, I did the only thing I could do. Hiding next to my brother behind the chair, I looked up the number of the local RCMP station.

By this time the monsters had reached the door and were banging on it, turning the knob back and forth. I knew at any moment they were going to get in and we'd all be dead! The phone at the police station only rang once. "Sir, there are two very big scary creatures at our door, and they're trying to get in and kill us."

The officer on duty was a good friend and hunting buddy of my father, and when he identified himself and asked for my name, intense relief washed over me at his familiar voice. "Are your mother and father home?" he asked.

"No, they're playing cards at Mr. and Mrs. White's house," I said, my throat constricted with abject terror.

"Listen to me now. Don't open the door," he said. "Stay where you are and we'll be right there." Hanging up the phone, I silently said the Our Father and Hail Mary over and over again, praying God wouldn't let those monsters get in the house.

After what seemed like an eternity of knocking and shuffling outside the door, we finally heard the sirens and saw the blue and red flashing lights on the living room ceiling. That was when the uninvited guests started slowly retreating down the stairs.

Unbelievable relief washed over me! We were safe and the monsters were going to jail. For a split second I imagined the ghouls overtaking the police and then coming back for us because we called the cops in the first place. But sneaking over to the window, I watched the two RCMP officers talking to the strangers.

And then the strangers removed their masks and I stared open-mouthed at two of my parents' best friends. Wanting to surprise my mother with a little touch of her east coast tradition, the two mummers had promised my dad they'd stop by that evening. Apparently Dad forgot!

Needless to say, I didn't get into any trouble for calling the cops on the mummers that night, but that was the last time mummers came to our house at Christmastime!

— Annabel Sheila —

That Was
Embarrassing

62

Green Salami

That is the best — to laugh with someone because
you both think the same things are funny.
~Gloria Vanderbilt

Sometime during the seventh grade two things happened to me. The first was that I got hooked on salami. Salami sandwiches, salami and cheese, salami on crackers— I couldn't get enough of the salty, spicy sausage. The other thing was that my mom and I weren't getting along really well. We weren't fighting really badly or anything, but it just seemed as if all she wanted to do was argue with me and tell me what to do. We also didn't laugh together much anymore. Things were changing, and my mom and I were the first to feel it.

As far as the salami went, my mom wouldn't buy any because she said it was too expensive and not that good for me. To prove my emerging independence, I decided to go ahead and eat what I wanted anyway. So one day I used my allowance to buy a full sausage of dry salami.

Now a problem had to be solved: Where would I put the salami? I didn't want my mom to see it. So I hid it in the only place that I knew was totally safe — under my bed. There was a special corner under the bed that the upright Hoover couldn't reach and that my mom rarely had the ambition to clean. Under the bed went the salami, back in the corner — in the dark and the dust.

A couple of weeks later, I remembered the delicious treat that was waiting for me. I peered beneath the bed and saw… not the salami that I had hidden, but some green and hairy object that didn't look like anything I had ever seen before. The salami had grown about an inch of hair, and the hair was standing straight up, as if the salami had been surprised by the sudden appearance of my face next to its hiding place. Being the picky eater I was, I was not interested in consuming any of *this* object. The best thing I could think of to do was… *absolutely nothing.*

Sometime later, my mom became obsessed with spring cleaning, which in her case meant she would clean places that had never seen the light of day. Of course, that meant under my bed. I knew in my heart that the moment would soon come when she would find the object in its hiding place. During the first two days of her frenzy, I watched carefully to judge the time when I thought she would find the salami. She washed, she scrubbed, she dusted… she *screamed!* She screamed and screamed and screamed. "Ahhhhhh… ahhhhhh… ahhhhhh!" The screams were coming from my room. Alarms went off in my head. She had found the salami!

"What is it, Mom?" I yelled as I ran into my room.

"There is *something* under your bed!"

"What's under my bed?" I opened my eyes very wide to show my complete innocence.

"Something… something… I don't know what it is!" She finally stopped screaming. Then she whispered, "Maybe it's alive."

I got down to look under my bed.

"Watch out!" she shouted. "I don't know what it is!" she said again. She pushed me to one side. I was proud of the bravery she was demonstrating to save me from the "something" in spite of her distress.

I was amazed at what I saw. The last time I had looked at the salami, the hair on it was about an inch long and fuzzy all over. Now, the hair had grown another three inches, was a gray-green color and had actually started to grow on the surrounding area as well. You could no longer tell the actual shape of what the hair was covering. I looked at my mom. Except for the color, her hair closely resembled the hair on the salami: It was standing straight up, too! Abruptly she got up and left the room, only to return five seconds later with the broom.

Using the handle of the broom, she poked the salami. It didn't move. She poked it harder. It still didn't move. At that point, I wanted to tell her what it was, but I couldn't seem to make my mouth work. My chest was squeezing with an effort to repress the laughter that, unbidden, was threatening to explode. At the same time, I was terrified of her rage when she finally discovered what it was. I was also afraid she was going to have a heart attack because she looked so scared.

Finally, my mom got up her nerve and pushed the salami really hard. At that same exact moment, the laughter I had been trying to hold back exploded from my mouth. She dropped the broom and looked at me.

"What's so funny?" my mom asked. Up close, two inches from my face, she looked furious. Maybe it was just the position of having her head lower than her bottom that made her face so red, but I was sure she was about to poke me with the broom handle. I sure didn't want that to happen because it still had some pieces of gray-green hair sticking to it. I felt kind of sick, but then another one of my huge laughs erupted. It was as if I had no control over my body. One followed another, and pretty soon I was rolling on the floor. My mom sat down — hard.

"What is so funny?!"

"Salami," I managed to get out despite the gales of laughter that I had no control over. "Salami! Salami!" I rolled on the floor. "It's a salami!"

My mother gazed at me with disbelief. What did salami have to do with anything? The object under the bed did not look like any salami she had ever seen. In fact, it did not look like *anything* she (or I) had ever seen.

I gasped for breath. "Mom, it's a salami — you know, one of those big salami sausages!"

She asked what any sane mother would ask in this situation. "What is a salami doing under your bed?"

"I bought it with my allowance." My laughter was subsiding, and fear was beginning to take its place. I looked at her. She had the strangest expression on her face that I had ever seen: a combination of disgust, confusion, exhaustion, fear—and *anger!* Her hair was standing on end, perspiration beaded on her flushed face and her eyes looked as if they were going to jump out of her head. I couldn't help it. I started to laugh again.

And then the miracle of miracles happened. My mom started to laugh, too. First just a nervous release, a titter really, but then it turned into the full-on belly laugh that only my mom's side of the family is capable of. The two of us laughed until tears rolled down our cheeks and I thought I would pee my pants.

When we finally were able to stop laughing, my mom shoved the broom into my hands.

"Okay, Patty Jean Shaw, *clean it up,* no matter what it is!"

I had no idea how to clean up something and not look at it or touch it. So, of course, I got my little sister to help me. I could get her to help with anything, as long as I bribed or threatened her. Since she didn't know what the object was supposed to look like to begin with, she didn't have much fear attached to helping. Between the two of us, we managed to roll it onto the evening newspaper (my dad never knew what happened to it). I *carefully,* carefully carried it outside and put it into the trash. Then I had my sister remove the remaining fuzz from the carpet. I had convinced her that I was too large to get into the small corner where it had grown. I ended up owing her my allowance for two weeks.

My mom never got mad at me for buying the salami. I guess she thought I had already paid a price. The salami provided a memory of shared, unrestrained laughter. For years to come, all I had to do was threaten to buy salami to make my mom laugh.

—Patty Hansen—

63

Bad Hair Day

Parents are embarrassed when their children tell lies,
and even more embarrassed when they tell the truth.
~Author Unknown

t was a typical Thursday morning: Crazy, naturally, but not unusual. Luckily, my daughters decided to take matters into their own hands — they did their own hair and picked out their own clothes and lied about brushing their teeth without any grumbling. My younger daughter asked to borrow something of mine. I nodded my approval as I tossed a still-frozen strudel at each girl. Breakfast was done, and we were out the door!

With only moments to spare, I pulled into their school and slowed the van down as they jumped out the side door. My younger daughter turned to blow me a kiss; her little side ponytail was starting to fall but she looked cute, nonetheless. I was so proud of her for doing her own hair. It's not every seven-year-old that can create her own side ponytail, you know! That kid was going to go places. I got weepy thinking about how much I loved that independent little world-changer.

That afternoon, however, the school sent home an entirely different kid.

As she crawled into the van, she cried out, "Momma, your leopard ponytail holder is CRAP. Absolute CRAP!"

"Excuse me?" I countered, hoping that my tone and word choice would indicate that I didn't appreciate such language coming from the mouth of my seven-year-old daughter, future CEO of some major international, multi-galactic corporation and caregiver of her tired and aged momma.

"You heard me — it's CRAP!" she continued, failing to notice that her audience (me) was completely lost.

"It was hard enough getting it to work right the first time, but then it came out in the middle of reading. So, I had to put my hair back up without a mirror because my teacher wouldn't let me go to the bathroom even though it wasn't my turn to read. Then it came out again when we were going to centers and I asked Bobby to help me, but he was NO help. He said he didn't even know how to put in a regular ponytail holder. He really couldn't do a complicated ponytail holder like yours. Then my teacher said she'd help me, but she didn't know how to work that ponytail holder either and she made me put it in my backpack. She said I couldn't wear it to school ever again. Thanks, Momma. Thanks for buying a leopard, stupid, no-good ponytail holder that's CRAP!"

Oh for heaven's sake! I had no idea what she was talking about. I didn't even have a leopard ponytail holder…. The only leopard print thing I owned was…

Oh geez.

Oh… well, she was right: Oh CRAP.

I felt all the blood rush to my face; I recalled the only leopard-print thing I owned.

I saw my innocent baby girl's second-grade teacher smile and wave really big as I drove by. I was mortified. From the back seat, my frustrated daughter pulled my leopard-print thong from her backpack and threw it into the front seat. "Here!" she huffed. "I will never wear that again!"

You and me both, baby.

— Heather Davis —

Damaged Goods

The only sure thing about luck is that it will change.
~Wilson Mizner

When you are over sixty, it is hard to find someone to date. In fact, it is nearly impossible.

I asked my friends to introduce me to their brothers, cousins, neighbors, anyone, but according to them, they didn't know any unmarried men. I didn't believe them and suspected they were hoarding all the single men for themselves.

I had joined clubs, gone to lectures, volunteered for practically everything, tried sports I hated, visited different church senior singles events and checked out the Internet. Nothing had worked. I think the last time I had a date Reagan was President. Okay, I could be wrong about that, but it had been a while.

My friend, Marsha, started dating a very nice man and was annoyingly happy. She said she'd met him at the grocery store between the carrots and green peppers. By the time they reached the checkout, he'd asked her for a date.

Well, that might be fine for Marsha, but I was hoping for something a little more romantic, like meeting him in a field of daisies or seeing each other across a crowded room and experiencing love at first sight.

Sometimes, you can wake up on a perfectly ordinary morning and feel like something wonderful is going to happen to you.

Thursday morning I woke up, went into the kitchen to make my coffee and promptly turned around and hit the left side of my face on a cupboard door that had swung back open. It only took a few minutes before my eye was black, puffy and nearly swollen shut. It also kept tearing up so that I had to keep dabbing at it to keep it from leaking down my face.

I also had a root canal scheduled that morning and the tooth happened to be on the left side of my face. The dentist was so repulsed by the way my eye looked that he laid a paper towel across my eye so he wouldn't have to look at it. He said he did it to protect my eye, but I think it was because he was repulsed.

After the root canal I decided I'd better stop at the store on my way home and get some soft food to eat that night. I was bending over the frozen dinners trying to find something that would require very little chewing when a man stopped beside me on my right side. I glanced up at him with my right eye. He was tall, in my age range, and wasn't wearing a ring.

"It's hard to find a frozen dinner that tastes better than the box it came in," he said. "When you live alone, it really isn't worth trying to cook a meal."

"Yes, you're right," I said. I'm a brilliant conversationalist.

"I get tired of frozen dinners but it's no fun to go out and eat alone. Sometimes it would be nice just to have someone to have dinner with once a week," he smiled.

My mind was racing. He's nice, he's tall, he's mentioned twice he is single. Marsha was right! You could meet a man in the grocery store. This was my lucky day!

"Yes, it would be wonderful to have someone to have dinner with, someone to talk to." I stood upright and turned to face him.

He stared at me.

"Oh, I'm so sorry, were you in an accident?" he asked.

I reached into my purse and took out my compact. My eye was black, swollen shut, and leaking tears. My jaw was the size of a baseball from the root canal and I was drooling just a little from the corner of my mouth because my lips were numb and swollen.

I looked like I should be ringing a bell in a tower. The only thing missing was a hunch on my back and the day wasn't over yet.

"I've had a bad day." I started to explain that I didn't always look like this but he was already backing away.

"Try the roast beef dinner; it's pretty good," he said and pushed his cart down the aisle as quickly as he could.

I decided to accidentally bump into him at the checkout to explain why I looked hideous but he was too clever. When I reached the tea and coffee aisle I saw his abandoned cart. He'd left without his bananas, onions and bread.

Well, his loss. He'd left behind his groceries and possibly the great love of his life. If all he cared about was superficial looks, then he wasn't the right man for me anyway. In another week my eye wouldn't be black and leaking and my cheek wouldn't be swollen and I wouldn't be drooling and even if I ran into him in the store again, I wouldn't speak to him. After all, I have my pride!

I think I'll call Marsha and ask her where she buys her groceries.

— April Knight —

The Smell of Love

The rate at which a person can mature is directly
proportional to the embarrassment he can tolerate.
~Douglas C. Engelbart

wanted to look my best, and it's hard to look one's best when it is thirty-three degrees outside. Stiff, insulated jackets are never elegant — at least, none of the ones I owned. And so it was with a martyr's heart that I bravely pushed aside my warmest jackets and selected a thinner, brown coat. Also, the color made my eyes look nice.

I was stuffing my purse with my cell phone and wallet when I heard a knock on the door. It rang through the small dorm room like church bells. Tim was here already? I checked my hair in the mirror and opened the door.

And there he was. My heart sputtered as Tim smiled at me. He was looking as nervous as I felt, and was dressed just as inappropriately for the cold December weather. Tim was a diehard summer fan and refused to wear anything other than a Hawaiian shirt. So here we were, me in my thin coat and him in his endearingly optimistic floral shirt, ready for our first date.

As freshmen college students living on campus, we didn't have cars. Instead, I had my trusty, hand-me-down mountain bike named Pegasus, and Tim had a gray street bike. We pedaled quickly through the streets to the movie theater. Our breath steamed behind us as we hurried. Once we were in the warmth of the theater, things would be different. At that moment, though, I was so nervous, it took all my concentration just to make my numb fingers grip the handlebars.

"It's a little muddy over here," Tim said as we approached the bicycle rack outside the theater. "You can take the far end. I'll park here." Like a true gentleman, he parked his bike in the dirt and let me take the clean space. I watched him dismount and step gingerly around in the mud. It was a very dark night, and the stars were bright in the sky despite the golden glow of the streetlamps. He laughed as he slipped a bit in the sludge, throwing his hands out for balance.

During the movie, Tim put his arm around me for the first time. The thrill of it! It would have been perfect except that, in the enclosed space of the theater, a child's dirty diaper began to flood the aisles with an unpleasant odor. Tim seemed unperturbed. (I learned later he had very little sense of smell.) I ignored it as best I could, breathing through my sleeve when a draft spread the smell too much.

After the movie, Tim took me out to eat at a burrito shop. The air was heavy with the smell of spices. Being a Friday, it was a full house, and so we were relegated to the corner by the bathroom. It wasn't long before the gentle stench of the lavatory began to creep its way over to join us at our table. I had to laugh to myself. This was the smelliest date I'd ever been on!

We rode back to our dorm rooms after dinner, and Tim walked me to my room and wished me good night. Just like that, our wonderful first date was over.

The next day, as I was walking through the halls to visit some friends, Tim's roommate Brian stopped me in the hall. "How could you stand it?" he said. "You must really like Tim to sit through all that."

"Sit through what?" I didn't understand. Not a single moment of the previous night had been a chore.

"The smell," he prompted. When I still showed no sign of comprehension, he laughed, long and hard. "When Tim came home last night," Brian told me, still wiping the tears from his eyes, "we had to kick him out and make him wash his shoes. He smelled like an open sewer. You had to have noticed. He had poop all over his shoes. He said he must have stepped in it while parking his bike last night. He thought it was mud at the time."

Looking very embarrassed, and with only socks on his feet, Tim came out of his room. He'd no doubt heard Brian and me talking about the date.

"I'm sorry you had to go through that," Tim apologized. "I really thought it was only mud. I couldn't tell the difference."

"Really, I didn't even notice it was you," I said truthfully.

Six years later, my husband still avoids suspicious mud patches for fear of recreating our first date.

—Rae Mitchell—

Click

As long as the world is turning and spinning,
we're gonna be dizzy and we're gonna make mistakes.
~Mel Brooks

heard a strangely familiar click as I rushed off my back porch
after my Greyhound, Holly, and Yorkshire Terrier, Caesar, to dis-
suade them from tag-teaming a panicked, fleeing rabbit. A few
seconds later they aborted the chase after the rabbit squeezed
itself through two planks of the wood fence.

The dogs returned to the porch empty-handed. Thankful that I
wouldn't have to snatch a squealing rabbit from a dog's jowls, I grabbed
the door handle to let them back inside. The door wouldn't budge.
The earlier "click" now made sense. Excited by the chase, my Belgian
Tervuren, Maxx, who had remained inside the house, had hit the
locking mechanism with his paw when he jumped onto the glass door.

Maxx wagged his tail as I jiggled the handle.

"Oh, come on," I pleaded, as if Maxx could turn the handle to
pop the lock. Holly and Caesar poked their noses into the corner of the
door in anticipation while I stood outside in a business suit, pantyhose,
and heels. Better than in my pajamas, I supposed.

For security reasons, I neither kept a key hidden outside nor
provided one for the neighbor for such emergencies. To complicate
matters, my husband wasn't due home from an out-of-town business
meeting for three more days, and our nearest relative lived 300 miles
north. I was on my own... except for the baby I was due to deliver

in four months.

Desperate to get back inside and to leave for work on time for a scheduled employee breakfast, I tugged on a nearby window—locked. Then I tried to open all the back windows—same result. Meanwhile, Maxx darted from room to room, peering through the curtains at me and playing a game of peek-a-boo. Since he remained interested, I planned to lure Maxx back over to the door, hoping he'd jump up and hit the handle and unlock the door.

"Come on, boy," I called from outside and darted to the back door. When I discovered him waiting for me, I thought my plan might work. I held out my hand and said, "Do you want a treat?"

His ears perked up. A good sign. I raised my hand in an upward motion and repeated the word "treat" in hopes of getting his front legs off the ground. Instead, he lay down as I had taught him whenever I rewarded him with a snack. Stupid obedience training.

Holly and Caesar also knew the word and lay down on the patio. Three dogs now stared at me, waiting for a make-believe reward. Whining commenced when I didn't produce the goods. A couple of minutes later, I turned to see Maxx walking toward the kitchen. The word "treat" must've awakened his hunger since he began sniffing the countertop where I had placed the cheesy egg-and-ham casserole for the employee breakfast. The jumping motion—which I had hoped to elicit earlier from Maxx—came to him with ease as he placed his front paws on the kitchen island to investigate the casserole dish.

I pounded the glass door. "Maxx, no! Leave it."

He turned his head sideways and nudged the tin foil, and the casserole fell to the ground. I continued banging as Maxx began to gorge. Knowing that I could never compete with breakfast, I decided it was time to call a locksmith. I headed over to the gate to walk next door to my neighbor's house but, unfortunately, the gate was padlocked and the key was stored in the garage. Why did I have to be such a safety nut?

I sized up the fence. What would be so hard about scaling a four-foot fence? The business suit? The heels? The protruding belly? I kicked off my shoes—those I could ditch without breaking the law—and started to climb. Once I reached the top of the gate, I turned around and started to lower myself down the other side. I hooked my toes on the cross boards; unfortunately, my toes weren't the only things hooked on the wooden planks. The front of my skirt had caught on the top of the gate and proceeded to rip until I could unhook it. Losing my balance, I hit the ground with a thud. With a torn skirt, toes peeking through tattered hose, a disheveled blouse, and a forehead beaded with sweat, I stood on my neighbor's porch and rang the doorbell.

"Cathi, what on earth happened?" she asked. "Are you okay?"

"Maxx locked me out of the house, and I need to call a locksmith."

After the laughter cleared, I made the call. Twenty minutes later, a white van pulled into the driveway. The man looked at me and asked, "So, what can I help you with?"

I pointed to my front door. "I need to get into my house. I've been locked out." I didn't have the energy to tell him the whole story. Not to mention, would he even believe it?

"Do you have some I.D.? You know, to prove that you live here before I just go and open the door."

I couldn't blame him for asking since I looked like a vagrant. I was certain that I'd appreciate his reticence once the ordeal ended. My mind flashed to my purse on the kitchen island.

"It's in my wallet inside the house," I said, and for the first time that morning, I began to cry. Pointing to my naked toes, my ragged skirt, and my protruding belly, I said, "Sir, I really just need to get inside."

"Will the neighbor vouch for you?" he asked, and I nodded.

Within fifteen minutes, I stood safely in the kitchen amidst an empty casserole dish and a sated Belgian Tervuren. I called my employer, and they graciously gave me the day off work. As I changed out of my ragged clothing and placed a bag of ice on my backside to ease the pain from my abrupt landing, I made a mental note to make a spare key for the neighbor. A sharp bark interrupted my thoughts: a reminder from Caesar that he still wanted his treat.

— Cathi LaMarche —

Badger Meatloaf

*Man is the only animal that can remain
on friendly terms with the victims he
intends to eat until he eats them.*
~Samuel Butler

T he freezer paper bore one scribbled line: Badger Meatloaf. I can't say it surprised me to find that in my own refrigerator but I was intrigued. It was a remnant from my brother-in-law's pet-sitting visit and not the worst thing I could have found from his bachelor's stay. Still, it was a little different than dried up pizza crusts or a quart of soured milk.

I'm a country girl who married an outdoorsman, so I have a skewed view of what's unusual. I have also discovered some things about truly fine dining over the years and have learned to savor the gifts from our own environs. For instance, I've watched my husband trim up a fresh batch of dandelion and wilt it into submission with hot bacon dressing from his grandmother's recipe. Thanks to my grandmother, I'm an expert at soaking the wild morel mushrooms in a pan of saltwater until all the little bugs come out and the mushrooms can be sautéed in real butter.

As far as I'm concerned, the finest cut of Angus beef can't touch a fresh venison tenderloin cozied up to a baked potato. I have dined on grilled trout from our local creek — rainbow, palomino and the brookies. I long ago learned how to wrap wild turkey and pheasant with bacon and slow roast them, to five-star family reviews. I've eaten rabbit casserole and rolled out dough for squirrel potpie. I also once used a package of Shake 'n Bake to cook up a rattlesnake plucked fresh from the garden. (It tastes just like chicken and goes well with a nice Bordeaux.) Elk, caribou, moose, frog legs, and turtle soup have all been on our menu. But badger meatloaf? That was new.

I remember unwrapping that brown chunk of leftovers with an open mind, but by the time I ran across it at the back of the fridge, it had definitely failed the sniff check, even by bachelor standards. As I tossed it into the trash, I also remember asking my husband if badgers were even native to Pennsylvania. He was watching football at the time so I doubt he really focused on my random inquiry.

The badger meatloaf was easily forgotten; it hadn't been odd enough in my world to have even become a story. Our fridge regained its former personality and the weeks went by until we all gathered for dinner with my father-in-law. Unlike us, he lived in a residential development and shared backyard boundaries with three other families. Conversations drifted to twenty years of neighborhood memories as it often did and he joined his two grown sons in regaling me with stories of the marvelous homemade dinners and fresh-baked breads frequently delivered by their friends next door, Don and Ellen.

Surrounded by my husband and the in-laws who loved me, I was instantly catapulted to family legend that night. The moment has survived more than three decades of storytelling. It was really my own fault for letting out the audible "Aha!" and recounting the tale of the meatloaf discovery with no thought to how it might haunt me. The light came on for me during story hour around that kitchen table and, of course, I still bear the brunt. The mystery meat I had tossed had been a gift — from Don and Ellen Badger.

— Mitchell Kyd —

Clueless

Before we work on artificial intelligence why
don't we do something about natural stupidity?
~Steve Polyak

The doorbell rang. My blind date, Mr. X, had arrived. I stood up, smoothed my shirt and headed to the door. We planned to grab dinner but it was early so I invited him in and offered him a beer. We talked for a bit, finished our beers, and decided to leave for the restaurant. Mr. X excused himself and headed to the bathroom.

As I watched him walk toward the bathroom I thought, "Huh. Great smile, polite, very personable... this guy has real potential. I'm so glad my friend set us up!"

When my dream date reached the bathroom he turned around, walked to my bookshelf and in one fell swoop took a huge 500-page book off the shelf and proceeded back into the bathroom.

Oh. No. He. Didn't!

Oh my god. I couldn't believe it. Did he just bring a book into the bathroom on our first date? Ugh.

Maybe I was being too harsh. Maybe it wasn't too weird. Just a smidge weird. And a smidge weird is okay. Heck knows, I did weird things sometimes too.

I subsequently perched myself on the edge of the couch and tried to appear busy. I looked at the quilt on the back of the couch, ran my fingers over the fabric and acted oddly interested in the design and pattern of my own quilt while I waited... and waited.

Next thing I knew, Mr. X had been in the bathroom for fifteen minutes. That may not seem like a long amount of time, but keep in mind that he was a visitor on his first date and he knew I was waiting for him. Fifteen minutes is longer than it takes to get your oil changed at Jiffy Lube.

It occurred to me that maybe he was sick. Poor thing! Or maybe he was embarrassed because the apartment was so small he was worried I would hear him. For that, I had a plan. I stood up and yelled in the general direction of the bathroom, "I forgot to get the mail this morning! I'm just going to run out to the mailbox and see if it arrived!"

I walked outside, purposely shutting the screen door loudly to inform him that I had in fact left the building. I walked over to the mailbox, opened it, and checked for mail. Empty. Obviously, because I had gotten the mail six hours before. I took my time heading back to the apartment so that he would have time to do his thing.

When I walked back inside I expected to see Mr. X sitting on my couch, but he was nowhere in sight. I glanced at the clock: 5:08 p.m. Man, was he really still in there?

The possibility crossed my mind that something was seriously wrong with him, but seconds later I heard his feet shuffling in the bathroom. And — I kid you not — I also heard pages turning. Boyfriend was just fine. And he was apparently enjoying his novel while I sat there for over half an hour waiting for him.

I walked over to the mirror to check my hair and make-up. I fluffed my hair and played with my shirt. I was torn between trying to look sweet or sexy. He did a ton of charity work, so I figured he'd probably be into sweet. I pulled my neckline up a little. But charity work or no charity work, he was a man. I yanked my neckline down a little. Up, down, up down, sweet, sexy, sweet, sexy... Argh! Whatever! None of this was going to matter if he never came out of that bathroom!

It was 5:34 p.m. (exactly fifty-four minutes) when I heard the bathroom door open and Mr. X emerged from the bathroom. I politely, but eagerly, awaited his explanation for his hour-long rendezvous in my bathroom.... "I have a digestive disease," maybe, or "I ate something bad on the car ride here." Anything.

But he didn't say anything. I was greeted by an upbeat Mr. X who placed the book back on the shelf, clapped his hands together and said, "All right! Ready to grab a bite to eat?"

Feeling shell-shocked after his spending an hour in my bathroom, I continued to wait for the explanation. But the reality hit me that it was his business and there was no reason for me to know anything more than that. Forgive, forget, move on.

"Yep! I'm ready for dinner, let's go!" I replied.

Then, Mr. X grabbed his jacket, turned to me and said, "That was a great dump!"

Screech! Stop the music! Did he just say the word "dump?"

I stopped myself from bringing it to his attention that I was not his brother, his friend, nor his doctor. I was his date. His disgusted date.

We still went to dinner because I didn't feel as though I had a choice, I felt backed into a corner. In that moment, I knew there was no chance of a second date, so I decided to get this one over with. Mr. X-Lax was welcome to continue his Book Tour elsewhere.

— Gretchen Schiller —

Field Trip Fiasco

Every day may not be good,
but there's something good in every day.
~Author Unknown

When I accepted the teaching position at the small private school in the Green Mountains of Vermont, I expected to be passing on my love of language to middle-school children with learning disabilities. I did not expect to be standing in a parking lot with a bleeding little girl surrounded by Vermont state troopers, hands at their holsters. But that was exactly my position at 11:25 AM one August day.

At seven years old, Sabrina was on her third set of adoptive parents when she showed up at Autumn Acres. Our little school only housed about sixty kids, but they were sixty kids who'd already seen more horrible things than most people ever see. Sabrina had it worst of all.

I wasn't with them at recess when it happened, but Sabrina managed to climb fifteen feet up a tree and then fall. When I came into work Monday morning, teachers huddled in corners, from which I could hear snatches of conversation: "… wasn't being watched… shouldn't be left alone… bit her tongue completely in half…."

Sabrina showed up for school on Friday with her jaw wired shut. They were able to re-attach the tongue, but there had been significant nerve damage, and it was questionable that she'd ever be able to speak normally again. Mr. Garrity, the principal, pulled me aside as I was warming up the van to take the kids on a field trip.

"Mr. Kaiser, we really want to get Sabrina reintegrated into the population as quickly as possible."

"Sabrina? I don't know if bringing her is a good idea. We'll be walking a couple of miles. If something should happen…"

"Look, Mr. Kaiser. Rather than punish her even more, I'd like you to take her along on the field trip today."

Of course they wanted Sabrina to go on the field trip. That way none of the administrators would have to deal with her back at the school.

I parked the raucous student-packed van in the handicapped spot at the Green Mountain Animal Sanctuary. Mrs. Bourne, the science teacher, got out of the van, and opened the back door to let the kids out to stretch their legs and eat the orange slices we'd brought for snack. The seven other teachers walked over with their lists. Each teacher would have eight students.

I heard a cough behind me, and there sat Sabrina alone in the van. I looked at my clipboard; she was not mine. Her blue eyes looked even bigger than usual, her face drawn and her jaw sticking out as if she was angry. I couldn't tell if she truly was, or if the wiring made her look so. I stepped into the van and extended my hand to her, and her big eyes became narrow slits. She shook her head vigorously. She didn't know me. To someone who'd experienced terrible things at the hands of those closest to her, a stranger must have looked like another predator. I stepped back and Sabrina extended a white, skinny arm to Mrs. Bourne.

Mrs. Bourne took her group straight to the skunk pen, outside of which was a table holding little metal cans. Each can had a perforated top, and everyone was invited to pick up a can and smell the skunk's musk. The badger pen was located near the skunk pen and the badger musk smelled like the worst armpit in the world according to one boy. He was right. I gagged after I lifted the can to my nose.

We continued on the winding tarmac to the hut housing the moles. When I stepped through the doorway I saw Sabrina standing perfectly still and staring up at a mole burrow behind the glass. Behind her was what looked like a giant captain's wheel, but with badgers and moles and skunks and mountain lions and other animals painted on it. When the wheel stopped, the animals would be lined up with either what they preyed on, or what preyed on them. But it was the wheel itself that preyed on little Sabrina, because when she took a step back, the wheel's wooden handle slammed right down on top of her head. She collapsed to her knees and I heard the haunting, muted cry of a child trying to scream through a wired jaw. Sabrina's lips were drawn back as far as they would go and her teeth were bared to expose the thin strips of metal running across her teeth, and blood seeped from between her teeth. She'd bitten her tongue stitches.

I radioed for help, and fearing she might choke on her blood, I stooped and in one motion tipped her over into my arms and stood. She immediately began kicking her feet wildly and thrashing and screaming as if she had a gag in her mouth. I began running the mile or so back to the van.

Sabrina was still kicking as I ran, and her attempts at screaming had jetted blood from between her teeth all over the right side of my head and face. Sabrina was only sixty pounds, but she began to get heavy as I plodded along, fetching strange looks from bystanders who saw a man running away with a screaming, bloody girl who sounded as if she'd been gagged.

The science teacher Catharine had heard my radio transmission and she was waiting at the van, with a little boy named Derek.

She said, "Do you want me to drive her to the hospital?"

"I can drive her. Can you just get her in the van for me? She doesn't trust me." I put Sabrina down and Catharine took both her hands and bent down, whispered something to her. Surprisingly, Sabrina stepped into the van and sat in the very back. Derek climbed in and even snapped her seatbelt on, then belted himself in too.

"Can I come?"

"Oh, um, actually that's not a bad idea, Derek." I started the van and heard movement behind me — Sabrina was trying to unbuckle her seatbelt, and Derek was holding her hands so she couldn't.

"Hip-hop!" cried Derek. "She likes hip-hop!" I tuned the radio to a rap station.

"Turn it up! Loud!" he cried. In the rearview mirror, I could see Sabrina smiling in her blood-sprayed white T-shirt, bouncing to the rhythm.

I called the school on my way to the hospital, but they gave me other instructions. Sabrina's parents did not want her brought to the small local hospital, but to Children's Hospital Boston, where she had her tongue sewed back on in the first place. I started to protest, but she did seem okay back there with Derek, so I agreed to meet Sabrina's parents in a parking lot on Main Street.

And it was there, with hip-hop music blasting, blood-covered Sabrina and Derek dancing, leaning against the driver's door myself covered with blood, that the three Vermont state police cruisers arrived and surrounded me.

They exited their vehicles and, gun hands at their hips, slowly began walking toward me. I was leaning on the car watching this unfold, thinking this was just what I needed to top off this wonderful day

"I've got a hurt kid here — I'm waiting for her parents to pick her up!" I yelled. They closed in, and I handed over my license. They seemed to think they'd caught me at something. Then I saw an older woman standing on her porch, peeking out from behind a post with a cordless phone in her hand. Of course I would probably have thought it suspicious too if I saw a man in his late twenties hanging out with a bloody little girl, having a hip-hop dance party in a parking lot. As it turned out, they thought I was a pedophile luring children with music.

When I look back at that day, my most stressful ever of teaching, what sticks in my mind is not being mistaken for a pedophile, or any animosity toward poor wounded Sabrina, but the kindness of that little boy Derek, who like so many good people who pass briefly through our lives, touched me with his goodwill and moved on before I let him know how grateful I was.

— Ron Kaiser, Jr. —

70

My White Christmas Sleigh

A good time to laugh is any time you can.
~Linda Ellerbee

t was the night before Christmas Eve, an ideal night for shopping, with large soft snowflakes floating down and Christmas music drifting from every doorway. The air was crispy cool and you could see your breath. Sidewalks creaked with every step and the coloured lights blinked a Merry Christmas greeting as the sparkling snowflakes blinked back at them.

If I was ever going to be in the mood for Christmas shopping this was the time! I still had last-minute gifts to purchase and I talked my husband into going with me. We began adventurously elbowing our way through the masses of shoppers.

Last-minute shopping was not my husband's idea of a great way to spend an evening, so he finally said he'd wait for me in the car. We owned a white Dodge 600 in those days and he had parked at the meter in front of the downtown department store where I was spending my last few dollars. I went about my task, humming along with the music, threading my way through the throng or waiting in long checkout lines.

Eventually I could buy and carry no more, so I decided to join my husband and head for home. I pushed open the doors, spotted the white Dodge with the patient male behind the wheel, and crawled in with my load of parcels. Reaching blindly over the top of the front seat, I unceremoniously dumped the packages on the seat behind me and proceeded to adjust the bungled fabric of my long winter coat. When I had it comfortably in place, it dawned on me that the key had not even been turned in the ignition.

"Well? What are you waiting for? Christmas?" I asked as I adjusted my over-wadded shoulder bag on my lap. Still no response. I turned quickly to look at — a stranger!

"Oh, no!! I thought this was our car," I blurted as, red-faced, I began to paw for the packages on the back seat.

The strange driver was looking at me with a peculiar half-smile on his face and it was obvious he was having difficulty holding back a chuckle. Two car lengths behind, my husband was sitting in our identical car splitting his sides with laughter. From this vantage point, he had watched the entire episode unfold in front of him from the moment I came out of the store.

— Joyce MacBeth Morehouse —

71

I Love Lucy

One of the things I learned the hard way
was that it doesn't pay to get discouraged.
~Lucille Ball

"**H**appy?" my brand-new fiancé asks. I smile and nod, pretty certain that I've never been happier.

Sitting mid-restaurant, puppy-eyed and giddy, we share a bottle of champagne and appetizers. It's all very Disney's *Lady and the Tramp*, minus the shared meatball. He tinkers with the sparkling diamond, which has found its home on my left hand in just the past twenty-five minutes.

I think through the past four hours, trying to rejoin reality... I want to remember it all!

I recall a phone conversation with my father; he had uncharacteristically failed to ask about my plans for the evening, and then sounded funny when I told him about them anyway. My boyfriend and I had reservations at the nicest steakhouse in town. I'd chosen a dress he'd never seen.

"Wow, you look great!"

"Thanks! You, too." Dockers and a collared shirt, an extra effort, very handsome!

We went to church before dinner and arrived at five-fifteen for our six o'clock reservation. A typical Saturday night in one of the hottest spots — people crowded the corridor, the bar, and the tables inside the restaurant area...

The hostess giggled as she seated us early, making it clear that she had chosen a special spot, all the while looking cow-eyed and adoringly at John.

"Do you know her?" I'd asked.

"No."

"She acts like she knows you; why would she seat us so early?"

"She didn't," he'd said, though she'd done so, just as we'd gotten drinks from the bar. John had handed the bartender his entire wallet in payment. Both weird, but I'd had no reason for suspicion. He claims now that he'd been nervous but I hadn't noticed.

By the time we got our appetizers, it was clear this was no typical evening: the most beautiful engagement ring I'd ever seen was brought out under glass.

John got down on one knee...

"Will you marry me?" he'd asked.

"Absolutely!"

He'd reached for the ring box to put the ring on my finger, found it empty, momentarily panicked, then realized I was already wearing it!

"I guess that means you like it?"

"It's PERFECT!" Tears blurred my vision.

Since we were already center stage, he stood up and announced to the entire restaurant that we were engaged. Pulling me to my feet, he threw our arms up in the air as if we had just won Olympic medals. People everywhere clapped. By that point, simultaneous laughter and crying had overcome me.

We called both families from the patio of the restaurant on John's cell and planned trips to visit them the next day.

As we'd returned to our tables, he'd said, "You can see now why I wanted to get that out of the way before the steaks came... so I could eat my dinner!"

He confessed:

- He had gotten to the restaurant before picking me up and made arrangements with the manager, hostess, and wait staff.
- The previous night, he'd left work early, headed to my dad's barbershop, and waited his turn for a haircut that

he never intended to receive.

- Dad had given "permission for my hand," a cliché that made me cry.

He had done everything correctly! It was all so romantic that it was hard to believe it was actually happening to me!

I heard myself babbling Lucille Ball-style... Nervous excitement had taken over. Relaxed, John ate his dinner as he'd hoped. Mine sat in a take-out box.

Now we're nibbling on fancy sweets. He's smiling like he's just won the lottery and playing with the diamond he's just put on my finger.

"You know," John says abruptly, snapping me out of the dream-night video playing in my head, "it's a little big; we need to get it sized as soon as possible."

"It's not that big!" I insist, waving my hand to prove that the diamond will remain on my finger.

As if on cue, it flies off and into a coin-size slot where the booth connects to the wall! Forgetting dress and heels, I wiggle to the floor and crawl around, searching like crazy. John meets me under the table and escorts me back to my seat.

"Oh, John, you scared me. Give it back to me."

"I don't have it, honey. It's not on the floor."

I look at him, through him, and try to laugh. "No kidding, give it to me!"

He's pointing to the tiny entryway. "Gina, we both saw that ring fly! It passed right by my face and slid into that slot! You couldn't make a shot like that twice! It's in the wall!"

The waitress comes over again to congratulate us and see if we need anything else.

"I LOST MY RING!" I hear the famous Lucy whine come from my side of the booth.

"You're not going to believe this," John says. "She waved her hand and the ring—it was a little big—flew off her finger and right here into the wall!"

"Are you sure?" She's as baffled as we are. She calls a busboy over, and he leaves and returns with a long stick of some sort. He is trying to swipe it toward the floor and out of the booth.

"You don't understand," John's voice quivers. "It's in the wall. I saw it. I'm sure it's in the wall."

Soon we are escorted to a different table where we watch busboys disassembling our booth.

People around us begin looking under their tables and passing the story amongst themselves. A woman in the crowd loudly accuses: "You'd think he'd get the right size!"

The manager comes over. "Are you sure you lost your ring? Could it be in your purse or in the bathroom or somewhere?"

John's voice is adamant. "It is in the wall!"

"Okay, then, when the dining room clears, we will take the booth apart from the wall. You are going to have to wait; we are already disturbing our customers enough."

We watch everyone slowly digesting meals. Time barely moves. We somberly swallow champagne and then dessert.

I ask: "Do you still want to marry me?"

"Yes."

(Whew!) "You know, my friends would say this was a typical 'Gina' thing to do. I can be a little *I Love Lucy*. You may be in for a lifetime of stuff like this."

He melts a bit. "Well, I guess I'm warned."

Eventually, only restaurant employees remain with us. The manager comes over holding a power drill. Two men pull out the booth.

Center wall, between plaster and paint, in the ridge that normally holds the booth's base, my diamond stares out at us.

The manager looks relieved. "And there it is!"

"Can I kiss you?" I ask, reaching for it, appreciating the man who has put all things right again with his hand drill.

"You should kiss *him*," he says, pointing to John.

John grabs the ring out of my hand and places it on my finger — and then we kiss.

— Gina Farella Howley —

Getting Catty

At the Mall

*Like a graceful vase, a cat even when
motionless seems to flow.*
~George F. Will

ith great ceremony my husband reached into his coat and pulled out my perfect birthday gift, a tiny grey Persian kitten. We had been married a few short months but already I was experiencing the "nesting" urge. Children were still a few years off and I needed something to cuddle and spoil. Dogs were not allowed in our apartment so a kitten seemed the answer to my maternal impulse.

Gilligan (named after my husband's favorite TV show) was a delightful addition to our life. We were careful to raise him with just the right mix of affection and discipline, insisting on the best food available and a regular play schedule. The lucky kitty was even allowed to sleep with us every night, usually winning the battle for my pillow. He was promoted from pet to family member when he began joining us on all our excursions, even though he continued to treat us with disdain. We loved him anyway.

My great pride in Gilligan was that he had learned to walk on a leash. Yes, it was certainly quite an accomplishment and had taken a great deal of diligence and persistence, requiring just the right amount of creativity and bribery—but it had paid off.

My favorite outing was taking him for walks in the mall. For some reason my husband never seemed to be available for this venture. It was before animals were banned in many public places, and pet owners were known to frequent the shopping center with their precious darlings on a regular basis.

As we sauntered casually through the mall, people would stare at Gilligan, making ooh and ahh sounds as we went by. I got quite used to the attention and was proud of my obedient and talented kitty.

One particular day I decided to dress him up for our usual stroll through the mall. The latest purchase was brought out and a comical struggle ensued as we proceeded to put on his new green, knitted, turtleneck sweater.

Now I know that a Persian cat has no need of a knitted turtleneck sweater but I had no one else to dress up. We arrived at the mall and began our stroll through the maze of people and stores. Again, everyone looked at Gilligan in amazement, whispering to each other behind their hands. I simply walked on, staring straight ahead but thoroughly enjoying the looks on their faces.

As long as I didn't feel any drag on the leash, or a sudden jerk, I just kept going. When he went around a pole on the opposite side, it took a few moments of unwinding and we would be on our way again.

This day seemed like any other day. Children smiled, adults commented to each other and groups of people stopped to stare, but it suddenly dawned on me that shoppers seemed to be getting more than the usual enjoyment out of our performance. Smiles were more like snickers and chuckles had elements of hysterics. There had been no drag on the leash, but I turned my head to do a quick check anyway.

To my horror, there at the end of the leash was the cat, lying flat on his back with all fours reaching to the sky. He looked relaxed and quite comfortable with the new traveling arrangements. I realized this entire time I had been slowly dragging my twenty-pound cat around on the mall's slippery floor, on his back, in a green sweater! Drat that cat.

With lightning speed, I picked up Gilligan and tucked him under my arm — making a beeline for the exit. That was also the end of the leash walking. I figured next time we might find my picture in the evening paper under the heading — "Believe It or Not."

I'm sure there is some kind of moral to this story but I can't think of a single one. All I know is that at many dinner tables that night the conversation probably started with, "You won't believe the woman I saw today at the mall."

— Heather Rae Rodin —

The Great Escape

*Fun fact: It is believed that in ancient Egypt killing
a cat incurred the death penalty because cats were
viewed as sacred beings.*

y best friend from kindergarten had become a flight
attendant and lived in Boston. We were on the phone
one night when she complained that she would have to
work a three-day trip to Paris.

"What a problem!" I said. "I'd love to be able to get away for a
few days!"

"Then come here," she said. "Bring Kathy with you, enjoy Boston,
and feed my cat. I'll leave the key with David next door." I wondered
if it could really be that simple. My husband told me to go and enjoy
myself, and my sister Kathy said her bags could be packed in an instant.
We were about to have an adventure!

We had a very easy drive to Boston and felt that was a good omen.
We arrived at Dave's apartment a half-hour early, and he was waiting
for us — another good omen. But he had this little smirk on his face
and, as he handed us the key, he said, "Lots a luck!"

"What do you mean?" we asked.

"I mean good luck with that cat. Jackie's my friend," Dave said,
"but I wouldn't go in there if my life depended on it. Here's the list
of instructions and some treats. You'll need them just to get in." He
chuckled, shook his head and closed his door.

Kathy and I looked at each other. Neither one of us cares much for cats, but that's partially due to allergies. We had taken our antihistamines. We'd be fine.

We walked next door reading Jackie's list. She didn't mention the cat's name, so we returned to Dave's apartment.

"What's the cat's name?" I asked.

"Jackie calls him Simon," he said. "I call him Psycho."

Kathy and I tentatively approached Jackie's door, reassuring each other that Dave was a nut. We put our ears to the door and heard nothing. We put the key in the lock, and then we heard him. The cat was purring, but very loudly. In fact, it was more of a growl than a purr. I was afraid to open the door, but Kathy urged me on. "Come on! It's only a cat...."

We opened the door, and as the cat bounded toward us, the treats came in handy! I threw them as far as I could across the room, and the cat ran after them. I saw on a table next to the door a bag labeled in big letters: "READ THIS!" I grabbed it and slammed the door.

Inside the bag was another note along with a jar of pennies and a spray bottle of water. The note said that if Simon was acting up, we could shake the jar of coins or spray him with the water. This was not a good omen, so instead of going into the apartment, we took our bags back to the car and went to dinner.

We ordered wine immediately. I told Kathy about my last visit to Jackie's, pre-Simon. She has a beautiful studio apartment. Every surface is covered with whimsical treasures gathered as she travels the world. The studio has an open living/dining area. Her bedroom is in an alcove with louvered, bi-fold doors that seal off the bedroom from the rest of the apartment.

We also talked about Simon's (or Psycho's) behavior. What we had seen in our very brief encounter was that the cat was a big ball of white fur and would have been considered pretty if not for its evil countenance and its size. I am no judge of cats, but I think this one weighed about thirty pounds. In any case, he was big. Fat. Huge. He had a furrowed brow, probably from frowning so much, and red eyes that made him look possessed.

Over a second glass of wine, we decided that when we returned to the apartment, Kathy would throw more treats at the cat, I would make sure his dish was full, and we would sequester ourselves in the bedroom.

We got back to the apartment armed for battle. Kathy held the jar of coins, and I had the spray bottle. We would be brave. I opened the door, and the cat leapt at us with a hiss that could be heard throughout Boston. Kathy shook her coins frantically. I held my water bottle aloft, waiting for an opportune time to spray. Kathy threw the treats as far as she could. I checked on the cat food, and we ran to the bedroom, slamming those louvered doors. The lock was a hook-and-eye, and I latched it as fast as my trembling fingers allowed.

We could hear Psycho eating as we got into our pajamas, laughing nervously about how silly we were. Kathy looked around, admiring Jackie's souvenirs. She also noted long, silky hair pretty much everywhere. As we got into bed, we saw the hair on the spread and the pillow. Oh my God, I thought, Psycho must sleep in this bed. We each gulped another pill — without water, of course, because we dared not go to the kitchen.

We told each other to relax and get some sleep, but as our heads hit the pillows we heard the first whump. Psycho wanted in and was throwing himself at the door. Thank God there was a door! Whump again. And again. And now a yowl, a cat sound somewhere between a screech and a wail. How long could he keep that up? Long enough for Dave to knock on the wall and say, "I warned you."

But then it stopped. Psycho had given up. It was quiet out there. So quiet that I could hear Kathy's asthmatic breathing along with my own.

Then a new sound. Glass tinkling and what I knew to be treasures being knocked off the cocktail table, the desk, the TV stand, and the bookcase as Psycho rose higher and higher and nearer to the bedroom door. Then an explosion! The hook and eye gave way against the tremendous thirty-pound force. The louvered doors blew open, and Psycho flew into the room like a Super Cat, a demon, and landed on our bed. We jumped up screaming. I used my water spray to keep him back. Kathy grabbed the bags, and we ran into the living room. I pulled an ottoman in front of the bedroom door, knowing it would never hold back the behemoth. We grabbed the key and, still in our pajamas, fled the apartment.

Passing by Dave's door, we dropped the key in his mailbox, and I swear I heard him chuckling. We got to the car and figured we could get back home by 2:00 a.m. I could see the apartment from the parking lot. We had left on the bedroom lights, but we didn't care. I worried briefly about Psycho's food, but figured he could live on his fat for a month. Besides, Jackie would be home in two days. I stepped on the gas and looked back to see the outline of a big, hairy cat sitting on the windowsill.

Adventure? You can have it. Next vacation, Motel 6.

—Eileen Melia Hession—

74

Yoga Cat

I have noticed that what cats most appreciate
in a human being is not the ability to produce
food which they take for granted,
but his or her entertainment value.
~Author Unknown

took up yoga two years ago, around the same time we got our cat. Having read that owning a cat and practicing yoga were both fail-safe methods to soothe troubled nerves, I envisioned a life filled with peace and inner reflection. Now two years wiser, I know that people who own cats do yoga simply to release the stress in their lives that exists because they own a cat.

My cat mocks me while I do yoga. As I sit on my padded blue mat, tangled up in a pose the human body, or at least my body, was not meant to perform, she'll sit beside me and perform the same pose flawlessly.

"Now, raise your right leg, keeping your left leg fully extended," coos my video yoga instructor. "Balance on your sitting bones, and raise the leg over your head."

Puffing and grunting, I try to extend my leg. Without breaking a sweat, the cat plops herself down beside me and raises her right leg over her head, making sure her back leg remains fully extended. I look over at her. She looks back and, pointedly, bends down and licks herself, without lowering the leg.

I find this insulting.

I decide I need more personalized instruction, and sign up at our local Y, paying $75 to have a certified yoga instructor twist me into painful and humiliating poses. But the cat is not there, executing a better version of "Downward Facing Dog" than me, so it's bearable.

"You're doing very well," says my instructor.

"Thank you," I say. "I'm trying to impress my cat." The instructor backs away, and avoids me for the rest of the class. But I don't mind. I am raising and extending my legs at an advanced rate. I can't wait to show the cat.

I return home and pull out my mat. The cat looks pleased. It's been a few days since she's humiliated me.

"Ha! That's only what you think is going to happen," I say. "Watch this!" I proceed to execute a flawless "Dead Bug" pose. The cat looks amused.

"That's not all," I say. "I can also do this!" I move into Downward Facing Dog, remembering to breathe, as my instructor said.

The cat ambles over, takes a seat next to my head, and stares at me. My arms begin to tremble, but I refuse to give up the pose. The cat continues to stare, glancing significantly at my now shaking torso. I am no longer breathing properly. In fact, I think I am close to hyperventilating. The cat begins to purr.

I can't go any further. I collapse onto the mat. I'm pretty sure I've strained something. I can't locate exactly where at the moment, because my entire body is trembling.

Now that I'm on the floor, the cat yawns and stretches, fully extending her front legs and arching her back. She holds the pose. And holds it. And holds it. And darn it all, she's breathing. Releasing the pose, she takes a deep cleansing breath. Her final word on the subject is to claw at my yoga mat before exiting the room.

The phone rings. It's my yoga instructor.

"I was wondering if you wanted to sign up for our next series of classes," she said. "You were making such good progress."

I think about the physical anguish and sweat of the yoga class. Then I ponder the money spent to experience this pain. I tell the instructor I will not be returning to class. If it's pain I'm after, I can get that at home for free.

I'll just do yoga with my cat.

— Dena Harris —

75

Tommy Bangs Shampoo

With the qualities of cleanliness, affection, patience,
dignity, and courage that cats have, how many of us,
I ask you, would be capable of becoming cats?
~Fernand Mery

didn't want Tommy Bangs. When my husband and I decided to adopt a cat from the local animal shelter, my choice was a gold and white Himalayan. But Larry liked an ordinary, shorthaired, white and gray tabby that was already curled in his arms.

My darling, regal Himalayan spat and swatted at Larry's arm. Larry's cat yawned and butted his chin.

I rolled my eyes. I already knew the outcome of this showdown. Sure enough, the tabby went home with us. I named him after a naughty boy in *Little Men*, Tommy Bangs, and left the males to bond. It didn't take long for my husband and Tommy Bangs to establish a routine. In the mornings and evenings after Larry returned from work, he'd trudge to the bathroom, the little gray and white cat trotting after him.

I didn't have to get up so early, so I'd drift back to sleep.

One morning, Larry shook me awake. "Kar, you have to see this."

I propped open an eyelid. "Now? Is it an emergency?"

Larry grinned and pulled off the covers. "It'll only take a minute."

Trailing a blanket, I trudged after him. I threw up my hands to shield my eyes from the brightness of the bathroom light. Tommy

Bangs sat on the sink, admiring his profile in the mirror.

I glared, first at the cat, then at my husband. At 5:38 in the morning, I need a cup of tea before I can think, talk or function. Smiling isn't even a possibility.

"The cat? You dragged me out of bed to stare at the cat?"

Larry patted the creature's head. "He's so smart. He washes himself."

Before I said something that I would surely regret, I staggered back to the bedroom. "Unless he's juggling balls and singing, I really don't want to know!"

A couple of mornings later, I nudged Larry out for early morning necessities. Tommy Bangs was in the tub. We ignored each other while I finished my business and washed my hands. In the mirror, I glanced behind me.

Tommy Bangs caught several drops of water in his left paw. Instead of licking them off as I expected, he slapped the water on his face and scrubbed away. I rubbed my eyes and stared. He repeated the process with the right paw, the right side of his face. He methodically shampooed his chin, the top of his head, and even his ears the same way. He'd pause for a drink, then continue.

People take showers. Raccoons wash their food. Elephants cool down with streams of water. With the exception of tigers, cats are not supposed to like water. Not only did Tommy Bangs like water, but he shampooed his whole head.

Was he imitating my husband? Next, would he be requesting a washcloth and soap on a rope? I wouldn't be surprised. I went straight to the source.

"Larry, you didn't tell me that Tommy Bangs was your shower buddy." I tapped my big husband's arm. He shrugged on a blue shirt, a small grin on his face.

"I tried to, honey, but you aren't exactly at your best early in the morning." He kissed my cheek and fumbled with his cufflinks. "Hey, boy," he said, calling to the little gray and white cat who jumped on the bed. Tommy Bangs purred and washed the rest of his body in normal cat mode.

I stroked the top of the cat's wet head. "You can't get any cleaner than a shower."

"Yeah. But I'm sure he's thirsty. His tea should be cool by now. He prefers green tea with honey." Larry snapped on black suspenders.

Normally, I would compliment Larry on his dapper appearance, but my mind froze. My hand tightened on the cup of tea I'd been sipping.

Cat tea?

See what you miss when you sleep?

Weirdness.

— Karla Brown —

76

Crazy Cat Lady

Most beds sleep up to six cats.
Ten cats without the owner.
~Stephen Baker

have three cats, so naturally people like to buy me cat-themed gifts, especially oversized mugs. It is a truth universally acknowledged that a woman in possession of a good number of cats must be in want of a good cat mug. Whether earthenware or bone china, these mugs all tend to feature frolicking felines with such captions as "Knit One Purr Two," "I've Got Cattitude," or "Chairman Meow."

I'm not sure if these gifts are intended to say, "Here's something I think you'll like," or, more likely, "Honey? You are one cat shy of being declared a crazy cat lady."

So how many cats does it take to tip you over the threshold? Five? Ten? Twenty-seven? When do you cross over the border between pet lover and crazy cat lady?

Just like the famous judge who said, "I know pornography when I see it," I can spot a crazy cat lady when I see one, and I've seen my share at the annual cat show at County Center. They're the women decked out in dangling cat earrings and cat-themed sweaters, hawking the homemade kitty condo towers covered in organic tree bark. It's not a far leap to imagining them lounging at home in a squalor of cats and uncollected newspapers, wearing puffy chenille bathrobes, cramming down Kit Kat bars and watching old Tom Selleck movies on the Hallmark channel.

Crazy Cat Ladies are such a cultural cliché that Amazon even sells a crazy cat lady action figure. She "has a wild look in her eye, offers all the fun without the allergies, and comes with six cats." There's even a Crazy Cat Ladies Society. According to their webpage, their mission is to appropriate the term "crazy cat lady" for themselves as a way to combat stereotypes about cat-loving folks. Their attitude: "You say crazy cat lady like it's a bad thing."

Isn't it strange that you never hear about crazy dog ladies? And who said cats are the sole province of women anyway? In Key West, Florida, Ernest Hemingway, that most manly of men, is fondly remembered as a famous collector of cats.

Hey, it's not as if I'm taking my cats out for a walk on a leash. I don't let them eat at the table with us often. (Kidding.) It's not as if I'm feeding the ferals down the street. Sure, I frequently forward cute cat videos. I've referred to our three cats as my "furry children." I confess to keeping a Kitsch Kittens calendar on my desk. I've posted a picture or three of my cats to Facebook, and maybe I've even been known not to answer a phone because I didn't want to disturb the cat sleeping on my lap. But when people try to tempt me with terrible tales of strays in dire need of homes, I always refuse. I'm not about to upset the cat equilibrium of our household. You know what they call a woman who houses twenty cats? A hoarder. But you know what they call a woman with twenty kids? A reality TV star.

In our complicated household, cats are the comic relief. They lower my husband's blood pressure, keep our autistic son company, and generally amuse and delight our human family of four. To have and to hold them, in sickness and in health… when all is said and done, our cats are family too.

One night at the dinner table my husband started to hiccup badly. Our son looked up in consternation. "Dad?" he asked. "Are you having a hairball?"

Clearly, we're all a bit invested in our cats here.

But please: keep the cat mugs and refrigerator magnets to yourself. Stop calling me a crazy old cat lady.

Because I'm not old.

—Liane Kupferberg Carter—

77

Frankie and Squirrelzilla

You can't be friends with a squirrel!
A squirrel is just a rat with a cuter outfit.
~Sarah Jessica Parker

Frankie caught his first squirrel at 7:08 a.m. on a crisp October day. In a directly related incident, he released his first squirrel at 7:08:13 that same morning, after a brief but terrifying tussle involving claws, teeth, growling, yowling and possible squirrel karate. Looking back on that pivotal moment, it would probably have been best for Frankie to stick it out, lick a few wounds, and declare a victory, no matter how brief. Instead, he yowled in a most panicked way, banged through the pet door (dislodging a curious Chihuahua in the process), and hid under the bed. The squirrel never forgot this and developed a pattern of feline abuse.

I should explain that Frankie, a tabby, was born a runt and matured with minimal growth. When the squirrel incident happened, he was a year old and only the size of a large kitten. Not only did this incident stunt his growth even further, but he may have actually shrunk.

Frankie took the squirrel incident as a lesson to never attack anything bigger than him, and for the next year busied himself with stalking bugs and attacking dandelions. Meanwhile, I had taken to feeding peanuts to the squirrels, a fact I hid from Frankie for he would never have forgiven me. Actually, I was just feeding one squirrel because a particularly large squirrel with a bad attitude declared the backyard feeding area as his own, not even allowing other squirrels in the vicinity. And woe be to the household pet who came too near; it would soon run away while the squirrel shouted squirrel obscenities from a low-hanging branch. The legend of Squirrelzilla was born.

Squirrelzilla was Frankie's declared nemesis, the undisputed champion of their encounter the year before. Whereas Frankie's size was stunted, Squirrelzilla grew to enormousness, at least by squirrel standards. Frankie avoided the feeding area (a picnic table) and the overhanging limb that the squirrel used as a guard post. The few times Frankie strayed, he was rudely threatened via angry chirps and growls from the squirrel.

I had never heard a squirrel growl like that, but this was no ordinary rodent. He had no fear and would come within a foot of me to get a peanut. My original intention was to try to hand-feed him, but after the growls I decided that we should forgo any actual contact lest he mug me for the remaining peanuts just inside the door. I suspected that he was only a missed nut away from being a man-eater.

But time heals all wounds, and even a squirrel fight eventually becomes a dim memory to a cat. While Frankie generally avoided squirrel encounters, he eventually decided to stand up for his right to snooze in the sunshine on the railing beside the picnic table. Squirrelzilla began to accept this arrangement grudgingly. Sometimes. But every so often, he would decide that Frankie should relocate and would lunge at him as if to charge. It worked. Terrified, Frankie would leap from the railing into the yard, seeking shelter under a nearby garage.

One day, though, Frankie decided that he'd had enough. I had long before decided that the safest approach was to throw peanuts toward the picnic table, and then run inside and watch through the windows. I also locked the door because one can't be too careful when dealing with rodents with bad attitudes. As was routine, the squirrel lunged from a few feet away, and Frankie leapt from the railing. But this time, he landed beside the picnic table and went no farther, instead looking up at Squirrelzilla from only a couple of feet away. Squirrelzilla took this as a great insult. He stood on the table, ignoring the nuts, and looked down at Frankie while chattering insistently. Their eyes locked. The katydids and crickets became silent. Then came the squirrel growls. Still, Frankie refused to budge. It was on.

Squirrelzilla leapt over Frankie, clearing the cat's head by mere inches. But instead of retreating in fear, Frankie stuck up a paw, slapping the squirrel in mid-flight. I saw a look of utter shock on the rodent's face as the cat's paw connected. Squirrelzilla hit the ground, tumbled, and then in a reversal of past history, ran up the tree with Frankie right behind him. I could only see about ten feet up the tree from the safety of the window, but I was content in knowing that Frankie had finally made a symbolic stand against bullies everywhere, or at least this particular squirrel.

It didn't matter that Squirrelzilla was almost his size, had threatened him on numerous occasions, laughed at him to his face, or even cursed him in Squirrelese. An era of rodent bullying was ending, and I was there to see it. They remained out of sight for several seconds, and my only fear was that Frankie would climb so high in his pursuit of the rodent that I'd be required to rescue him later. I shouldn't have worried.

Falling chunks of bark were my first clue, and then I saw a panicked tabby scooting down the tree trunk at a speed I didn't think was possible while going backwards. The squirrel followed close on his heels. Frankie hit the ground butt first, bounced once, and then charged through our pet door, disappearing into the confines of the great indoors. Fearing an invasion, I blocked the pet door as Squirrelzilla stood just outside of it growling. I'm not exactly sure what he was saying, but I do know I couldn't repeat it in a family-oriented publication anyway.

I soon found Frankie under the bed in his safe space. He was terrified, but his close encounter had taught me an important lesson in life: Stand up to adversaries, but also know when to stand down. And never forget: Nuts will always be involved in life's trials and tribulations.

— Butch Holcombe —

78

Guilty Steps

Every day I will find something to laugh about.
~Richard Simmons, The Book of Hope

n my on and off battle against the bulge, the bulge was winning to the tune of twenty pounds. Okay, twenty-five pounds. That didn't mean I was waving the white flag and giving up. No, I simply retreated to the couch with my honor guard, a six-pack of donuts, to decide on my next step.

Step? Of course, that was it. I'd walk myself thin. I would become, pardon the pun, a foot soldier in the battle against fat. And I would start immediately. Well, immediately after I finished eating my faithful troops. After all, I was going to need the energy for my walking.

To put my program on a scientific footing, I went out and bought an electronic pedometer, a device that counts every step you take. Now, as long as the batteries held up, I would have a daily record of my progress.

I even bought a calendar and a bright red pen to write down the number of steps I took each day. I put the calendar on the fridge where I would see it every time I opened the fridge. That way the calendar and I would be seeing a lot of each other.

Then I opened the package and took out my nifty pedometer. I felt healthier just holding it. Although the instructions were obviously written by someone whose first language wasn't English, I finally figured out which little red buttons to push to make the thing work.

I held my breath, sucked in my stomach, stretched out the

waistband of my pants, and popped the gizmo on. I slowly released the waistband, hoping nothing would explode. But my pants and the gizmo looked fine.

So, I got off the couch and started walking around the house. Then I remembered to turn it on and started walking again.

Ten steps from the couch to the fridge, twelve steps from the couch to the bathroom, twenty-five steps from the couch to my bedroom. The fact that I kept using the couch as my reference point told me I hadn't bought the gadget a minute too soon. But as I watched those little numbers add up, I felt a surge of optimism.

This was going to be easier than I thought.

That night I put the pedometer next to my bed so I would remember to put it on as soon as I got up. The next morning I rolled out of bed, popped the gizmo on my pj's and started walking. Let's see, go to the bathroom, feed two cats, go upstairs, give third cat medicine, go back downstairs, walk to the closet and get clothes, get dressed, go back upstairs. Oops, run back downstairs, take gizmo off pj's and put it on pants.

By the end of the day I had logged 954 steps. By the end of the week my calendar was filled with little red numbers, each day showing a bigger total. I admit some of the increase was when I discovered I could have my cake and eat it too. Instead of sitting down to eat, I ate while walking around the house. By the way, don't try it with soup.

The more I ate, the higher my little red numbers went. I figured the steps canceled out the calories. The scale, however, took a different view.

Unfortunately, in the middle of the third week the cats found the pedometer on the night table. It took me two days and a lot of crawling around on my hands and knees before I finally found it under the couch hidden behind old candy wrappers, elastic bands and enough cat hair to knit another cat.

Based on the tiny teeth marks I found on it, I think the cats hoped it was food, then decided it was a toy. Or maybe they also tried the eat-and-walk program.

Although I felt I had gotten a lot of exercise crawling around, technically it wasn't walking. I wrote those two days off which meant two blank days on the calendar. I promised myself I would get right back on the bandwagon the next day and I did. And the day after that.

Then came the fateful day. I had every intention of walking, really I did, but it was raining outside and the couch looked so inviting and I was reading a good book and the cats all decided to sit on me.

One thing led to another, or in this case didn't lead anywhere. By the end of the day the number on the pedometer was so dismal that I didn't have the heart to write it on my calendar — I just left the square blank.

That was the beginning of the end. Every time I walked into the kitchen to look at the calendar and saw those blank squares, I felt a little pang of guilt which led to chocolate cake guilt, ice cream guilt and potato chip guilt. The guilt just got bigger and bigger and so did I. I finally realized I had to do something about the guilt or I would end up the size of my refrigerator.

I ripped the calendar off the fridge and went back to my couch.

All was not lost. I gave the pedometer to the cats who have been running and batting it all over the house and the numbers just keep growing and growing. I'm pretty sure two of them have lost a little weight.

You know something else? Now that I don't feel guilty, I've lost five pounds.

— Harriet Cooper —

79

Trick or Feat

Where there is no imagination there is no horror.
~Arthur Conan Doyle, Sr.

Sebastian, my tuxedo cat, dashed through the living room, with me in hot pursuit. He went into capture-and-conquer mode every time I used the feather duster. His fascination for it grew beyond merely taking it from me. Finding its newest hiding place had become one of his favorite pastimes.

I caught up with him by the sofa and grabbed the duster. "You can't have this." I sat on the sofa and dropped the tempting cleaning tool next to me.

He hopped up and swatted at the feathers.

"No." I shoved the duster under my sweatshirt. "I don't have time for this."

In addition to my regular housecleaning chores, this was Halloween. I had to finish dusting, sweeping, and mopping before I could set out the pumpkins, scarecrows, and candy.

Sebastian flipped his tail expectantly.

I laughed and stroked his black and white forehead. "You understand every word, don't you, boy?"

I carried the duster, still hidden within my clothing, from room to room, searching for a nook or canny my clever cat hadn't yet discovered.

"Aha. He'll never think to look in here." I glanced back into the living room. Sebastian sniffed and pawed at the sofa, where he had last seen his catch of the day. I tossed a couple of toys in his direction, hoping to distract him. It worked.

"Now," I said to myself, "time to finish my chores. Trick-or-treaters will be here before dusk."

After the last costumed child begged his treat, I locked the front door and turned off the porch light.

Sebastian toyed with his favorite catnip mouse as I watched TV. The feather duster was tucked safely in its latest hiding place.

Later that night, I sat in bed with my book, hoping to finish at least one chapter. The first paragraph blurred on the page. "I'll have to wait until tomorrow to find out who done it." Sebastian curled up next to me as I set the novel on the nightstand and scooted between cozy sheets. I turned off the lamp and was fast asleep in minutes.

A creak, thump, and scrape woke me in the middle of the night. The LED numbers on my clock radio read 1:45.

I had lived alone for many years, so normal household sounds rarely disturbed me. But those strange noises made my blood run cold. Had some goblin invaded my home?

I climbed out of bed and, following the sounds, tiptoed into the kitchen.

TV cop shows taught me not to turn on a light when investigating a noise. If it was a burglar, I wanted to see him before he saw me.

My eyes strained in the darkness. I could barely make out the half-opened pantry door.

Another creak, thump, and scrape came from the pantry. I crept forward and opened the door all the way.

Movement on the top shelf caught my attention. I could barely make out a small, strange creature with a crouched torso. Two silvery-green eyes glowed from the Medusa-like head rolling back and forth in a wavy motion. A muffled growl sent shivers down my spine. I couldn't move.

The creature lunged at me. I screamed when the monster landed on my shoulders, its claws digging into my flesh. Something hard hit my cheek. Then the creature emitted a familiar purr before leaping to the floor.

I turned on the light.

"Sebastian?" The nightmarish beast was my cat, his size enhanced by the feather duster protruding from his mouth. He dropped his prey and meowed his conquest.

I looked at the pantry. How did he open the door? The top shelf was eight feet high. He couldn't have climbed up there without knocking everything off the four shelves beneath it. Did he really jump from the floor to the top? And how did he know the feather duster was up there?

I turned to my acrobat cat. He stretched up a paw as though expecting a high-five. With his amazing top-shelf flight, I considered giving him one, or at least a good boy treat.

I scooped up Sebastian. "Back to bed, little guy."

He jumped out of my arms and grabbed the feather duster in his mouth, padding toward the bedroom.

"Uh, no. I'm not sleeping with a feather duster," I said to his retreating backside. The ceiling fan caught my eye. Hmmm, ten-foot ceilings. If I taped the duster to the top of the blade? I laughed at myself. You're getting desperate, girl.

Two o'clock in the morning was no time to match wits with a tricky cat. I took Sebastian's booty from him and put it in the refrigerator. As I headed back to bed, he sat staring at the refrigerator door. I shook my head. Wouldn't surprise me in the least if he found a way to open it.

— Janet Ramsdell Rockey —

80

A Tale of Two Suckers

There's a sucker born every minute.
~P.T. Barnum

y cousin Becky isn't easily rattled. She is, after all, head nurse on the oncology ward of a prestigious hospital. She's as capable as they come. Calm, controlled, in charge. She is not, in any circle, considered a sucker.

But one very hot day at her home in central Indiana, even Becky lost her cool. She was washing dishes when her daughter Jenny raced into the kitchen.

"Mom! Mom! There's something wrong with the kitten!" she said frantically.

Becky dried her hands and followed her six-year-old outside. The kitten lay in his customary spot, his calico fur warm in the sun. He looked content so Becky leaned closer, and then recoiled, pushing Jenny behind her to shield her from what she had seen. On the kitten's soft abdomen was a rounded protrusion — a rusty chocolate color, like old blood. Becky had been a nurse a long time and knew that a dog must have savaged this kitten, for its abdomen had been torn open and its intestines exposed. Periodically, the poor beast bent to lick the wound, and then flopped onto his side as if he were completely spent.

"Find your brother! Hurry!" Becky said.

Attica was sixty miles away, and Becky knew the kitten probably wouldn't make it to the vet's. It was too badly hurt. In spite of all the things her job demanded of her, Becky couldn't help this kitten. Indeed she couldn't even make herself examine the gaping wound. She ransacked the house for a way to transport him, finally settling on an old Nike shoebox. Then she wrapped him in a dishtowel and placed him in the box, lid ajar.

"The kitten's going to be okay, right, Mom?" her son, Jamie, asked as he and Jenny peered into the box.

Becky put on a brave face, not wanting her children to know the gravity of the kitten's condition. She didn't want to lie, but for now, she had to.

"Sure, honey! He'll be fine," Becky said. "But we have to hurry. Get in the car."

They hadn't gone a mile when the cat started to scream out in pain, its voice muffled by the box. Becky looked into the rearview mirror at the kids. Their eyes had gone wide.

"Don't let the kitty out, sweethearts. He might hurt himself some more." Becky shuddered, visions of cat guts smeared on the car's interior popping into her mind. What would that do to the kids? She stomped the gas pedal hard.

The cries continued, now accompanied by raking sounds as the frantic cat tried to break free. Jenny clamped down the lid, eyes wide, for the kitten's agony seemed to have given it Hulk-like strength. Suddenly, the lid popped off, and the cat dashed for freedom, careening across the back seat, into the front, then the back again.

"Roll up the windows! Quick! Before he jumps!" said Becky.

The kitten raged through the car, bouncing off windows, howling, hissing, and finally retching. Becky wanted to join her daughter and cry too. Finally, the kitten came to rest on the floor, exhausted, panting, only bending once to lick the bloody bulge.

"Should I pick him up and put him back in the box, Mom?" Jamie said tentatively.

"No!" said Becky. "He's fine where he is, honey. Just let him rest."

But the kitten wasn't ready to rest. He scratched at the back seat, then shinnied under it until he was beneath the driver's seat, his wailing harmonizing with Jenny's. If this cat didn't die on the way to the vet, it would have to be put down. An animal that sounded like that was too injured to survive. How would the kids take it? In the back seat Jennifer had begun to whine.

"Mom! Mom! I'm hot, Mom!" said Jenny, raising her T-shirt to show Becky her tummy covered with angry pink pinpoints. Jenny had prickly heat.

The vet's office was both efficiently modern and cozy. After wrestling the cat from the car, he was now lying on the exam table, the wound exposed to Doc's professional scrutiny, purring as if he hadn't a care in the world. Apparently, he didn't know he was dying.

"Becky, come here," Doc said.

"Just do what you have to do," she said, shooting a quick look at the children. "Kids. Go outside." She watched them leave and then turned to Doc. "I know you can't save him. I know how badly he's hurt. I mean, for God's sake, his guts are exposed!"

"Becky, come here," the doctor said again.

"Not exactly a medical word, guts, but you know what I mean. Just do what you have to do. It'll be fine. I'll be fine. I'll explain to the kids, though I don't know how," she said and started to cry.

Doc had been around for a long time and seen it all. Becky had known him for years. He knew all about her career. He knew her children, her husband. More importantly, he knew her parents, and when Doc spoke, Becky was inclined to obey. But this time she just couldn't. "Just put the poor thing out of his misery!"

Doc kissed the kitten's calico head and sighed. He turned to Becky and crossed his arms over his chest.

"Someone needs to be put out of her misery today, but it sure isn't this kitten," he said. He took Becky by the arm and dragged her to the examination table. She squeezed her eyes shut.

"Open your eyes, Becky."

Slowly, she did. The kitten gazed up at her, eyes at half-mast as he succumbed to sleep. The poor thing was still purring. Doc turned the kitten over so Becky could get a better look at the exposed intestines. A feeling of surprise washed over her. Then relief. Then the most pained embarrassment of her nursing career.

"You can take this kitten home," he said. For there on the kitten's abdomen, where earlier Becky believed she had seen protruding intestines, was a half-eaten Tootsie Roll Pop—chocolate, in fact. She watched the kitten bend over and give the sucker a long, satisfied lick.

—Leslie C. Schneider—

81

This Is Who I Am

A cat has absolute emotional honesty: human beings,
for one reason or another may hide their feelings,
but a cat does not.
~Ernest Hemingway

The first time he did it, we thought it was a one-time thing. My husband and I were cooking dinner, and we heard this guttural screaming coming from the bathroom. We ran to see if Boo Boo Kitty was okay, only to find him dragging a towel he had taken off the rack. He had it in his mouth and was tripping over it as he carried it through the kitchen. He was howling like a fire alarm.

Boo Boo was a crazy cat that we adopted from our local shelter. Every animal we've had came with its own bit of kookiness, but Boo Boo was by far the most unusual. He didn't pay much attention to us at first, apparently because he had this obsession with dragging anything fabric through the house. He would get into our closets and pull shirts, pants, and sweaters from the hangers. He would grab blankets off our beds and run through the house screaming, as if to say, "I'll save you. Come with me!"

Boo Boo didn't care who saw him do it, and I knew it could happen at any time. That's what made him so lovable. One afternoon, I was lying on the couch watching a movie with him curled up on my chest when the doorbell rang. Boo Boo took off because the doorbell always scared him. It was my day off, and I hadn't cleaned the house yet, but at least I was dressed and looked decent enough to answer the door.

My neighbor had a big smile on her face as she handed me a plate of her gorgeous cookies. "Are you busy?" she asked.

"Hi, Anna! No, of course not. How sweet of you to bake for me!" I motioned for her to come in while saying a silent prayer, "Please, God, help Boo Boo Kitty be on his best behavior."

Anna, a lovely older woman, lived across the street. She would often invite me over for tea and some of her homemade Italian cookies. Her teacups looked like they should have been in a museum, as did everything else in her house. On the other hand, I liked to think of my house as having that "lived-in" look — comfortable, like an old pair of sneakers.

Anna never had a pet, so her house didn't have scratched-up furniture or fur balls hiding in all the nooks and crannies like ours did. She did everything with grace and perfection, so I was always a little hesitant to have her in *my* house.

I saw Boo Boo Kitty run into the bedroom as I invited Anna to sit down. Unfortunately, the bedroom was where he got into the most trouble.

We were having a delightful conversation at the kitchen table when I heard the howling begin. I tried to ignore it even though I knew what was coming.

"How's your garden doing this summer?" I asked Anna. Boo Boo's howling was getting louder and closer to us.

"My tomatoes are bigger than last year," she said, trying to hide her obvious concern over what she was hearing.

"Oh, nothing better than homegrown tomatoes," I said. I could feel the sweat beading up on my forehead.

Boo Boo was now emitting his primal scream as he dragged a pair of my husband's pajama bottoms into the kitchen. He must have grabbed them off a shelf. This particular day, of all days, he had the pajamas I had given my husband for Valentine's Day — with Cupids and hearts all over them.

I still tried to act like nothing out of the ordinary was happening even though I felt like I was having an out-of-body experience. I kept babbling, "Boy, you'll have to give me the recipe for these cookies, Anna. They're fabulous!" She was, of course, ever the polite lady and thanked me for the compliment while shifting her eyes toward the cat. Boo Boo dropped the pajamas at her feet as if to say, "Here is a wonderful gift for you, Anna!" He looked so pleased with himself. Meanwhile, I was trying to figure out how to explain this situation to a woman who seemed perfect in every way.

We continued to chat as I tried to hide my embarrassment. I snatched up the pajamas and was pretty sure my face was redder than the hearts that covered them. I explained that Boo Boo was a shelter cat, and we had saved his life by adopting him. I went on to say, "I really love pets, but sometimes they can be kind of quirky." I just kept chattering, and I think I even told her about all my childhood pets. I couldn't stop talking. At this point, Boo Boo was rubbing on Anna's leg, leaving a large patch of gray fur on her crisply ironed, navy slacks.

While I was embarrassed, Boo Boo was just the opposite. He was unabashedly sharing himself, with all his quirkiness. He didn't care that he was dragging pajamas around the house and screaming. It was as if he wanted to say, "This is who I am, and I want you to know me."

I thought later to myself, *What a great way to be.* Boo Boo taught me a lesson about not trying to be someone you aren't. I shouldn't have been embarrassed just because I had a weird cat.

My neighbor stayed for quite a while that day, and I thought she would never come over again, but she did several more times. I'm assuming she liked coming over because she could let her hair down and relax a bit in our way less than perfect home. She seemed to enjoy Boo Boo's crazy antics. I know he liked her, too. He wouldn't have given heart-covered pajamas to just anyone.

— Marijo Herndon —

Chapter 9

Senior Moments

82

A Dog's Prayer

Animals are such agreeable friends —
they ask no questions, they pass no criticisms.
~George Eliot

ecember 2003 was a very hard time for my family. My teenage daughter had missed a week of school due to a hospitalization and was saddled with a lot of makeup work. At the same time, my husband had the first of two surgeries. This particular surgery was a total hip replacement, and it was to be followed by a total knee replacement a few months later.

My parents drove up from South Carolina to Kentucky to spend a few days with us to help me out during this difficult time. They came to help around the house and watch my younger child, allowing me to spend time at the hospital with my husband and help my daughter get caught up in her studies.

My mother is no animal lover, but my husband is. We had three dogs at the time, and my husband might have wanted more if I hadn't insisted that three was my limit. My poor mother spent those few days trying to keep the house clean, stay up to date on the laundry, and cook meals for all of us.

She also fed the dogs and let them outside when they needed to go out. One particular day, it had rained the night before, so the back yard was quite saturated. All of our dogs tracked in mud that day, causing my mom extra work on the floors and carpet. One of my dogs, who loved to chew on wet grass, then proceeded to throw up this partially chewed, wet grass all over the family room carpet. My mother patiently cleaned that up, too.

That was the day my husband came home from the hospital, so by late afternoon we were all home. At dinnertime, he felt up to joining us at the table. As we sat around the dining room table preparing to eat the delicious meal my mother had lovingly prepared, we all bowed our heads to ask for the Lord's blessing on our food. It has always been my parents' custom to hold hands when they pray before a meal, so we all did that.

That night, my father said, "Let us pray." Then he bowed his head, closed his eyes, and extended his hands out to the person on his right and on his left. We all bowed our heads, closed our eyes, and reached our hands out for the hand of the person next to us, too.

When the prayer was over, my mother, with her hand still stretched out, lifted up her head, looked at my six-year-old son and asked, "Ty, why is your hand wet?"

"My hand's not wet," he replied. Then, lifting both of his hands out from under the table so that we could all see them, he added, "Grandma, you are not holding my hand."

My mother bent her head back down and looked at her right hand, which was still outstretched beneath the table. She let out a startled scream and jumped up from her seat.

When she finally regained her composure, she told us she had apparently been holding the nose of our dog — the very same dog that had been so much trouble to her all day!

Ty burst into laughter! He said he had watched it all happen and wondered why his grandmother had chosen to hold the dog's nose instead of his hand. It seems that when my mother reached out to hold his hand, this funny dog of ours stuck his nose in my mother's open palm. Ty said he reached his hand out to grab his grandmother's hand, but then saw her wrap her hand over the dog's nose instead, so he just put his hand in his pocket.

My mother's perspective was quite different. She reached her hand out after she had already closed her eyes and then felt what she thought was Ty's wet hand. She just assumed he probably had a good reason for it being wet. He was just a six-year-old, after all. So, she closed her hand around what she thought was the little, wet hand of her sweet grandchild.

I think maybe the dog was trying to make up to her for all the trouble he had caused her that day by patiently letting her hold his nose, for reasons he probably figured only she knew.

—Harriet E. Michael—

83

Another Mega-Sized Idea

Three wise men — are you serious?
~Author Unknown

As a baby boomer, I find myself inundated these days with attractive offers for the perfect retirement location:

"It's Baja for Blue Hair, Bingo and Beans."

"Rise Again in Phoenix's New Viagra Timeshares."

"Retire in Witness Protection Program, Arizona. We Have Great Sicilian Food."

"Arkansas: Trailers welcome."

But just recently I found the perfect retirement location that has everything a guy could possibly want.

"Welcome to Costco. I have an opening right here in the middle."

"Thank you," I said to the sales guy. Then I eased my butt down into a Galaxy D3000 Acupuncture Point Deluxe Air Massage Chair.

"Remote?" I asked.

"You bet." The sales guy handed me the throttle to decadence. I fired it up. A groan of ecstasy instantly escaped my now vibrating torso.

"Yeah, you got that right," the guy beside me said. He was fully reclined in an Eclipse D4000 with built-in MP3 player.

"Nice slipper socks," I said. "Get them here?"

"Of course," he said. "I spotted them when I was looking for the forklift guy, to see if I could get that television moved closer in time for the game."

He pointed at the humongous plasma TV, which now featured a commercial advertising something that required a close-up of more-than-ample cleavage.

"Ever do any rappelling?" another guy asked.

"No and I've always regretted it. Maybe when I retire."

"My wife wants to travel when we retire, which always screws up my digestive system."

"I know what you mean," someone said.

Two new guys moved into the chairs to my left. When they got the speed set properly, they passed around a pillow-sized bag of pretzel nuggets and a cheese block the size of a foreign car.

I was thinking about retirement and the odds of getting a massage chair. My wife's not big on furniture that requires extension cords. I found that out when I tried to pass off a refrigerated wet bar as a coffee table.

"You know," the guy beside me said, "it's too bad we couldn't just retire here."

"What? You mean in Costco?"

"Sure. Think about it. This place has everything." We were interrupted by a saleslady passing out free barbecued mesquite chicken wings. "See?" the guy said.

Another guy agreed. "There's enough beer and wine here for the entire baseball season, plus they must have three hundred pounds of tri-tip steaks. Not to mention desserts up the wazoo."

"We could take turns cooking. They've got a gas grill over there could easily hold enough for a dozen of us at once."

"I do a mean charbroiled fish," one of the new guys said. "And they just brought in a truckload of tiger prawns."

I reversed the kneading function on my Galaxy D3000 and turned up the back heat. "What about recreation?" I asked.

"They got a twenty-foot inflatable water slide that looks like a lot of fun, plus we could clear a few aisles and easily set up a tennis court."

"Or put down a couple hundred throw rugs and make a fairway."

"Plus, we could set up a couple of tents and sit around one of those tables with the fire pit in the middle and play poker."

"The wife says you're supposed to get cultural stimulation when you retire," one guy said.

A group of purple-haired teenagers walked by followed by an Asian couple, a family of Pakistanis and two large women speaking Russian.

"No problem."

"Maybe we could buy, like, timeshares."

"Wow!" we all said.

"We should pitch this idea right now," I said. "See if we can get a group rate."

We called the chair sales guy over and told him our plan and he immediately left to talk with management. We began planning.

"First we should set up a computer so we can download all the sports schedules, then get some beer and start in on some rotisserie chickens. Maybe drag in some patio heaters for when it cools down later."

The sales guy returned. "The manager loved the idea of you wanting to spend more time here," he said. "So he gave me these."

He handed us all job applications. There was a huge sound of deflation, as if the air was being let out of the Goodyear blimp.

"You know," one guy said, "I've heard good things about Baja."

"And Arkansas," I said. Then I shut off my Galaxy D3000 and headed home.

— Ernie Witham —

84

The Great Escape

A smile is a curve that sets everything straight.
~Phyllis Diller

om thought it seemed like a good idea at the time, going for a little drive with our family friend, Helen. What fun it would be to get out of the house for a coffee klatsch and gossip with Aunt Margaret in the next town. Little did my mother know the chain of events she would set off with this simple action.

My mother had been living on the farm alone since my father's death years earlier. She walked with a cane and had stopped driving a few years earlier. With twelve children (nine boys and three girls), we divided up jobs to keep her safe, mostly healthy and living at home. One of the compromises she made was to agree to the "Help, I've Fallen and Can't Get Up" button. This made us feel better about her being alone on the farm — that, and one of my brothers lived only a mile away so he was first on the call list.

One lovely summer day, the phone went out at the farm. This was actually not that unusual in our area, but Mom worried about not having contact and decided it would be a good idea to press her "button" to inform them her phone was not working. Mom's lack of knowledge about anything technical made her unaware that the "button" actually needed a working telephone to communicate with the "button people." After several minutes of no answers from the "button people," she gave up and started on Plan B.

This was before cell phones were common, and most of us would probably just have waited a few hours to see if the phone company got it fixed. Well, not my mother. She decided she really needed the phone repaired ASAP, and since driving wasn't an option, she was determined to come up with a plan.

Her plan was simple. Cane and all, she would drag a folding chair to the end of the driveway, almost a football field in length. Then she would sit alongside the road and wave her cane at cars driving by to get someone to stop. Once she got them to stop, she would talk them into driving into town, going to the phone company and informing them her phone wasn't working.

I can't imagine how she pulled off dragging that chair to the road. And I can't shake off the image of her shaking her cane at strangers driving by. They must have thought she was a crazy, old woman yelling at them for driving on her road!

According to her, it took a few cars before someone stopped, and she was able to convince them to do this task. However, not really trusting the first driver, she decided she would wait for another one to stop — just to be safe. Only a short time later, she snagged her second driver, who agreed to her request. She was in business.

Just as she was getting ready to drag her chair back to the house, Helen drove up on an impromptu trip to visit Mom. Mom was itching to get out and about, so she convinced Helen to drive into the next town where they would visit my mom's sister, Margaret.

Remember that "button" she pushed? Yup, you guessed it — the phone came back on, and the people on the other end of the "button" were notified that Marie needed some help. But she wasn't answering. And then the phone calls began. My brother who lived the closest couldn't be reached, so the next one on the list was my attorney brother living about thirty miles away. His response? "Call the sheriff's department."

Within thirty minutes, the farm was swarming with sheriff's deputies, EMTs, and several of my brothers looking in ditches, cornfields, barns, and the house. When they had arrived at the farm, all they found was an empty folding chair at the end of the driveway. Had she been kidnapped? Was she dead in the ditch? She couldn't walk that far, so had someone taken her? The search was on, and my brothers were frantic — but apparently not frantic enough to call me. I sat at work not having a clue.

After nearly an hour of combing the ditches, my mom and Helen drove slowly up the gravel road, totally oblivious to the chaos they had created. I can hear them now, screaming "Oh, crap!" as they came over the hill and saw sheriff's cars, an ambulance and even a fire truck at the farm. Right then and there, they knew they were in a sticky predicament.

How were they going to get out of this one? Helen was particularly concerned since she had worked at the courthouse for years and was on a first-name basis with most of the deputies. She would never live this one down. So she did the only thing she could figure out: She drove down the back side of the driveway behind the garage, had my mom do a tuck-and-roll out of the car and then ditched her. Well, she probably stopped the car and helped her out, but she skedaddled as fast as she could, hoping she wasn't seen by all the hubbub.

Oddly enough, I really never heard what my brothers said to my mom — probably a bad nursing-home threat and something about leaving a note when she left the farm. She probably said, "Okay" and then said something sassy under her breath. I thought it was hysterical when I finally heard the story later that night. Go, Mom, go! My brothers — not so much!

Thereafter, whenever Mom left the house, she always left a note written on a paper plate that she tucked in a kitchen cabinet door. It read only, "Here is the note."

— Mary Lovstad —

85

The Reluctant Triathlete

*If God invented marathons to keep people from doing
anything more stupid, the triathlon must have taken
Him completely by surprise.*
~P.Z. Pearce

"How shall I spend my retirement?" I said, thinking out loud in my wife's company, a frequent error on my part.

Retirement would mean earned relaxation. Absence of exertion. Gentle challenges like crosswords. Time to remember, to reflect, to meditate, to ponder. A chance to put competitiveness to one side.

"Triathlons," she said.

"What?" said I, dumbfounded by the non sequitur, but not that dumfounded — wives specialize in non sequiturs, as anyone who has been married for more than a few milliseconds well knows.

"Swimming, cycling and..."

"I know what a triathlon is," I interrupted, lying, but knowing that whatever it was, it would hurt. "I just don't know what relevance it has to my retirement."

"Something... to... do," she said, enunciating the words as if my age were closer to six than sixty.

"I have plenty to do." She had given me a list of what seemed like several thousand things to do around the house, things that had been pleasant suggestions while I was working, but now hung over me like menacing threats to our continuing relationship.

"I mean a real challenge, something to aim at, something to achieve," she said.

"I can't swim."

"Yes, you can."

"I mean I can't swim more than a length without getting exhausted."

"If you can swim a length you can swim a mile," she said — no, she declared as an uncontestable fact, like a proven theorem — a veritable Pythagoras, my wife.

"I can jump in the air a few inches. Does that mean I can fly to the moon?" I said, waiting to see how Pythagoras would handle an encounter with W. C. Fields.

"With practice, I mean," she said, reverting to the talking-to-a-six-year-old-tone.

"With practice I can fly...."

"With practice you can swim a mile!" she interrupted, before I could complete my lampoonery, the smirk dying on my face as I began to feel uneasy, cornered, threatened.

And that's how it started. She threw down the gauntlet, and down is where it stayed, on the floor of my mind, ignored; until three days later I found myself Googling "triathlon," and that, as they say, was that.

"Elderly man dies doing first triathlon!" screams the tabloid headline I imagine whenever I consider my own death being reported in the press — not that it ever will be, but one can at least aspire to posthumous fame even if one never manages to acquire any of the prehumous variety. "He should have known better — says medical expert!" the fictitious press account continues. "He might just as well have taken up Russian Roulette — exciting certainly, but inevitably short-lived."

"I Googled 'people dying in triathlons' and got 24,000 hits," I told my wife.

"People die doing anything. Reading. Having sex," she said. We looked at each other for an uncomfortable few seconds. I don't know why it was uncomfortable, but I suspect it wasn't related to reading, and before I could work it out she carried on talking.

"Think of all the people who'll live longer because they're getting fit to do triathlons," she said.

"Do you want me to live longer?"

"Of course."

"Longer than you?" I asked.

"Yes," she said. "One second longer."

I had to think about that one too. Did she mean that she...? I stopped myself. Don't go there. Stick to the subject.

And I did. In fact I stuck to it so effectively that a month later and $2,000 poorer, I was the owner of a wetsuit, updated running shoes, a carbon fibre road bike and endless other accessories and bits and bobs I didn't know existed until I entered the world of triathlons.

Don't ask me why I had to have a carbon fibre bike rather than an any-old-other-fibre bike; people just told me I did. Ditto this wetsuit rather than that wetsuit. Ditto just about every item I would have chosen, which needed to be replaced by what someone else suggested, the one common denominator amongst the replacements being they were more expensive, a lot more expensive. It was like joining an esoteric cult where "all will be revealed" at some future time, that is, during your first triathlon, when you'll understand all your own, uninformed choices of gear would have proven idiotic, laughable, disastrous, fatal even. Thus it is you blindly follow the advice of the cognoscenti.

Like many of her gender, my wife finds the act of buying clothing, any clothing for any person, as stimulating as eating chocolate. She accompanied me when I went to buy my wetsuit, which serves to illustrate the strength of her addiction.

"I didn't know your stomach stuck out until I saw you in that," she remarked, helpfully, after I had levered myself into the first suit I tried on.

"Well, there's not exactly anywhere to hide it," I quipped, "unless I can squeeze it up to my chest."

"Yuck, don't do that. You'll look even more grotesque."

Her remark didn't offend me, which only goes to show either (a) how close we are, or (b) how little we value each other's opinions.

At this point the shop assistant yanked up the zipper to complete the fitting process. Garroting couldn't be more painful.

"He's gone purple," my wife said. "Is that normal?"

"Only if it doesn't go away in five minutes."

"I think it's too tight," I managed to wheeze out of lungs compressed to the size of shriveled lemons.

"It has to be tight," said the assistant. "You only want a thin layer of water between you and the suit to keep you warm."

"But I can't move," I managed to groan. "How can I swim if I can't move my arms and legs?" Ironically, as if in a taunt, the shop began to swim before my eyes, and as I tottered towards a faint the assistant yanked the zipper down. An elephant had stepped off my chest.

I tried another. Comfortable, but too loose. And another, which nearly cut my testicles in half.

"I've had enough," I said, panting. "Let's come back another day."

"How do you expect to do a triathlon if you haven't even got the energy to buy a wetsuit?" asked my wife.

"It's you who expects me to do a triathlon," I told her, not sure what point I was making.

"I do," she said. "You will." No doubt the point she was making.

Fast forward a year. I have completed four triathlons. They weren't easy, but they weren't that hard either, once I'd decided I was going to complete them. My wife is proud of me. I'm a little proud of myself. I'm still alive and convinced that despite age, even the most absurd challenges can be met if you (and your partner) think you can make it — particularly your partner, because she has no incentive to fail and, however mysteriously she acquired it, no reason to doubt your aging body still has life in it.

We live by the judgments of others, so why not let them set our challenges from time to time? Perhaps they know us better than we know ourselves, particularly as we grow old together.

— Brian Staff —

86

The Other Toy Story

Just about the time a woman thinks her work is done,
she becomes a grandmother.
~Edward H. Dreschnack

For those of us raised in a gentler time, visiting a toy store in today's world can be a daunting experience. It's not that we didn't have our own difficulties a generation ago — we stood in line for the latest shipment of Strawberry Shortcake dolls, waited to adopt a Cabbage Patch or kept up with the latest Atari game. Still, those hurdles were nothing compared to what we experience now when we go in search of toys for the grandkids.

Years ago, a barrage of television commercials around the holidays helped us a little. Children wanted whatever flashed across the screen, and for us, an actual image and name we could pronounce was a good start. Today, we're on our own.

Being told, "Get them anything — they like whatever you choose," may be well-intended advice, but useless, nevertheless. Sure, they'll like anything. That's why there are rows of different lunch boxes, a myriad of craft projects and board games, miles of train sets and shelves of different action figures. After I insisted I needed clearer directions, my daughters were more specific: "It has to be a Game Boy Advantage 2, not just Game Boy or Advantage 1, but 2 and not a Game Cube; she wants pink first, then black but definitely not blue; it's the one that turns into a jet plane, not a tank or helicopter, but a jet; if you can't get the duck, then get the monkey, then the kitten, then the frog, but not the dog, she already has the dog." I jotted down the instructions as quickly as possible.

Armed with the shopping list I'd run by my daughters several times, I set out on a Tuesday (the day with the fewest shoppers) and as early in the morning as possible. Hanging on to a shred of pride, I walked past the young man in the red shirt. I was not ready to admit defeat, not within a few feet of the entrance.

Starting with the easy items, I headed for the doll section. All I needed was a simple doll stroller. How hard could that be? Thirty years ago, there was one choice; today, I could opt for the walking/running stroller, an umbrella stroller, a stroller for twins or the super-model with the rod of learning beads and balls to entertain the passenger, and — when that passenger is tired — can be folded back into a bed. Did someone forget the passenger is just a doll?

And, speaking of dolls. Today, they eat, wet their diapers, speak full sentences, change facial expressions — everything but pay for themselves. One realistic newborn started wailing whenever I walked near it. I stood there, pleading with the doll, "Please, stop that, be quiet, shhhhh. Please..." Looking over my shoulder for witnesses, I slipped away, feeling guilty that I had disturbed that sleeping chunk of plastic. Whatever happened to the plain, empty-eyed, curly-haired dolls that did nothing but lie there?

I was elated to find one item sitting right at the front of its section. The joy, however, was short-lived as I realized the item came in a box, unassembled. From the sound of 100 different parts rattling around inside that box, I knew the words "easy to assemble" applied to those with MIT engineering degrees. The devil on my shoulder urged me to buy it anyway and let my son-in-law deal with the hours of frustration. Maybe supplying the "batteries not included" would help me look a little better.

The final stop was in the electronics department. Confident I had this one down, I marched up to the counter and read off my list, which sounded something like "Pokamong Peekachu Venge da Nivia." Tilting his head, the clerk looked me square in the eyes and asked, "Huh?" I tried the name a few more times until he figured out what I was trying to say. When he informed me he thought the store was out of stock, my face began to tighten, then twist; I could feel heat working its way from my neck to my hairline as I growled through clenched teeth, "Look again." He scurried into the supply room and found one.

An hour and a half after starting my search, I was back in the car with the toys safely stored in the trunk. I had weathered this venture, fortunately finding every item on my list. My heart rate had returned to almost normal, and the beads of perspiration had begun to dry. Although I was proud of myself for tackling this feat and felt a sense of achievement in braving the maze of a modern toy store, next time I will grab that kid in the red shirt as soon as I push through the doors.

— Alison Shelton —

87

What Goes Up

An hour with your grandchildren can make you
feel young again. Anything longer than that,
and you start to age quickly.
~Gene Perret

ur ten-year-old grandson scrambled up our backyard maple tree like King Kong scaling the Empire State Building. He stood on a limb, grabbed the one above him, and bounced. Hapless young leaves dropped under his onslaught as the branch bobbed up and down.

My breath caught in my throat, a regular occurrence for a grandparent of an active boy. "Asher, be careful. You haven't broken any bones yet. Let's keep it that way."

He stopped bouncing and plopped onto the limb. My lungs resumed their normal rhythm. "Grandma," he called in a cajoling tone, "climb up with me. Please."

I eyed the old tree. Asher and I considered it our private fortress, but the branch I normally used to boost myself up had broken off in a recent storm. Getting into that tree would take more upper-arm strength than I possessed. "Honey, I don't think I can climb up there anymore."

Asher's eyes widened as if I'd uttered a blasphemy. "But, Grandma, it's our special place. You have to try." His stricken look prompted me to grab a branch, but I was struggling. "Pull harder, Grandma. Boy, you should really start working out. You're getting pretty weak."

After multiple tries, I hefted myself onto the lowest limb and lay panting against the rough bark. Slow maneuvering brought me to a sitting position.

"See, Grandma, I knew you could get up here." Asher grinned and scooted next to me. We sat together on the branch, our feet dangling. A cool May breeze held the insects at bay as Asher told me about his school day.

I silently thanked God for the opportunity to spend time with this beloved grandson. My husband Jake and I relished our time with him. We'd forged a special bond over the years with this child.

As sunset streaked the sky, the breeze died down, and mosquitoes began attacking us. "Okay, sweetie, let's go in. Your grandpa will be home soon."

Asher shimmied down the trunk like a competitor in a lumberjack competition. I swung my leg lower, feeling for the limb I always used to descend. "Be careful, Grandma," he warned. "Your climb-down branch is gone, remember?"

I surveyed the hard surface below. Our new river-rock-and-brick landscape edging mocked me. I couldn't figure out how to get myself down safely.

"Hurry up, Grandma." Asher bounced on the patio.

"Sweetie, I'm having trouble."

Asher stopped jumping and peered up at me. "Grandma, are you stuck in the tree?"

The knobby bark bit into my protesting backside. I cautiously shifted my weight on the branch. "I don't want you to worry, but…"

"Are you *really* stuck?"

"Yes, Asher, I'm really stuck."

His eyes gleamed with excitement. "Can I call 911?" he asked hopefully.

"No, not 911. Call your grandpa."

Asher ran inside for the phone. A tiny gnat, the size of a pinhead, landed on my arm. I jerked at its needle-jab sting, and then fought to keep my balance. A red, dime-sized welt appeared where the gnat stung me. I swatted away another Mutant Robo-Gnat that was dive-bombing my face.

Asher ran back, waving the phone like a prize. "Are you sure I can't call 911?" he asked again. I could see his mental wheels turning. A fire truck or two, perhaps a rescue squad on stand-by, would make a great story at school.

"Dial your grandpa and put him on speaker," I commanded.

Jake answered on the second ring. "Grandma's stuck in a tree," Asher announced cheerfully.

"What?"

I rolled my eyes and swatted another gnat.

"Grandma told me to call because she's stuck in a tree."

I heard a long pause before my husband asked, "Is Grandma really stuck in a tree?"

"Yeah, and she wants you to come home and help her down," Asher enthused.

Jake's hysterical laughter flowed through the phone line.

"You're on speaker. I can hear you," I shouted from my perch. "Now stop cackling, come home, and get me down."

Between bouts of laughter, Jake said, "Tell Grandma to hang on. I'll be there soon."

"Okay, bye Gramps. I'll take care of things until you get home." Asher laid the house phone on the patio table and ran back inside. I smashed a Robo-Gnat attacking my leg as Asher burst through the patio door, his new cell phone in hand. "My grandmother is stuck in a tree," he said in his best news-announcer voice.

"Who are you talking to?" I asked.

"Nobody, Grandma."

Asher resumed his spiel. "My grandmother is stuck in the tree. She can't get down. Grandma, would you like to say a few words?"

The splintery wood dug into my palms. I tamped down exasperation. "Say a few words to who? Who are you talking to?"

"I'm not talking to anyone. I'm recording you. See?"

He flipped the phone around and held it up for me to view. Sure enough, a video played on-screen. A middle-aged woman wearing silver loafers, dark-washed jeans, and an exasperated glare hunched in a maple.

"Give me that!" I made a feeble swipe at the phone. Asher pulled it back and tapped buttons furiously. I wobbled on the branch before regaining my balance. Asher peered up at me through the deepening twilight. "Be careful! You almost fell. Grandma, are you really, truly stuck?"

My heart softened at his evident concern. "Yes, sweetie, but I'll be all right. Don't worry."

"Oh, I'm not worried," he said. "I just posted this online. The video already has two 'likes.' You've gone worldwide."

—Jeanie Jacobson—

88

Personal Magnetism

Humor is just another defense against the universe.
~Mel Brooks

y great-grandma lived to be 102. She was stubborn and never gave up on things. When I tried to wear Great-Grandma's antique pearls, I discovered that I must have inherited her sticking power.

One of my nephews was getting married. Where I live, in the Pacific Northwest, clothing is mostly casual — think flannel shirts and blue jeans. I'm okay with casual, but I relished the chance to dress up.

The ceremony took place in early fall, when Oregon trees put on a spectacular show that rivals East Coast fall splendor. The couple had chosen a garden setting to take advantage of the changing leaves. In October, the garden blazed with striking reds, oranges and yellows, contrasting with a backdrop of dark green firs and Indian summer sky. I settled on wearing a dressy cranberry-colored pantsuit, which would go perfectly with my great-grandmother's pearls.

If Great-Grandma was as far-sighted as I've become, there's no way she could have put on that necklace by herself. The pearls were gorgeous, but the findings were intricate and tiny. I'd had trouble hooking the clasp even before I started wearing bifocals.

Now, even with a magnifying glass, the fastener looked microscopic. I knew I'd never get the necklace hooked on my own, and I lived alone, not counting my fifteen-year-old cat Oliver. Then I remembered something I'd seen in the drugstore.

Like a lot of drugstores, this one had an entire section devoted to products for older people. Canes, walkers and raised toilet seats vied for my attention, along with pill splitters, pill boxes and pill organizers to help people remember to take their morning and nighttime meds. They had long poles for grabbing out-of-reach things so you wouldn't have to bend over. They sold cell phones with oversized buttons, and a lamp that turned on automatically, so robbers wouldn't know you lived alone.

Then, on a display hook I spotted what I was searching for. Hiding behind the eyeglass repair kits — complete with the world's tiniest screwdriver and a packet of tinier screws — hung the perfect solution for fastening necklaces like my string of pearls. For those of us with arthritic hands or dimming eyesight, the package promised no less than a miracle.

I knocked off all the eyeglass kits getting it, but finally dug out a miracle necklace helper and examined the package's contents, which included a couple of small magnets. All you did was connect a little magnet to each end of the necklace. That was it. I was expecting something more dramatic, but the package promised to fasten any necklace and save my eyes. I bought several sets.

The day of my nephew's wedding, I donned the cranberry pantsuit and the pearls. I looked stunning — if I may say so — and proudly allowed one of the groomsmen to usher me to the family section. The metal folding chair wasn't the most comfortable seat, but I reminded myself that this was a "Northwest Casual" wedding, not a formal affair in a basilica.

The wedding march began — not the traditional one, but a flute and guitar version of the Beatles' "Here Comes the Sun." During the processional, the bridesmaids, in wine-colored satin as colorful as surrounding trees, did that special walk up the aisle. My nephew looked handsome in his suit and pink tie.

The big moment arrived. The bride was beautiful, in a cloud of white chiffon that complemented her long auburn hair. Everyone rose.

Everyone except me.

I tried to stand but felt intense pressure on my neck. I put a hand to my throat, as the pearls pressed against my neck. The pearl necklace's magnets clung to the back of the metal chair. I was stuck.

I couldn't ask for help, lest I call attention to myself. I sat there smiling, hoping no one would notice my face turning the same shade of red as my outfit.

By the time I'd discretely disconnected myself from the chair, my nephew was kissing his bride. I was too embarrassed to explain why I didn't stand for the bride that day, or why my neck had pearl-like rope burns. Besides, I'm stubborn too. If I make it to age 102, I'll attribute my longevity to my great-grandmother's good genes and my own personal magnetism.

—Linda S. Clare—

89

Tunnel of Love

When a child is born, so are grandmothers.
~Judith Levy

"Levi, go get your daddy!" I implored my three-year-old grandson. Off he ran, his tiny bare feet slapping the wood floor. I cringed a bit as I heard him holler to my son-in-law: "Grandma 'tuck!" I squirmed a bit as I listened to Johnny's approaching footsteps, and forced a smile as Levi came back into view. He pointed a tiny finger at me.

Grandma was indeed stuck. It was completely my own fault. Levi and I had been engaged in a jolly game of hide-and-seek. We'd taken turns hiding. He was always easy to find. He'd cover his head with a corner of the rug and consider himself well hidden. Or he'd wriggle under his bed, leaving his toes vulnerable to a tickling when I'd find him. I have my usual places to hide: behind the shower curtain, the couch or the laundry room door. But today I had spotted a new place to try! Levi had a springy play tunnel that he loved to crawl through. My good judgment took a temporary break as I slithered into it like a snake. My upper body fit well; it was my mid-section that met resistance. Somehow, I was able to wriggle most of myself in and patiently waited for Levi to find me.

It didn't take him long since it was a 5' tunnel and I'm a 5'4" grandma. He giggled with excitement, shouting, "I found you!" I laughed with him and declared him a clever boy, indeed. It was time to exit, so I began to wiggle my way forward. I advanced an inch or two but my hips seemed to be wedged. I decided to back out. I put more vigor into my wiggle, twisting with all my might. Levi sat down cross-legged to watch the show.

I could not get out. Since I had entered face first and worm-like, my arms were trapped at my sides. Red-faced and damp with exertion, it was then that I had sent Levi for help.

At first, Johnny stood speechless. What do you say to a pair of adult feet sticking out of a child's toy? He walked around to the other end and peered in. I could clearly see the smirk that he was trying to hide.

"Don't ask questions; just help me out!" I said.

What followed was probably the most comical fifteen minutes of my life. Since he couldn't pull or push me, he somehow managed to get both the tunnel and me into a standing position. That part is a blur. I do remember chanting a prayer. From that point, he slowly eased the tunnel down the length of my body, folding the spring downward until I was finally able to step out. Levi clapped as I hugged my hero.

This event probably would have never happened if it weren't for my ample waistline. My athletic, slender daughter would have shimmied out of that tunnel in seconds. And twenty years ago, I would have, too. With middle age, my shape transformed from a French fry to the whole potato. I fought against this shift at first. But trying different exercises and diets didn't work for me. Worrying about my clothing size was making me unhappy. Life is too short to be sad!

One day when Levi was an infant, I sat in the rocking chair with him. He was snuggled up and sound asleep, his body resting cozily on my stomach. "I guess you like my mattress," I whispered, stroking his hair. My attitude began to change a bit toward my "curves."

As Levi grew, I adored playing with him. I learned which slides at the park I fit on, and we "whooshed" down together. I could fit through the door of his playhouse, and accepted each invitation inside. I learned which little chairs I could sit on without snapping them to bits like Goldilocks.

I was a large playmate, but I was always eager and available. Together, Levi and I make memories. I want him to remember his Grandma as a happy, smiling friend.

I may be a sphere instead of a cylinder, but there's more room for joy inside me. I'm as soft as a teddy bear and enjoy many loving squeezes. We share plenty of adventures and I hope he remembers each one, even the day I got 'tuck!

— Marianne Fosnow —

90

A Second Chance at Love

A bargain is something you can't use
at a price you can't resist.
~Franklin P. Jones

M y mother's home has a revolving door. Not really, but she loves to shop and then she needs to give things away since her house gets too full. It's a constant battle for her. She needs to get rid of stuff but she's not able to resist buying things. Fortunately, she likes to shop at tag sales, thrift stores, and Goodwill, since she doesn't like to spend a lot of money — and every day there are new things to buy!

Although her house is jammed with stuff, she is diligent about getting rid of it — since she has also acquired all the books about organizing, throwing out, and the joy of living with less! We've tried to help her rein in her shopping habits over the years, but the bottom line is that she can afford it, it gives her enormous pleasure, and it keeps her busy. The rest of us just shake our heads when she comes in excited about her new purchase.

One day when I was at her house she showed me a small, beautiful bone china pitcher that she had just bought at one of her favorite haunts. Although it was mostly white, the bone china had a delicate pattern, and it was hand painted with a green decorative line, small tulips and other flowers.

I looked more closely at the pitcher. It actually looked very similar to one that I had seen before at her house.

"Mom, don't you already have one just like it?" I asked.

She stopped and looked at it. She thought for a moment. "Huh, yes, I guess you're right," she replied. "But I gave it away."

I looked at her wondering if what I thought had happened, had in fact happened.

She burst out laughing. "You know, I think I might have bought back the pitcher I gave away!"

"Yes, Mom, I think you did," I said, incredulous.

I waited a beat before I continued, "So much for that bargain. You bought it twice!"

"Don't look at it that way," she replied, happily. "I just fell in love with it all over again!"

— Gwen Daye —

91

Road Trip

Sometimes the most scenic roads in life
are the detours you didn't mean to take.
~Angela N. Blount

y mom is a road warrior with whom I've journeyed many miles. She and Dad were snowbirds who followed sunshine and seventy-degree temperatures between Pennsylvania and Arizona. Maintaining their lifestyle required four road trips annually, and I was their driver for many of those years.

We knew the route by heart, but Mom still insisted on giving me turn-by-turn directions from their trusty *Rand McNally Road Atlas* while Dad read or napped in the back seat. Dad's objective was to arrive at our destination in the fewest number of hours possible, despite Mom's suggestion to take a scenic detour or stop at the gift shop shaped like a giant candle.

In the glove box, Mom also kept a travel log and a sharp pencil with which she'd note the car's mileage and our precise time of departure. She'd jot down what time we passed each landmark, how long we'd stopped, the price of gas, the weather, what we ate, and our arrival time. I always attributed her attentiveness to the strong black coffee, which she'd sip continually, even after it had marinated for two days in the big Stanley Thermos. Mom's journal served as a ready review of each motel, hotel, breakfast bar, or public restroom we'd ever patronized. And her memory, in those days, was impeccable.

"Don't pull into that station!" she'd warn. "I remember the last time we stopped there, I saw roaches, and the door wouldn't lock. It was 1954."

"I don't remember that one, Mom. I wasn't born yet."

"Well, why take chances?"

Mom often read aloud from notes of previous trips, as well. "Last year, we left the house at 4:07 a.m. and passed this same exit at 5:35." Then she'd look at her watch and sigh. "It's already 7:00." At times, I felt like a contestant on *The Great Race*, one of Mom's favorite shows.

After Dad passed away, traveling our old familiar route was like a yellow-brick road of memories, and a 1,000-mile ribbon of mourning, too. So, Mom and I began to venture on roads less traveled, stopping along the way. Only then did she allow my GPS to navigate our route, but the *Rand McNally Road Atlas* stayed close at hand.

When Mom downsized to one small home in the Midwest, we began to enjoy shorter adventures closer to home. Somehow, in the shuffle, the atlas went missing. But on a spontaneous weekend trip to Hot Springs, Arkansas, we sure could've used old Rand McNally.

The reason for our weekend jaunt was two-fold: to enjoy the fall foliage and to relocate an old friend of Mom's. We meandered through the Ouachita Mountains and over black iron bridges that carried us across gushing white streams. We strolled along Bathhouse Row, enjoyed dinner at a historic hotel, and found a cozy room overlooking Lake Hamilton.

The following afternoon, I chose a more direct route for our return trip. Forests and valleys glowed crimson and gold against a deep blue sky. Our car handled the mountainous highway without incident until I shifted into reverse after stopping at a rest area outside of the Ouachita National Forest, and the transmission hesitated. A few miles down the road, the "check engine" light came on.

I pulled onto the first wide shoulder available, activated the car's flashers, and dialed for help on the car's built-in emergency-service provider. A woman's voice responded to my SOS.

"My check engine light is on," I offered. "Feels like the transmission."

"I can help you, ma'am. I just need to ask a few questions first."

Mom's eyes targeted me. "Who are you talking to, honey?"

"I'm speaking to you, ma'am," the voice answered her. "Are you in a…"

"Who's talking…?" Mom interrupted.

I pressed a finger to my lips while pointing to the car's speaker, and then asked, "Could you repeat the question, please?"

"Are you in a safe spot while I run diagnostics on your vehicle?"

I glanced at the steep ledge, trying not to sound frightened. "Yes."

"No," Mom chimed.

"Which is it, ma'am?" the voice asked.

"We're fine," I conceded. While on hold, I gave Mom a layman's tutorial on satellites and navigation systems. Within minutes, the voice returned.

"Your check engine light is on, ma'am, indicating your vehicle's transmission may be affected."

Seriously? Mom's eyes rolled. "That's what my daughter just told you!"

"Thanks," I piped up. "Can you tell me where we are and how far to the closest garage?"

"You're in Booneville, Arkansas."

Booneville? We hadn't passed any signs for Booneville, and neither my smarter-than-me phone nor my fading-in-and-out GPS showed Booneville on our route. I assumed the mountains were to blame. "Are you sure we're in Booneville?"

Mom unbuckled her seatbelt. "Where's that atlas?" she mumbled as she leaned toward the back seat.

"I'm sure you're in Booneville," the voice replied. "You're eight miles from the closest dealership that can provide service. I can program turn-by-turn instructions over your radio, or I can transfer you to roadside service. Which would you prefer?"

A logging truck roared past, shaking our vehicle. "I think we're safer on the road than teetering on its shoulder. I'll drive to the dealership. Eight miles? Straight ahead on Highway 71?"

"The dealership is on Broadway Street, ma'am. Not Highway 71."

"You said eight miles straight ahead."

"Yes, Ma'am. You're not on Highway 71. You're in Booneville. I can send you directions."

"Miss," Mom interjected, "we most certainly are on Highway 71. Didn't you see that truck?"

"I can't see you, ma'am," the voice answered.

Mom directed her gaze at me. "You told me she could see us."

I gave Mom's hand a gentle squeeze and further queried the voice. "Are you absolutely certain we're in Booneville? Can you actually see our location?"

"I know where you are, ma'am. You're in Booneville. The dealership is eight miles straight ahead on the right. Would you like me to program your turn-by-turn directions or not?"

I inferred "or not" to mean "or else," so I didn't press the issue. Soon, another female voice, more automated and less condescending, told us to continue our route.

Within moments, however, we passed a Highway 71 marker, confirming my suspicion. I swerved into a quick mart, veering from the pre-programmed directions, which initiated an onslaught of recalculated directions from the radio's speakers.

"Cancel," I instructed, while also explaining to Mom why I was stopping.

"Recalculating. Please follow directed route."

"Cancel."

"Recalculating. Please follow…"

"Cancel!" I repeated, irritation rising in my own voice. I knew I was listening to a computer, but apparently Mom did not.

Like a gunshot, my mother's hand smacked the car's dashboard, startling me. "Miss," Mom yelled at the radio, "would you please be quiet and let my daughter drive!" Then she pointed a finger inches from my nose and scolded me with her best "mom look."

"I told you not to get rid of that atlas!"

— Julia M. Toto —

Chapter 10

It's All Relative

Catastrophe

Life is either a great adventure or nothing.
~Helen Keller

f I were a betting woman, I would have said the odds were overwhelmingly against my mother going to a tattoo parlor, but there she was. Growing up, my mother taught me many things, mostly by example, and today was proving no different.

Today's lesson was about ingenuity, a trait she cherished. When she first told me her plan, calling it her last option, I decided I'd better go with her. That's how we both came to be standing on the threshold of Wicked Ink.

A cheery bell signaled our arrival. The clerk behind the counter greeted us with a wave and asked for a moment while he finished rolling what looked like a poster for a customer. I'm not sure who I expected to be working in this shop, but his welcoming eyes and nice smile were not only a pleasant surprise but also a comfort. I mean, this was my mother we were talking about.

While we waited, Mom pretended to admire the samples that covered the walls in dizzying rows, everything from fierce dragons to colorful butterflies. And skulls. I saw her eyes go wide.

"You still think this is a good idea, right?" I asked her. "Because we can leave."

"We're here, let's see it through." She fumbled in her purse for a Tums. "I'm at my wit's end."

The shopper left and we couldn't delay any longer. I put a firm hand on her back and propelled her forward. She tightened the scarf that covered the lower half of her face, mortified that anyone might see her, and made her way over to the clerk on shaky legs.

"Hello, how can I help you?"

"I'd like to speak to someone about —" she hesitated, "a problem," she finished in almost a whisper.

"You'd like to get a tattoo?"

"No. Definitely no," Mom said quickly. "I'm a kindergarten aide," she added, as though that explained everything.

"I see," he said, but of course he really didn't. "And?"

I could tell that she was fighting the urge to bolt. "I figured you guys were ink experts, so you'd be able to help me."

He leaned his elbows on the counter. "That's true. About the ink. So, do you want to tell me about it?" When she didn't respond, he pointed to a curtained-off section and added, "We could go in the back if you'd like."

Mom let out a grateful breath. "Yes, please."

We followed him to the area and she settled herself in an artist's chair. She didn't seem to know whether she should put her legs up on the recliner part or not. She tried it both ways, and settled for sitting sideways and ramrod straight. He seemed to sense her fish-out-of-water moment and waited patiently. She slowly lowered her scarf, a simple act that I knew took all her strength.

I had to give him credit. His eyes widened but he didn't gasp or say anything. I was sure he'd seen worse. He snapped on a light and stepped closer. "That is impressive," he finally said.

Mom could tell from the look on his face that he was holding in his laughter. "Don't you dare laugh at me," she said in her best teacher voice.

His eyes twinkled. "I'm more of a dog man myself, but those are great cat whiskers. May I?" he asked, as he lifted a hand. At Mom's nod, he gently examined her face. "Let me guess, indelible ink?"

"Yes." She flashed him an embarrassed smile.

"Your cheeks are quite red. What have you been doing?"

"My daughter went online and looked up ways to remove ink.

We've tried everything: hand sanitizer, rubbing alcohol, even hair spray. They're not as dark as they were, but even make-up won't cover them."

"How did this happen, if you don't mind my asking?"

"Today my class was doing face painting, and we were having a great time. The kids wanted to do my face, so I let them. I shut my eyes so I wouldn't get anything in them, and when I opened them… well, as you can see, I'm now a cat. I didn't even know there was a marker in the box of paints." Mom tucked a loose strand of gray-streaked hair behind her ear. "I've washed it and creamed it. It won't come off."

"Don't worry; it will wear off in a week or so," he said.

"Oh, no," she wailed. "I can't be a cat for a week. Open house is tomorrow night."

He snapped his fingers and his face lit up. "You're Mrs. Somers. My nephew is in your class. Jacob Murphy?"

"Yes, we've got Jacob this year. He's a great kid."

The thought of her class made my mom's face light up despite her situation. When my daughter started kindergarten, my mom wanted to be a part of it so she signed up to help. She read books, helped with the arts and crafts programs, and generally assisted the teacher. She loved it and had been in that classroom for three years.

He leaned back against the supply counter and crossed his arms. "I don't think I can help you."

At the look on her face he quickly added, "No, I mean I can't help you because I don't work here."

I suddenly realized he didn't have a single tattoo himself.

"Len, my uncle, owns this shop." He held out his hand. "I'm Ethan. I come in and do his books. He'll be right back. He ran to the bank. I'm sure he'll know what to do."

"You think so?" Relief flooded her face and for the first time since it happened she began to relax. "It is a little funny," she admitted.

Just then the doorbell dinged. It was Len, who proved to be as charming as his nephew. I noticed when they were introduced and shook hands that he held mom's a few beats longer than necessary. Sure enough he had a remedy. As he applied the remover with gentle dabs of soaked cotton, he flirted shamelessly. It made me smile to see Mom laugh and even get a bit flustered at his attention. Fifteen minutes later, Mom was appreciative and whisker-free. Len insisted on walking us out to the car, opening the doors for both of us. Mom settled herself in the passenger seat and turned to thank him once again.

"If you're free this Saturday night, I'm playing guitar at the art café around the corner," he said. "Any interest in coming with me?"

She was very interested.

"Make sure they don't ink stamp your hand to get in," I teased.

"Don't you worry about it," she said as we pulled away. "If they do, I know a man."

— Jody Lebel —

93

Papa's Arms

In the eyes of their grandchildren, grandfathers are
professional pranksters and veteran comedians.
~Author Unknown

My granddaughter, Lilith, had reached that scary but important age when her baby teeth were beginning to loosen and come out. As one would expect, it scared her. She would try to hide the fact that she had a loose tooth, not wanting us to touch it to see how loose it was or, even worse, attempt to pull it out.

No amount of sweet talk about how it wouldn't hurt would make her open her mouth to let us see it. No stories concerning the beautiful Tooth Fairy coming by at night when she was asleep would comfort her. Each loose tooth was a traumatic experience.

Eventually, she became used to the process, accepting it as a natural part of growing up from a toddler to a little girl. In fact, she began to look forward to the Tooth Fairy's visits and the coins that showed up under her pillow. She would proudly display the hole from each missing tooth like a badge of honor.

One day, after she had pretty much passed through that childhood phase, we were standing next to each other, and I noticed her looking at my arm.

"You see how my arms are longer than yours?" I asked her.

"Yes," she said.

"That's because these are my grown-up arms."

She looked down at her arms.

"Stick your arm out straight," I said, and she did.

I stooped down and stuck my arm out next to hers.

"See," I said. "Mine are longer."

I didn't realize that my wife had walked up behind us and was listening to this entire conversation. I stuck my other arm out straight, parallel to my other arm.

"Do you know why mine are longer?"

"Because you're bigger," she said.

"You're right. I'm an adult, and these are my adult arms."

Her big eyes looked from my hands to my shoulders, taking it all in.

"When you get a little bigger," I said, "and your baby arms fall off, you'll grow adult arms like me."

She took one look at her own arm sticking out and ran off screaming. I laughed and turned around to see the scowling face of my wife.

"You're paying for the therapy," she admonished, and went off shaking her head to comfort our granddaughter.

— Del Howison —

What's So Funny?

*A little girl at a wedding afterwards asked her mother
why the bride changed her mind. "What do you
mean?" responded her mother. "Well, she went down
the aisle with one man, and came back with another."*
~Author Unknown

t was a beautiful wedding. The dresses, the candles, the flowers — especially the flowers. They were wonderful. The candle glow and smell of roses heightened the intensity of the ceremony.

"And do you, Peggy, take this man..." the pastor began.

Yes of course I do. He's sweet and gorgeous and...

"I do," I said.

"And do you, Dickey, take this woman, Peggy..."

Yes, of course he does.

"Please kneel. Father, we ask your special blessing on this husband and this wife," the pastor continued.

Wait, is someone giggling?

"Bless their union..."

Who is giggling?

It's his mother! Why is she laughing? What does she know that I don't?

"And all of us gathered here promise to offer support..."

Now his mother's laughing out loud. And so is everyone else. Wait! May I ask a question before we continue?

"I now introduce Mr. and Mrs... ," the pastor concluded, although he seemed a little confused, too.

They're still laughing.

But the music swelled and this man I was no longer sure of whisked me out of the church.

"Wow!" I said with a catch in my throat. "They all seemed to enjoy the service." I turned to Dickey, fishing for an explanation.

Dickey had a look of suspicion on his face as he leaned against the wall. He lifted one shoe and then the other.

"My little sister! I'm going to get her!" he groaned, shaking his head. Then he showed me the bottom of his shoes.

Written in big red letters were the words "HELP ME!"

— Peggy Purser Freeman —

95

The Wrinkled One

A happy marriage is a new beginning of life,
a new starting point for happiness...
~Dean Stanley

Thirty years after my last date, I re-entered the dating scene. I nervously joined a matchmaker service, but expected to meet few, if any, wonderful men. I was wrong.

"Hi, are you Patt?" The question was posed by a man waiting near the reservation podium wearing the striped tan polo shirt and glasses I was told to expect. His easy smile relieved the usual awkwardness of a first date.

Our conversation was lively and nonstop. When I ordered ostrich, he did not freak out at my weirdness. After dinner in the parking lot, we sealed our deal with the still unforgettable kiss he planted on me. I discovered my soul mate and so did he.

Over the next several months, I renewed my acquaintance with internal butterflies and that special tingle. Life was again a glorious mystery worth exploring. We jointly proposed and planned a party to celebrate our mid-life love — at the dog museum.

Although I had "been there," I had not "done THIS." Mid-life love was new! Even shopping for a traditional wedding dress with my daughters was different and proved hilarious. Automatically, well-intended salesclerks steered me in the direction of "mother's dresses" and riddled my daughters with bride-type questions.

"Hello and welcome... When is your big day...? Wow, that's

great… How many bridesmaids…? Where is your wedding…? What type of gown do you have in mind?"

We conspired and tag teamed in a comedy routine.

"Talk to the wrinkled bride," my daughters would reply sternly with an open hand and palm forward.

I continued the merriment by grinning broadly with raised arm and pointing a finger downward to the top of my head. Not intending rudeness or embarrassment, we invited them to laugh with us — and they did.

I was fifty-one. Numerous excursions and try-ons yielded zero possibilities until finally my daughters heartily endorsed a sequined halter-top number and a long, slick white satin skirt with a train. The dress was perfect. The ensemble subtracted years and pounds while highlighting my "assets."

Each of our combined five children agreed to be in our wedding party — tuxes, fancy dresses, and flowers — the works. Time zoomed forward to our big day and the typical tizzy of mini-disasters. That day brought the unexpected repair of an overnight flat tire, which was soon upstaged by a wardrobe malfunction.

My younger daughter's last-minute snacking splattered stains on the top of her shimmery two-piece chartreuse gown. Unrattled, we spot cleaned it. She hung the semi-wet garment by hand out the van window. Fortunately, she did not lose her grip as it flapped dry in the wind while we sped to the dog museum.

When we made our late entrance, the nearly 100 guests were milling about the museum, fascinated by dog memorabilia. Our canine enthusiast guests commended us for our "dogtastic" location.

Although the minister performed a lackluster service, I delighted in the warm support family and friends showered on our celebration of love. Soon the glorious scent of cheese-filled mushrooms, beef tenderloin, hot rolls, and assorted goodies swirled in waves around us.

After dinner, the karaoke DJ was a resounding hit, highlighted by our newlywed dance. Joined by an eight-year-old nephew wearing a plastic monkey mask, my husband and I donned dog masks — Dalmatians because our ages totaled a bit over 101. Of course, the theme song was,

"Who Let the Dogs Out." Guests cheered and barked to the music.

Although we requested "the gift of your presence only," my husband's poker-hunting-fishing crowd (whom he has known for decades) cooked up delightfully bizarre surprise gifts. After our honeymoon, we gathered family and a few friends for the opening.

As we unwrapped the first gift from the group, my husband and I exchanged quizzical looks because it was a... toaster? Mmmmm, yes — not just something else packed in a toaster box. As I grabbed the second package from the men and their wives, my husband and I locked eyes and telepathed a shared observation, "These packages are exactly the same size."

In fact, not only were they the same size packages — they were seven identical toasters with UPC codes conscientiously cut away! So much for cashing in on returns. Amidst uncontrollable laughter, we posed for the friendly paparazzi with seven toasters stacked vertically between us.

Remarkably, we found greeting cards featuring toasters and sent them as notes of thanks. One month later, the same pranksters bestowed seven individually gift-wrapped loaves of bread on my husband as birthday gifts. (I was slow to catch the extended joke.) Our tale of seven toasters and loaves lasted for years as we discovered a series of creative ways to re-gift the toasters — even some back to the group itself.

We plan to grow older together and will not let things grow old between us — with our wedding as the benchmark for surprises, laughter, and spice. Our mid-life marriage extends beyond a simple approach to the sunset years or a boring rerun of past mistakes or pleasures. As Dean Stanley wrote, "A happy marriage is a new beginning of life, a new starting point for happiness..." — at any age.

— Patt Hollinger Pickett —

96

A Traditional Norwegian Christmas

The bond that links your true family is not one of blood,
but of respect and joy in each other's life.
~Richard Bach

It was going to be my stepfather's first Christmas Eve without his kids, and he was in a funk. My little brother, David, and I didn't call him "Dad" yet. He was still just "my mom's boyfriend" or "Mr. Leiren," but we were hoping he'd soon be more than that.

Mr. Leiren had four daughters and, like most divorced dads, he had to figure out how to schedule his holiday season. Mom asked Mr. Leiren how we could help him have a happy Christmas. He explained that his tradition as a Canadian parent was to open presents Christmas morning and have a family dinner that night. But he was born and raised in a small town in Norway with a name that's pretty much impossible to pronounce unless you're Scandinavian. Mr. Leiren explained that in Norway they opened presents and had the festive feast on Christmas Eve. So Mom offered to create a traditional Norwegian Christmas Eve. Then, the next day, he'd get to see his kids after their presents were opened.

Like many North American Jewish kids, our Hanukkah wish was to celebrate Christmas. Instead, we had to settle for dreidels, latkes and eight days of candles. But my mom wanted to help Mr. Leiren enjoy his holiday, so she asked what one served for a traditional Norwegian Christmas meal.

The feast started with lutefisk — dried cod treated with lye. The main course was a rack of lamb accompanied by raspekake — huge grey potato balls, which were pretty much the anti-latke. This was served with lots of smør — my favorite Norwegian word: butter.

Dessert consisted of krumkakes — thin, crispy, pastry horns stuffed with whipped cream mixed with cloudberry jam. My mom had to search everywhere in the city and the suburbs to find a proper Norwegian "krumkake iron."

Mom made the lamb and the dessert. Mr. Leiren cooked the fish and potatoes. And our traditional Christmas feast was delicious — except for the lutefisk, which was an acquired taste one apparently needed to be born in Norway to acquire.

My mom completed the festivities by putting up a small tree, and that year Hanukkah presents became Christmas presents.

Mr. Leiren spent the night smiling, laughing and telling us how this was the perfect Norwegian Christmas. From that year on, he and Mom would prepare the traditional Norwegian delicacies every Christmas Eve (minus the lutefisk).

After my first year of university, my friend Bob and I went backpacking through Europe. One of our stops was Stamneshella, the village where Dad grew up. I met his relatives, and we swapped stories about Dad, Canada, Norway and the correct way to pronounce "Leiren" as everyone served us platters overflowing with Norwegian treats.

One afternoon, Dad's cousin arrived with a plate of krumkakes. She was delighted and shocked that I not only knew what these were, but pronounced the name — not quite correctly, but close enough to be recognizable as Norsk.

She wanted to know how I knew the word. I explained that I knew the names of all the foods that were part of a traditional Norwegian Christmas feast. She looked puzzled and asked me to tell her about the rest of the meal. The more I told her, the more confused she looked until, finally, she started to laugh. "That's not a traditional Norwegian

Christmas dinner," she said. "Those are just your dad's favorite foods."

I thought about whether I should ask Dad about this, or at least mention it to my mom. But as I finished the last of the whipped cream from my krumkake, I realized something with perfect clarity: My dad's cousin didn't know anything about Norwegian Christmas traditions.

— Mark Leiren-Young —

97

All's Fair...

We don't stop playing because we grow old;
we grow old because we stop playing.
~George Bernard Shaw

It's the same every Christmas. My extended family gathers, we share a festive meal, and the kids open their gifts. Soon after, the fighting starts:

"You cheated!"

"No, you did!"

"That's mine! You can't take it!"

Surprisingly, it's not the kids who are yelling at the tops of their voices or wresting gifts from each other's hands. It's the adults.

My family's been playing the Gift Game — also known as Yankee Swap — for more than twenty Christmases now. To play, everyone over age eighteen places a gift in the center of the circle and takes a seat. I pass around a bowl of folded, numbered paper slips. Then the game begins.

Number 1 goes first. He unwraps a gift and displays it for all to see. It might be a can of nuts, a puzzle, or some other generic item. At this point, we all make appreciative noises or polite comments: "Mmm, looks tasty!" or "That's a pretty puzzle." After all, the game hasn't gotten going yet. But it will. Just wait.

Now it's Number 2's turn. She has choices: She can open a new gift, or — if she wants to get this party started — she can steal Number 1's gift. If she does, Number 1 might make a mild protest like, "Hey, I liked that!" or "That's not fair!" But unless it was a really good gift (read: gift card), facial expressions and voice volumes are still appropriately calm at this point. No one has lost control… yet.

If Number 2 does opt to steal, Number 1 — now gift-less — chooses a new gift from the pile. And the game continues with Numbers 3, 4, and so on. One important rule is that a person whose gift was stolen can turn around and steal someone else's; then that person can steal someone else's and so on down the line. So the fun really starts once we reach the middle numbers. By the time we reach 8, 9, and 10, gifts are being lost left and right, everyone's shouting, and people holding the desirable gifts are shielding them with chairs, pillows, and even bodies. The kids have left their new toys to stand around our circle, gaping and giggling at the crazy adults putting on a show.

We're normally a quiet family. But this game brings out the savage in some of us. My sister Lisa, a respectable, well-behaved mother of eleven, has been known to cackle triumphantly while stealing her own offspring's gift! Lisa and her husband José must be watched closely because another rule of the game is this: If your gift has just been stolen from you, you can't turn around and steal it right back. But several years ago, Lisa and José introduced a new twist to the game — the two-way steal.

Say Cousin Cheryl steals Lisa's Caribou Coffee gift card. Lisa can't take the card back from Cheryl, but she can steal her husband's twenty-pack of AA batteries. Then he can steal the Caribou card back from Cheryl. So at the end of the game, Lisa has power in a box and José has two large, decaf turtle mochas. All they have to do is switch with each other.

The game reveals our competitive streaks, too, as each of us strives to bring the most coveted gift. Before gift cards became popular and we raised the spending limit to ten dollars, my mom held the record two years straight for her box of clementine oranges. (The third year, Aunt Sonya topped her by wrapping up *two* boxes of clementines.) Other favored gifts have been a wooden puzzle box (containing a gift card!), an animated butterfly in a jar, and a dissect-your-own-owl-pellet kit. (Some might consider bird vomit undesirable, but as a homeschooling mom, I loved this ready-made science experiment.) People have gotten creative in their choice of container, as well. In recent years, my brother Paul became notable for his prank "Earwax Candle Kit" gift box and his "Mobile Foot Rub" gift-card holder.

Then there was the most notorious gift. Several years ago, when my husband Jory's number came up, I nudged him toward a particular flat package. I was sure it was the candy my mom had told me she was going to buy. However, instead of his favorite almond bark, the box contained an Elvis Christmas ornament. A *singing* Elvis Christmas ornament.

Jory begged every subsequent number to steal his ornament. He displayed it ostentatiously and extolled its (nonexistent) virtues with Vanna-like flourishes. He even kicked it into the center of the circle each time someone stood to pick a new gift! But, shockingly, no one wanted a sparkly tree bauble that blared "Blue Christmas" at the touch of a button. At the end of the night, most of us had useful or edible gifts. A few lucky ones had gift cards. But all my husband had was Elvis. Cousin Dave finally confessed to having brought it, and Jory still hasn't forgiven him.

Even though our game always brings fun to our Christmas gathering, I never thought much about what it means to me. In fact, there were years — back when my twins were infants and I was low on energy — that I suggested forgoing it. But then, two Octobers ago, Aunt Sonya died. The next Christmas, my puzzle-loving aunt wasn't there to steal another player's jigsaw, and I felt her absence in a new way.

Suddenly, I realized that the Christmas Gift Game won't always look the same. People might move. Families with grown-up kids might splinter off to hold their own celebrations. Eventually, our number of players might shrink to the point where the game's not fun to play anymore, and we'll go back to exchanging soap-on-a-rope or salami sticks like we used to. And I will be sad because our game is more than a holiday pastime. It's tradition, togetherness and laughing so hard that my stomach aches and my eyes tear up. In fact, the game has given me some of my best Christmas memories.

In light of that, I will play the game hard while I can. I will wrap my presents cleverly. (Just wait until next Christmas when Paul sees the "Motorized Rolling Pin" gift box I found!) I will train my two daughters in the art of the four-way steal so that when they come of age, they'll be ready to compete. Heck, I might even throw caution to the wind, buy an Elvis — or Elton John, or Justin Bieber — ornament, and wrap it up in classic-car paper, in hopes of enticing hot-rod-loving Cousin Dave to pick it out of the pile.

All's fair in love and Christmas gifting!

— Sara Matson —

Canadian Winters Are Not for Fashionistas

*There's no such thing as bad weather,
only unsuitable clothing.*
~Alfred Wainwright

At twenty-something, I was ever so fashionable and cute. I donned a meticulously selected outfit, hat, footwear and accessories for every event. The effect of the look was the priority, not its comfort or practicality, which was all too obvious one winter night in Ontario's cottage country.

I jumped in my little red sports car, heading north for New Year's Eve at my family's cottage in Haliburton. Only a sprinkling of snow dusted the ground in Toronto as I began my two-hour journey north. The traffic was clear and the roads dry, until I turned onto the cottage road from the highway, just thirty minutes south of Algonquin Park.

Without snow tires on my sports car, I felt the car veering closer to the deep ditch of the single lane road, without guardrails to protect my fall. I felt my carefully applied make-up dripping down my face as the sweat began to show my fear. I dropped into low gear, pumped the brake and prayed. Like a puppy walking on ice, I made it to the bottom of the road and arrived at the lakefront cottage.

I took a deep breath and assessed the situation. I was fine, and the car was in one piece. One look in the rear-view mirror and I saw my make-up was the only casualty. Some powder and lipstick did the trick. I jumped out of my car, feeling stylish in my short, leather boots with three-inch heels, tight blue jeans, a leather blazer and sleek blond hairdo peeking from under a fashionable hat. I was too cool for a scarf or gloves.

With my first step out of the car, I knew I was in trouble. My boots sunk through a foot of snow and had absolutely no traction to get me up the icy stairs to the deck where I could make my entrance. I held my arms out for balance, took tiny steps, cursed a few times and made it up the stairs and to the front of the deck. Family and friends were skating on the lake and visiting on the front deck. It was hard to tell who was who since their entire bodies were covered in winter wear that was clearly not going to be seen in the pages of *Chatelaine*.

"I'm here," I announced as I struck a pose to show off my coolness. "Hey there," "You made it," and other welcomes rang out. One voice could be heard above others — my older brother — as he took in my "look" and began to laugh, saying, "Good luck with that," and nodding at my attire. With stubbornness that only a baby sister can muster up, I stuck out my chin and said, "I'm tough. Besides, you won't catch me in an outfit like yours!" I grabbed my first beer and headed off to join the others.

In less than ten minutes it became very clear that the boots had to go. The wet snow had seeped through and I was losing feeling in my toes. I went inside the cottage and borrowed a pair of Ski-Doo boots, lined with 3/4-inch felt. They almost reached my knees and had enough tread to scale an iceberg. Off I went — again. Another fifteen minutes passed and my fingers were turning red with white blotches. I went back in the cottage for lined mitts that reached my elbows, and another beer — to keep me warm.

A little more time passed and my ears begin to sting. Off I went again, but this time, I noticed the snickers from onlookers. My sister guided me by my arm back into the cottage. As the baby sister who is more than a decade younger than the other three siblings, space was often provided to make my own mistakes, but this sister decided enough was enough. Out came the balaclava and a full ski suit from neck to ankles. I stepped back out on the deck, greeted with cheers from the group for my warm attire. I heaved a sigh for my lost coolness, leaving it behind while my great hairdo got crushed and my perfect make-up rubbed off on the inside of the balaclava. I rang in the New Year taking active pleasure in the fun — with warm limbs, no surface skin and fully functioning digits.

— Sheri Gammon Dewling —

99

Glam-ma's Red Christmas Suit

In order to be irreplaceable one
must always be different.
~Coco Chanel

My sister was thrilled when I told her we were going to make the trip to her house for Christmas. She explained the Christmas tradition she had started shortly after Mom passed away. "We're lining the walkway around the house with luminaries. We'll light a candle as we call out the names of our loved ones who have passed on. When we're finished, we'll have a moment of silence. Then, in unison, we'll say the short prayer that I've printed out. Finally, we'll sing the first verse of "Silent Night," and then go in to have our Christmas Eve dinner. Dress warm because we're expecting snow."

She was so excited that we were coming. After Mom passed away, we had gotten into a nasty fight and didn't talk to each other for a few years. Now that we had finally put aside our differences, it seemed as if we couldn't get enough of each other. We had spent Thanksgiving together and now, for the first time in years, we would also be spending Christmas together. I was just as thrilled as she was.

While running around to pick up last-minute gifts, I came across a two-piece outfit that I thought would be perfect for staying warm during the outdoor ceremony. It was bright red, and the jacket had a hood. It fit me perfectly. I couldn't believe how lucky I was to find such a warm, fuzzy, beautiful red Christmas suit when I wasn't even looking for one. I loved everything about it.

As we prepared to leave, I put on my red suit with a white turtleneck. I looked great. When my husband came in, I asked excitedly, "How do you like my outfit?"

He stopped short, and then he said, "Well, well, I… Yeah, it's nice. We better get going. We have a long ride ahead of us."

When we finally drove up my sister's long driveway, I was excited to see my sister, brother-in-law, nephew and another family member smiling and waving. I pulled up the hood of my jacket so I wouldn't get cold, and then got out of the car with open arms, yelling "MERRY CHRISTMAS!" For some reason, everyone looked completely shocked!

Still smiling but somewhat confused, I repeated, "MERRY CHRISTMAS!" My sister walked over and gave me a hug, and then stood back. My brother-in-law stood with his head tilted to the side. My nephew looked like he was half smiling, half smirking.

Finally, my sister broke the silence by yelling, "WHAT THE HECK DO YOU HAVE ON? IT LOOKS LIKE SHAG CARPET!" Before I could say anything, she bombarded me with questions. "WHERE DID YOU GET THAT THING? YOU LOOK LIKE AN ELF. NO, YOU LOOK LIKE A BIG RED SHEEP. All YOU NEED IS A TAIL! DO YOU SHEAR, VACUUM OR WASH THAT THING?" Then everyone burst out laughing. I tentatively joined in the laughter but thought to myself, *You ought to be glad I'm not an elf because I'd be helping Santa put some names on his naughty list right about now.*

Slowly, I walked over to my very tall nephew, who hugged me. With my head barely reaching his chest, I looked up and whispered, "What's wrong with them? Is my suit that bad?"

He broke out in a laugh and said, "You look like Elmo!" I should've known better than to ask a nineteen-year-old.

The luminary ceremony was touching and absolutely beautiful, but for some reason everyone burst out laughing before we even finished singing "Silent Night." I've often been told that I'm a Glam-ma, but even Glam-mas are allowed to make fashion mistakes. And according to everyone's reactions, I made a big one.

I must admit, that Christmas was one of the best I ever had. I knew we were going to have a great time, but I had no idea that my warm, fuzzy and beautiful red Christmas suit would add to the merriment.

—Francine L. Billingslea—

100

Grandparents' Day

A grandparent is old on the outside
but young on the inside.
~Author Unknown

I enter the elementary school cafetorium crowded with grandparents. We're invited here to be honored at Grandparents' Day. This is a rare role reversal, since we're usually focusing on our adored grandchildren, who exist because we raised their parents.

Soon, the stage fills with awkward kindergartners preparing to sing. The audience chuckles at the little girl in the front row who pulls up her dress with one hand and waves with the other.

After several grade levels perform, the fifth-grade chorus takes the stage and bursts into a lively rendition of "Rockin' Robin." Grandparents come alive and sing the familiar lyrics from the fifties, transporting us back to the sock hops and proms we attended decades ago. Bulging waistlines rock and happy heads roll to the rhythm, while hands dotted with age spots clap and wrinkled faces beam.

When the performances end, my seven-year-old grandson, Kyle, appears and escorts me to his classroom. I sit next to him and he hands me the papers he prepared for my visit. On one sheet he's written things he likes to do with me: bike riding, going places, fishing, and making pancakes.

On another sheet he writes my answers while he interviews me.

"Where were you born?"

"Michigan."

"What were your favorite toys as a child?"

"Dolls."

"What did your family like to do for entertainment?"

"Raise a garden."

"What is your favorite grade-school memory?"

"Riding horses."

"What do you enjoy doing now?"

"Being with my grandchildren."

"What is your favorite place in the whole world?"

"My home."

"What inventions have changed the way you live?"

"Television and computers."

"What one thing do you wish had not changed over the years?"

"My age."

Before I leave the school, Kyle and I sit at a picnic table outside and eat the lunches my daughter has packed for us. I share my appreciation for the wonderful Grandparents' Day and mention several observations.

"I noticed something too," he says.

"What?" I ask.

"I can tell when a lady is a grandmother."

"How?"

"Her hair turns blond."

— Miriam Hill —

Manners Mishap

*Politeness is the art of choosing
among one's real thoughts.*
~Abel Stevens

We bundled up in our coats, mittens and hats to head out the door to Grandma's house. We loaded the wrapped gifts into the trunk and I saw that the kids were all buckled into their car seats. As we began to pull down the driveway, the kids were animated in their discussion of what awaited them at their grandparents' house.

"I bet Nana made cinnamon rolls!" Kyle said.

"And Grandpa will probably get out some shrimp later!" said Karen, matching his anticipation.

There's not much that's more heartwarming than listening to eager children on Christmas morning. Before they got too much further into their holiday chattering, I thought it would be a good time to launch into my annual conversation about good manners. "Be sure to say 'please' and 'thank you' at Grandma's today — at all of the meals and when you open your gifts — even if you don't like something," I lectured.

"Okay," they responded, as if they were wondering how I could be thinking of something as boring as manners on an exciting day like Christmas.

"How grown-up of me!" I chuckled to myself.

We finally arrived at the house and the kids dashed inside. They would only ask fifty times when it would be time to open gifts and I would only remind them fifty times to mind their manners.

Finally, the moment they'd somewhat patiently waited for arrived. We all gathered in our designated spots. The kids helped their grandmother and various aunts and uncles pass out the gifts. Then it was time to unwrap the gifts, one at a time as everyone watched.

Every year, my grandmother created handmade gifts. This particular year, she had knitted rainbow-striped cardigan sweaters. My daughter's was made with beautiful pastel yarns and my son's was made with primary colors. As they opened their sweaters, I watched as my young, elementary-aged son pulled his out of the box, held it up with an awkward look on his face, and said, "Thank you! Even though I don't like it!"

I was mortified as giggles broke out around the room. I couldn't really discipline my son because he'd done exactly as I'd instructed him. He said thank you even though he didn't like the gift. He just missed the context a bit.

Oh well! Out of the mouths of babes. Even my grandmother got a good laugh out of it and commented later that maybe the colors weren't quite suited to a young man. Kyle gave the sweater to his sister, who was very grateful to have two! Her enthusiasm for the sweaters and the group's laughter more than made up for my son's unfiltered but obedient comment.

— Stephanie Davenport —

We are pleased to introduce you to the writers whose stories were compiled from our past books to create this new collection. These bios were the ones that ran when the stories were originally published. They were current as of the publication dates of those books.

Meet Our Contributors

Heidi Allen is the founder of the Positive People Army. What began as a blog has rapidly become a positive social media global movement with thousands of people from all over the world working together to make a positive difference.

Teresa Ambord is a business writer and editor, working from her home in rural Northern California. What she loves best is writing family stories. Her posse of small dogs serves as her muses. They inspire her writing and decorate her life.

Cindy D'Ambroso Argiento lives in North Carolina with her family. She is a freelance writer and has published a book entitled *Deal With Life's Stress With "A Little Humor."* To purchase a copy and read her work, check out her website at www.cindyargiento.com or e-mail her at cargiento@aol.com.

Francine L. Billingslea is a retired "Glam-ma" who has found a passion for writing in her later years. She is proud to have over sixty-three publications including several in the *Chicken Soup for the Soul* series. She loves writing, traveling, shopping, and spending quality time with her loved ones.

Jan Bono taught school for thirty years on the Long Beach peninsula in Southwest Washington State. She now works as a life coach, writing coach, Law of Attraction presenter, and freelance writer, with numerous articles and several books to her credit. Check out her blog at www.daybreak-solutions.com/blog.

Caleb Jennings Breakey is self-conscious about writing in the third person. He thinks it's a little weird. But he should still tell you that he's a writer, youth mentor, and crazy lover of Jesus. He and his sweetheart, Brittney, passionately teach writing and character at high schools, colleges, and conferences. E-mail him at calebbreakey@gmail.com.

Ilah Breen delights in teaching fourth grade in warm and sunny Florida. After spending many years in the cool, foggy lands of Humboldt County, California, she celebrates life by spending time with her family, playing with grandchildren, writing, gardening, and painting.

Sally A. Breslin is a copy editor and writer whose award-winning humor column, "My Life," was published weekly from 1994–2016 in several New England newspapers. She has authored three novels, including *There's a Tick in My Underwear!*, a humorous look at camping back in the 1960s. E-mail her at sillysally@att.net.

Karla Brown is married and lives on the outskirts of Philadelphia, PA. She loves swimming, British movies, chocolate and gardening. She also writes paranormal romantic suspense, YA and middle grade, and hopes one day to be a novelist.

After seventy-plus years of misbehaving, **Robert Campbell** settled into humorous reminiscences of his youth in Boston, sailing adventures in the Caribbean and elder age in Florida trying to amuse his wife with such stories. As a cancer patient, writing keeps his pulse on the value of humor.

Liane Kupferberg Carter is a journalist whose articles and essays have appeared in many publications, including *The New York Times*, the *Chicago Tribune* and The Huffington Post. She writes a monthly column for *Autism After 16*. She wrangles cats with her husband and two adult sons.

Jane McBride Choate received her Bachelor of Science degree from Brigham Young University. Writing is a dream come true for her, especially appearing in the *Chicken Soup for the Soul* series.

Linda S. Clare is the author of several books, including *The Fence My Father Built*, (Abingdon Press 2009). She teaches and coaches writing for George Fox University and Lane Community College. She lives with her family in Eugene, OR. She blogs at GodSongGrace.blogspot. com, or e-mail her at Lindas352@comcast.net.

Sharon Love Cook lives in Beverly Farms, Mass., with her husband and herd of cats (currently no dogs). She writes a humor column and draws cartoons for *The Salem News*. She is seeking a publisher for her humorous illustrated gift book about men and cats. E-mail her at Cookie978@aol.com.

Harriet Cooper is a freelance writer, editor and language instructor. She specializes in writing creative nonfiction, humor and often writes about health, exercise, diet, cats, family and the environment. A frequent contributor to *Chicken Soup for the Soul*, her work has also appeared in newspapers, magazines, newsletters, anthologies, websites and radio.

D'ette Corona is the Associate Publisher for Chicken Soup for the Soul Publishing, LLC. She received her Bachelor of Science in business management in 1994. D'ette has been married for eighteen years and has a thirteen-year-old son.

Steph Davenport is a nationally published writer and previous contributor to the *Chicken Soup for the Soul* series. Her stories about food, health, relationships and spirituality have appeared in magazines, collaborative works and newspapers. Steph enjoys life in the Midwest and is passionate about agriculture and creativity.

Heather Davis has a finely tuned snarky side that she uses to save her sanity. *Oversharing My Life*, a collection of humorous essays, is due to be released in April 2013. She and her family live in Oklahoma, where she chronicles her life at www.Minivan-Momma.com. Yes, she drives a minivan. Really.

Gwen Daye is a wife, homemaker, dog rescuer, parent of two teenagers, and is thrilled to have her second piece accepted into the *Chicken Soup for the Soul* series.

Sheri Gammon Dewling, a former software executive, runs a small consulting business, while raising two small children in Markham, ON. Sheri aspires to turn her life lessons into stories that will inspire others. E-mail her at sheri@justmomsense.com.

Jeannie Dotson is a middle school language arts teacher in Powell County, KY. She enjoys writing nonfiction and is currently working on a nonfiction picture book for children.

Jane Marie Allen Farmer works at both private and homeschooled children's enrichment facilities. She enjoys horseback riding and hiking. She and one of her four dogs, Leala, work as a pet therapy team. She received her BS in Wildlife/Fisheries Science, BFA in Art and MS in Education from University of Tennessee.

Manley Fisher has a Bachelor of Education degree and has taught English classes to adults for nearly twenty years. He lives in Spruce Grove, Alberta, and enjoys cross-country skiing, fishing, and, of course, writing. His other work includes pieces for professional publications and hopes one day to be an inspirational speaker.

Marianne Fosnow resides in South Carolina. She was thrilled and honored to have a story included in *Chicken Soup for the Soul: The Spirit of America*. She's an avid reader and also enjoys photography.

Peggy Purser Freeman is the author of *The Coldest Day in Texas*, *Swept Back to a Texas Future*, *Cruisin' Thru Life: Dip Street and Other Miracles*, and *Spy Cam One*. Her experience as a magazine editor, student writing workshop teacher and her many published works in magazines across Texas inspire readers. Learn more at PeggyPurserFreeman.com.

Kathleen Gerard has shared her life with Yorkshire Terriers since she was nine years old. Her love of the breed inspired *The Thing Is*, a novel about a therapy dog named Prozac who rescues a woman in grief. Kathleen's writing has been widely published and anthologized. Learn more at kathleengerard.blogspot.com.

Pamela Gilsenan is the mother of five adult children whose names all begin with "J." She is a Rocky Mountain regional writer and graduate of Stephens College. She has written and published two children's books and several specialty cookbooks. Her upcoming cookbook is *Rhubarb! Rhubarb!*. Please e-mail her at p_Gilsenan@hotmail.com.

Patty Hansen co-authored many of the most beloved stories in the

Chicken Soup for the Soul series. She was one of the founding executives of Chicken Soup for the Soul and responsible for its early successes.

Dena Harris is the author of several hilarious books on cats including *Lessons in Stalking* and the upcoming *Kiss My Kitty Butt: More Life With Cats*. She spends her days plotting how to sneak more cats in the house without her husband noticing. Visit www.denaharris.com or contact her at dena@kissmykittybutt.com.

Marijo Herndon's stories appear in numerous *Chicken Soup for the Soul* books as well as many other anthologies and publications. She enjoys writing from her home in New York where she lives with her husband, Dave, and two rescue cats, Lucy and Ethel.

Eileen Melia Hession is a former teacher and publisher's representative whose writing has appeared in various publications. She has one daughter and enjoys running, yoga and ceramics. She believes there is a need for more levity in life and her writing reflects that belief.

Miriam Hill is a frequent contributor to *Chicken Soup for the Soul* books and has been published in *Writer's Digest*, *The Christian Science Monitor*, *Grit*, *St. Petersburg Times*, *The Sacramento Bee* and Poynter Online. Miriam's manuscript received Honorable Mention for Inspirational Writing in a Writer's Digest Writing Competition.

Hailing from Acworth, GA, **Butch Holcombe** dreamed of being a published author. Those dreams became reality and he went on to create *American Digger Magazine*, now in its fifteenth year of publication. He considers himself a cat/dog person, but admits an affinity for squirrels. Please don't tell Frankie… it would crush him.

Joei Carlton Hossack has been a travel writer for over twenty years, specializing in solo RV travel. She is a motivational and inspirational speaker and storyteller. She enjoys photography, teaching and recently discovered her love of beadwork. She lives in Surrey, B.C.

Del Howison, along with his wife Sue, is the creator and owner of Dark Delicacies in Burbank, CA. He is an award-winning editor and author having won the Bram Stoker Award for which he was nominated four times. He has also been nominated for the Shirley Jackson Award and the Black Quill Award.

Former teacher **Gina Farella Howley** currently lives out her dream Mom career. Her three boys, all under seven years old, consume much of her time. When they are not awake, she is thinking about them, writing about them, and looking to make a name for herself as an author someday.

Cindy Hval's work has appeared in numerous *Chicken Soup for the Soul* collections. She's currently working on her first book *Love Stories From the Greatest Generation*. She's a columnist and correspondent for *The Spokesman-Review* newspaper in Spokane, Washington where she lives with her husband, four sons and one cat.

Jeanie Jacobson is on the Wordsowers Christian Writers leadership team. She's been published in *Focus on the Family* and *Live* magazines, the *Chicken Soup for the Soul* series, and other anthologies. Jeanie loves visiting family, reading, hiking, and dancing. Grab her book, *Fast Fixes for the Christian Pack-Rat* online. Learn more at JeanieJacobson.com.

Robin Jankiewicz lives a happily married life in Los Angeles, CA with her husband and two children. She looks forward to visiting Florida again someday.

Ronald W. Kaiser, Jr. received his master's degree in English Literature from the University of New Hampshire. He lives and teaches English in New Hampshire's Lakes Region. Writing stories is his second passion, next to his radiant wife. And then of course there are his two terriers.

Ann Denise Karson has an English/Writing degree from the University of Colorado. She lives in the D.C. area, but loves to get back to Colorado when she can. Denise's interests include writing, reading, traveling, cooking, yoga, and she especially loves spending time with her family.

Shannon Kernaghan has published two books as well as hundreds of stories in anthologies, journals and newspapers. She's still waiting to find that "singing clock" in her Christmas stocking! Connect with her at www.shannonkernaghan.com.

April Knight is a frequent contibutor to *Chicken Soup for the Soul* books. She is also the author of several books about Native Americans, including *Crying Wind* and *My Searching Heart* and others written under her tribal name, Crying Wind.

Tina Koenig is a writer and technology entrepreneur. In addition to exploiting her family for fun and profit, Koenig is the author of the historical middle-grade mystery novel, *A Case of Considerable Consequence*. Links to other humorous stories about family, holidays and travel may be found at tinakoenig.com.

Kimber Krochmal lives in rural North Carolina. She has a large family consisting of not only her own children but other children she "adopted" over the years. They keep her young and are a constant source of inspiration.

Mitchell Kyd wrapped up a thirty-year career as a Fortune 500 PR professional and is enjoying life as a wordsmith and storyteller. Her stories often reflect the joys and poignant moments of small-town living and she is a frequent contributor to the *Chicken Soup for the Soul* series. Visit her at www.mitchellkyd.com.

Joyce Laird is a freelance writer living in Southern California. Her features have been published in magazines including, *Cat Fancy*, *Grit*, *Mature Living*, and *Vibrant Life*. She contributes regularly to *Woman's World* and to the *Chicken Soup for the Soul* anthology. Joyce is also a member of Mystery Writers of America.

Cathi LaMarche is the author of the novel *While the Daffodils Danced* and has contributed to numerous anthologies. She currently teaches composition and literature. Living in St. Louis, she shares her home with her husband, two children, and three spoiled dogs.

Monika LaPlante is a marine biologist and environmental scientist with a Bachelor of Science degree from Northeastern University. She is currently a graduate student at Pace University studying Computer Science. Monika is an avid scuba diver and underwater filmmaker. Check out her films on her website at www.monikalaplante.com.

Carrie M. Leach is a missionary wife and mom-of-many in Eastern Europe. When she's not homeschooling, folding laundry, cooking, gardening, or working among the Gypsy children of her area, she is writing. Her goal is to write a book about her experiences. E-mail her at cmleach5@gmail.com.

A court reporter by day, **Jody Lebel** mainly writes romantic suspense novels. Her book *Playing Dead* was released by The Wild Rose

Press in 2012 to excellent reviews. Jody was raised in charming New England and now lives with her two cats in southern Florida.

Karen M. Leet writes from Lexington, KY, heart of the Bluegrass, where she enjoys reading, family time, and writing.

Mark Leiren-Young is the author of two comic memoirs: *Never Shoot a Stampede Queen* and *Free Magic Secrets Revealed*. Based in Victoria, BC, Mark is an advocate for the Southern Resident Orcas. He's the author of *The Killer Whale Who Changed the World*, director of *The Hundred-Year-Old Whale* and host of the Skaana podcast.

Delia Lloyd is an American writer/journalist/blogger based in London. Her essays have appeared in *The International Herald Tribune*, *The Christian Science Monitor*, and Mothering.com. She blogs about adulthood at www.realdelia.com.

Barbara LoMonaco has worked for Chicken Soup for the Soul as an editor and webmaster since 1998. She has co-authored two Chicken Soup for the Soul book titles and has had stories published in various other titles. Barbara is a graduate of the University of Southern California and has a teaching credential.

After twenty years of teaching college level Information Technology, **Mary Lovstad**, an Iowa farm girl, now runs a farm wedding venue and writes a cooking blog. She aspires to write a cookbook featuring vintage recipes. Erma Bombeck is her writing hero and she regularly participates in the Erma Bombeck Writer's Workshop.

Cheryl MacDonald has written, co-authored or edited nearly forty books on Canadian history as well as numerous articles and essays. When she's not researching or writing, she can usually be found talking about history or at a War of 1812 re-enactment. E-mail Cheryl at heronwood@execulink.com.

Gail MacMillan is a graduate of Queen's University, Kingston, Ontario. She is the author of three books on the Nova Scotia Duck Tolling Retriever, one of Canada's unique dog breeds. Gail enjoys reading, writing, and walking her dogs. She lives in New Brunswick, Canada with her husband and three dogs. E-mail her at macgail@nbnet.nb.ca.

David Martin's humor and political satire have appeared in many publications including *The New York Times*, the *Chicago Tribune* and the *Smithsonian Magazine*. His humor collection, *My Friend W*, was published in 2005 by Arriviste Press. David lives in Ottawa, Canada with his wife Cheryl and his daughter Sarah.

Sara Matson and her family live in Minnesota, where Christmases are cold but cozy. She's especially looking forward to this Christmas, when she plans to unveil her story to her family during the annual game of Yankee Swap! Visit her website at www.saramatson.com.

Shannon McCarty received her Master's in Rehabilitation Counseling from the University of Texas Medical Center in Dallas in 1994 and currently resides in Austin, Texas. She writes humor pieces about parenting, and receives much of her inspiration from her twins, Tess and Tabitha, and son, Riley. Please e-mail her at smccarty@austin.rr.com.

Jennifer McMurrain has won numerous awards for her short stories and novels. Her novels, *Quail Crossings* and *Winter Song*, are now available on Amazon. She lives in Bartlesville, OK with her husband, daughter, two diva cats, and two goofy dogs. Learn more at www.jennifermcmurrain.com.

Raised in Africa as the child of missionaries, **Harriet E. Michael** is an author, freelance writer, speaker, wife, mother, and grandmother. When not writing or speaking, she works part-time as a substitute teacher. Her books can be found at amazon.com/author/harrietemichael. Read her blog at harrietemichael.blogspot.com.

Janell Michael's first book, *Fairytales Redeemed: A Woman's Study on the Power of Love, Forgiveness, and Reconciliation*, was published in 2018. Recently, she and her husband moved 2,400 miles to live closer to their children and grandchildren. Since retiring from teaching, Janell hopes to continue her writing career.

Rae Mitchell graduated from the University of California, Davis with bachelor's degrees in Comparative Literature and Linguistics. She is currently married to the wonderful Mr. Mitchell who has always been a source of inspiration and support for her writing. They currently live in Washington with their son.

After a life of school teaching, **Joyce MacBeth Morehouse** decided to put down some funny episodes that had occurred over her lifetime. As a twelve-year-old, Joyce published her first poem, and poetry has always been a "first love." Over the years, several writings have found their way into periodicals.

Mike Morin co-hosts a morning radio show at WZID-FM in Manchester, New Hampshire. In addition to his forty years as a radio and TV personality, Mike writes humor columns and features for New England newspapers and magazines. He enjoys baking artisan breads for local charity auctions. Please e-mail Mike at Heymikey@aol.com.

When **Gail Molsbee Morris** isn't chasing after God's heart, she chases rare birds across America. She can be reached through her nature blog, godgirlgail.com, or Twitter @godgirlgail.

Rachel Dunstan Muller is an author, storyteller, and personal historian. She and her husband of twenty-eight years continue to have adventures from their home on Vancouver Island, Canada. They have five children and three grandchildren. Learn more at www.racheldunstanmuller.com.

Toni-Michelle Nell lives with her husband Martin in Metro Atlanta. She enjoys being with those she loves and sharing in laughter, something the world needs more of. Toni-Michelle is currently enrolled at the University of Phoenix where she maintains a 4.0 GPA and is working on her AA in Psychology with the hopes of continuing on to get her Master's degree. Please e-mail her at tmnell@comcast.net.

Barbara Nicks grew up in lower Wisconsin and now resides in East Texas. She has been teaching for twenty-five years, spending two of them in Portugal. She enjoys traveling with her husband and two teenage sons, sewing, reading, and learning about technology. E-mail her at barbnicks@gmail.com.

Katie O'Connell writes from the heart. She believes in the healing power of dark chocolate, a good laugh, and living an authentic and meaningful life. Her essays have been featured in *Reader's Digest*, *Sasee*, *Patheos*, and several *Chicken Soup for the Soul* books. Follow her blog at blog.heartwiredwriting.com.

Emily Oot is a junior at Georgetown University and a Spanish major. She completed her semester abroad in Chile in the fall of 2008 and went on to a spring semester in Madrid, Spain. She greatly enjoyed sharing her abroad adventures in *Chicken Soup for the Soul: Campus*

Chronicles. This is her first published story.

Marta A. Oppenheimer, the oldest of four sisters, was born and raised in Puerto Rico. She has degrees from Clark University and Pratt Institute of Art in New York City. She is an art director, freelance writer, and event planner for an animal rescue group. She lives in Miami with her rescued pets in an old house packed with art, books, and Converses.

J.M. Penfold lives in Portland, OR. Please e-mail him at penfol35@ yahoo.com.

Patt Hollinger Pickett, Ph.D., a licensed therapist and certified life coach, writes with humor from a warm, no-nonsense perspective. Dr. Pickett draws from her personal life blended with over twenty years in practice as a relationship expert. She has a book ready for publication. Contact Patt through www.DrCoachLove.com.

When **Becky Lewellen Povich** was a young girl, she always enjoyed reading, but didn't begin to write until she was almost fifty years old! This is her fifth story published in the *Chicken Soup for the Soul* series. Her motto, by George Eliot is: "It's never too late to be who you might have been." E-mail Becky at Writergal53@gmail.com.

Felice Prager is a writer and a multisensory educational therapist from Scottsdale, AZ. Her essays have been published locally, nationally, and internationally in print and on the Internet. She is the author of the book, *Quiz It: Arizona*. To find out more, visit www.QuizItAZ.com. To find more of her essays visit www.writefunny.blogspot.com.

Kim Reynolds received her B.A. degree in Journalism from Concordia University in Montreal. Her fiction and essays have appeared in newspapers and the fiction anthology *The Company We Keep*. She lives in Ottawa, Canada with her husband, two children, a quiet dog and a noisy cat. Contact her at kimreynoldscreative.ca.

Janet Ramsdell Rockey is a freelance writer living in Tampa, FL, with her Realtor husband and their two cats. Her dedication to writing survives the demands of a full-time job, her husband's constant home improvements, and her furry feline "children." See her Amazon Author page at www.amazon.com/author/janetrockey.

Heather Rae Rodin is mother to six grown children and serves as

Executive Director for Hope Grows Haiti. She and her husband Gord live with their Great Dane, Bogart, near Peterborough, Ontario. Family needs, charity demands, speaking and writing keep her schedule full.

John M. Scanlan is a 1983 graduate of the United States Naval Academy, and retired from the Marine Corps as a Lieutenant Colonel aviator. He currently resides on Hilton Head Island, SC, and is pursuing a second career as a writer. E-mail John at ping1@hargray.com.

Gretchen Schiller courageously continues to date while Mr. X-Lax continues his Book Tour elsewhere. Gretchen is an ex-wife, ex-pediatric nurse, ex-resident of Guatemala and ex-member of Weight Watchers. (Cake is simply too yummy!) Gretchen's humorous website, www.sassysinglemom.com, includes topics about motherhood, adoption, healthy co-parenting after divorce and of course, dating!

Leslie C. Schneider grew up in Montana where she and her husband of forty years raised their two sons. She has four grandchildren and currently resides in the Denver area. E-mail her at Leslie@airpost.net.

Annabel Sheila grew up in a picturesque little town in Newfoundland. She writes poetry and stories about nature, the ocean, love, and life, embracing the gentle nudge of her muse with passion. She loves to travel and spend time with her family, especially her adorable grandson.

Alison Shelton received her B.A. in English and history and her Master's degree in education. She taught high school for thirty years and, since retiring, has enjoyed traveling, art classes, writing workshops and especially her five grandchildren. Alison is a columnist for a senior magazine and also has published several articles in other magazines.

Mary Shotwell is the author of short stories and debuted her small-town romance novel *Christmas Catch* (Carina Press) in 2018, receiving a starred review from *Library Journal*. She lives in Nashville with her husband and three children and loves holidays — especially Christmas. Learn more at maryshotwell.com.

Brian Staff was born in England, has travelled throughout much of the world, and now lives in California. He has published a novel and a collection of stories/essays. His works in both fiction and non-fiction have also appeared in magazines and anthologies. Find more of his work on www.wordisworth.com.

Michael Sullivan is an award-winning writer, a storyteller, and a pediatric nurse. He has performed songs and stories throughout the country in libraries, schools, bookstores, and museums. He lives in Richmond, VA, with his wife and two children. For more information, please check out his website at www.msullivantales.com or www.eyeballinmygarden.com.

Tsgoyna Tanzman is a get-started later-in-life wife and mother. A former fitness trainer and speech pathologist, she now credits writing as the ultimate therapy for raising an adolescent. Her stories and poems can be read in *Chicken Soup for the Soul* books, *The Orange County Register* and online at More.com. E-mail her at tnzmn@cox.net.

Julie Theel lives in sunny Rancho Mirage, CA with her husband, two teenage daughters, four furry dogs and two fluffy cats. When not busy shuttling the girls to their many activities, Julie spends her time rescuing animals and running her business selling the Rippys, her patented rip-apart toys for dogs.

Julia M. Toto shares stories of hope, forgiveness, and second chances. She's a published author of inspirational fiction and a previous contributor to the *Chicken Soup for the Soul* series. Learn more at www.juliamtoto.com.

Adrienne Townsend received her BA in Secondary Social Studies and Master of Education in Secondary from Texas Christian University in 2007. She teaches high school U.S. History and World Geography in Texas. Adrienne enjoys traveling abroad, reading, and spending time with her family. Please e-mail her at Adrienne.L.Townsend@gmail.com.

Ernie Witham writes the humor column "Ernie's World" for the *Montecito Journal* in Montecito, CA. He is the author of two humor books including *A Year in the Life of a "Working" Writer*. His stories have appeared in more than a dozen *Chicken Soup for the Soul* books. He is also a humor workshop leader at several writers conferences.

Meet Amy Newmark

Amy Newmark is the bestselling author, editor-in-chief, and publisher of the *Chicken Soup for the Soul* book series. Since 2008, she has published 174 new books, most of them national bestsellers in the U.S. and Canada, more than doubling the number of Chicken Soup for the Soul titles in print today. She is also the author of *Simply Happy*, a crash course in Chicken Soup for the Soul advice and wisdom that is filled with easy-to-implement, practical tips for enjoying a better life.

Amy is credited with revitalizing the Chicken Soup for the Soul brand, which has been a publishing industry phenomenon since the first book came out in 1993. By compiling inspirational and aspirational true stories curated from ordinary people who have had extraordinary experiences, Amy has kept the twenty-seven-year-old Chicken Soup for the Soul brand fresh and relevant.

Amy graduated *magna cum laude* from Harvard University where she majored in Portuguese and minored in French. She then embarked on a three-decade career as a Wall Street analyst, a hedge fund manager, and a corporate executive in the technology field. She is a Chartered Financial Analyst.

Her return to literary pursuits was inevitable, as her honors thesis in college involved traveling throughout Brazil's impoverished northeast region, collecting stories from regular people. She is delighted to have come full circle in her writing career — from collecting stories "from the people" in Brazil as a twenty-year-old to, three decades later, collecting stories "from the people" for Chicken Soup for the Soul.

When Amy and her husband Bill, the CEO of Chicken Soup for the Soul, are not working, they are visiting their four grown children and their three grandchildren.

Follow Amy on Twitter @amynewmark. Listen to her free podcast — Chicken Soup for the Soul with Amy Newmark — on Apple Podcasts, Google Play, the Podcasts app on iPhone, or by using your favorite podcast app on other devices.

Sharing Happiness, Inspiration, and Hope

Real people sharing real stories, every day, all over the world. In 2007, *USA Today* named *Chicken Soup for the Soul* one of the five most memorable books in the last quarter-century. With over 100 million books sold to date in the U.S. and Canada alone, more than 250 titles in print, and translations into nearly fifty languages, "chicken soup for the soul®" is one of the world's best-known phrases.

Today, twenty-eight years after we first began sharing happiness, inspiration and hope through our books, we continue to delight our readers with new titles, but have also evolved beyond the bookshelves with super premium pet food, television shows, a podcast, video journalism from aplus.com, licensed products, and free movies and TV shows on our Popcornflix and Crackle apps. We are busy "changing the world one story at a time®." Thanks for reading!

Share with Us

We all have had Chicken Soup for the Soul moments in our lives. If you would like to share your story or poem with millions of people around the world, go to chickensoup.com and click on Submit Your Story. You may be able to help another reader and become a published author at the same time. Some of our past contributors have launched writing and speaking careers from the publication of their stories in our books!

We only accept story submissions via our website. They are no longer accepted via mail or fax. Visit our website, www.chickensoup. com, and click on Submit Your Story for our writing guidelines and a list of topics we are working on.

To contact us regarding other matters, please send us an e-mail through webmaster@chickensoupforthesoul.com, or fax or write us at:

Chicken Soup for the Soul
P.O. Box 700
Cos Cob, CT 06807-0700
Fax: 203-861-7194

One more note from your friends at Chicken Soup for the Soul: Occasionally, we receive an unsolicited book manuscript from one of our readers, and we would like to respectfully inform you that we do not accept unsolicited manuscripts, and we must discard the ones that appear.

Chicken Soup for the Soul

101 Feel Good Stories

Laughter Is the Best Medicine

Amy Newmark

Paperback: 978-1-61159-999-2
eBook: 978-1-61159-299-3

More humor, love, and laughs

Paperback: 978-1-61159-977-0
eBook: 978-1-61159-277-1

Because truth is stranger than fiction!

Chicken Soup for the Soul

for the Soul

Changing the world one story at a time®
www.chickensoup.com